Collective and Corporate Responsibility

COLLECTIVE
and
CORPORATE
RESPONSIBILITY

PETER A. FRENCH

New York Columbia University Press *1984*

Library of Congress Cataloging in Publication Data

French, Peter A.
Collective and corporate responsibility.

Includes bibliographical references and index.
1. Industry—Social aspects.   2. Corporations—
Corrupt practices.   3. Business ethics.   4. Social
ethics.   5. Criminal liability of juristic persons.
I. Title.
HD60.F74   1984   658.4'08   84-3226
ISBN 0-231-05836-5 (alk. paper)
ISBN 0-231-05837-3 (pbk. : alk. paper)

Columbia University Press
New York   Guildford, Surrey
Copyright © 1984 Columbia University Press
All rights reserved

PRINTED IN THE UNITED STATES OF AMERICA

*Clothbound editions of Columbia University Press Books are
Smyth-sewn and printed on permanent and durable acid-free paper*

CONTENTS

Preface   *vii*

CHAPTER ONE   Types of Collectivities: A Preliminary
Sorting   *1*

CHAPTER TWO   Crowds and Corporations   *19*

CHAPTER THREE   The Corporation as a Moral
Person   *31*

CHAPTER FOUR   Corporate Internal Decision
Structures   *48*

CHAPTER FIVE   The Power of the People in Groups and
Corporations   *67*

CHAPTER SIX   Kinds and Persons   *78*

CHAPTER SEVEN   Plato, Bradley, Rousseau, and the
Corporate Personality   *94*

CHAPTER EIGHT   Tribes   *112*

CHAPTER NINE   The Medical Profession   *120*

CHAPTER TEN   What Is Hamlet to McDonnell-Douglas or
McDonnell-Douglas to Hamlet:
DC-10   *129*

CHAPTER ELEVEN   The Principle of Responsive Adjustment:
The Crash on Mount Erebus   *145*

CHAPTER TWELVE   Intention and Corporate
Accountability   *164*

CHAPTER THIRTEEN   Corporate Criminality and the Model Penal
Code   *173*

CHAPTER FOURTEEN   Punishing the Criminal
                   Corporation   *187*
                        Notes   *203*
                        Index   *213*

PREFACE

Ethical theorists commonly hold that a minimal conception of morality must involve the idea of a moral community, an aggregate of those persons about whom moral judgments are made, on whom moral requirements of action are laid, and to whom moral admonitions are directed. But who is to be counted as a member of that important collective? A definitive answer to that question is not going to be deduced from moral principles or derived from moral theories alone. Moral community membership is essentially a premoral, a metaphysical, matter.

For centuries the standard minimal entrance qualifications for membership in the moral community have included being a natural person (a human being), being a rational animal capable of voluntary actions, and having the ability to appreciate the moral status of those actions. Only individual human beings possessed of a certain level of rational intelligence were to be recorded in the census of the moral community. Almost all Western moral philosophers have approached the subject of responsibility armed with the assumption that the only interesting and important things to be said on that topic must be about individual human beings. If ascriptions of moral responsibility appeared to be about groups, organizations, or corporate bodies, they were either nonsensical or they were reducible to statements about individual human beings. Kant, after all, had said that "moral worth is the worth of the person as such," and he certainly had individual human rational agents in mind, not business corporations or collectivities.

The foundation stones of our theories of moral responsibility were laid, their superstructures constructed, their walls raised, and their rococo ornamentation affixed centuries before the contemporary socioeconomic world emerged. The grand individualist tradition that characterizes much of our moral thought has its taproot in Western religion's conception of personal salvation. This tradition, therefore, insists, with the kind of rigidity generally reserved only for doctrine, upon the reduction of all group and organizational social structures to individual natural-person component members when anyone is about the serious business of moral evaluation, blaming, punishing, or praising. Hence, corporations, clubs, nations, etc., are to be treated as mere fictions, figments of the imagination, the moral world's equivalents to the physical world's ghosts and hallucinations. Morally, organizations and collectives do not exist and, mutatis mutandis, the notions of corporate and collective responsibility are illusionary. Sentences that appear to hold a group or a corporation responsible are merely shorthand devices for ascribing responsibility to each of or at least one of the human beings who comprise the group or are associated in the corporation. Rudyard Kipling wrote the warning of the Devil to poor Tomlinson, but it had echoed in the literature of ethics for centuries before he took up his pen.

"And carry my word to the Sons of Men or ever ye come to die:
That the sin they do by two and two they must pay for one by one."[1]

The very idea of collective responsibility has been anathema to the myriad of followers of this tradition. They have found worthy of imprecation the thought that a business firm, a mere artifact, in no way a natural human being nor the simple conjunction of human beings, could itself be a nonreducible subject of a moral judgment. Tradition dies hard!

The twentieth-century individualist, however, resides in a social world the forefathers of the theory could not have even imagined. The doctrine of the tradition rides a collision course with the reality of corporate entities that today define and maintain human existence within the industrialized world. Ours is a world of business corporations, of large organizations that cannot be ignored or fictionalized by moral theorists. As Kenneth Goodpaster has clearly put it,

> It is as if we have just begun to realize that the ships in our social harbor (a) include more than the ship of state and the little dinghies of individual thoughts and actions, and (b) are captained by teams of decision makers who are fast becoming as reflective as they are ambitious.[2]

Business firms in this century occupy social positions roughly equivalent to the prominent posts held in other eras by the church, the nobility, the army, even the feudal lords. They dominate the lives of all but a few members of the community. They control the financial and economic aspects of society and are possessed of monetary power far greater than the world's governments. America's largest corporations annually handle revenues that are better than eight times those of the federal government and five times the total of all government revenues. Corporations today enjoy the prestige associated with creating and maintaining the scale of worth against which the majority of adults in Western societies judge their own accomplishments and personal value. Most Americans, we are told by researchers, decide whether or not they are successes or failures in life primarily on the basis of their attainment of some corporate status. The position, rank, or office they hold within a corporate enterprise is their gauge of worth. Although this widespread phenomenon may be decried by philosophers, social psychologists, priests, and the withering remnants of the flower children of the sixties, and not without reason, it is an index of the prominence of corporations in virtually every aspect of twentieth-century community life.

Corporations are accused of polluting the environment, blamed for destroying the economic structure of a community, praised for community service projects, credited with providing jobs for members of oppressed minorities, and indicted for felonies. Corporations are far from being social fictions. A moral theory that must treat them as such is sadly impoverished.

In an address to an American Law Institute–American Bar Association symposium, legal theorist Alfred F. Conrad effectively expressed the dramatic and unanticipated differences between our world and that of those centuries in which the standard conception of membership in a moral community was developed. A little more than two hundred years ago the American colonists were declaring independence on Lockean-style political principles, and Hume and Kant were writing treatises on ethics.

> If Ben Franklin and Tom Jefferson could be with us today, I do not think they would be astounded by the executive jet that flew us here. I expect that Jefferson would pull a couple of sketches out of his saddlebag to show that he was thinking of a lighter-than-air machine to move tobacco from Charlottesville to Newport News. Ben would say it was in the back of his mind when he flew his kite. But I think they would be really amazed to discover how the life of America—its means of feeding, clothing, and sheltering itself, its work ways and work places, its culture and ideals—has come to be centered around the institution of the business corporation.[3]

One point of Conrad's address was that the political, economic, and social theorists whose works are usually identified as the cornerstones of our most important conceptions in politics, economics, and ethics, e.g., John Locke, Adam Smith, and Immanuel Kant, could have had no clearer or more useful conception of the place of business corporations in our society than a cloistered seventh-century monk could have had of the emergence of the nation states of the Renaissance.

Social import and power, of course, do not constitute moral personhood. The reductionists do not deny that corporations wield enormous social and political power. They deny that corporations qualify for treatment as proper subjects of moral indignation, disapprobation, blame, or credit, and their position ought not be taken lightly. We seem to be naturally inclined to reductionism and have grown comfortable with what John Danley has aptly called "anthropological bigotry." The burden of proof should fall on the revisionists, on those of us who would argue that corporations should be admitted to full-membership in the moral community. Corporations will have to satisfy the standard tests of accountability applicable to all members of the moral community if they are to be admitted to membership. If corporations fail such tests, the community's most powerful entities will avoid the scrutiny and control of moral sanction. That would not be much of a concern if it were always just to hold individual human beings responsible for corporate actions. Part of my analysis will show, however, that corporate actions cannot be identified with the actions of individuals, and so it will not always be just to blame a human being for a corporate moral or legal offense.

We must reject any strategy that amounts to a legislation of ad hoc tests of moral personhood just to catch corporations in the moral net. Our primary interest is in moral not legal personhood and the question of whether corporations can pass standard tests of moral responsibility is not a matter of institutional rules. It involves metaphysical problems of identity, agency, and the like. Attention must be directed to those questions, if the moral-person status of corporations is to be settled.

My interest in the metaphysical foundations of a theory of moral community was not originally directed to the business corporation. In the aftermath of reports about Vietnam War atrocities, especially the My Lai massacre, I began to examine the notion of collective responsibility. Claims were being made at that time, even by the perpetrators of the atrocities, that the soldiers of Charlie Company bore no individual guilt for their actions, that only the American people considered collectively could be held morally responsible. Similar condemnations of whole populations followed the fall of the Third Reich. Although at first I was anything but persuaded that collectivities could be held morally accountable, preferring with my professor, H. D. Lewis, to regard the very idea of collective responsibility as a barbarous notion. Further investigation and analysis of common blaming practices, however, began to sway my opinion. In those days I began to draw the sorts of distinctions among collectivities that are developed and defended in the early chapters of this book.

These attempts to distinguish types of collectivities seemed inexorably to be directing me to the business corporation. Here were organizations about which we typically make all manner of what appear to be moral judgments, and yet they are structurally unlike other groups or such collectivities as army units. "Exxon" names an entity that is not much like the collective named "the American people."

At about the time I was beginning to develop what I take to be the foundational theory of corporate responsibility, the subfield of ethics called business ethics began to emerge and gain some credibility among academic philosophers. My work on corporate responsibility was often identified within the literature of business ethics, but it was far removed philosophically from much of what was published about whistle-blowing, deceptive advertising, discriminatory hiring practices, etc. In fact, business ethics, like so many of the newly created fields of applied philosophy, was adrift in a conceptual Sargasso Sea without a defined course and with no anchor.

I am convinced that the primary problem of business ethics is not to identify ways of applying the traditional moral theories and principles in order to evaluate the actions of corporate managers. That, unfortunately, has been the characteristic approach in the field. Instead, the concept of the business corporation needs to be examined metaphysically and, I am convinced, the outcome of such work will not be an attack on the old moral principles. It will be the innovative application of those principles to the corporation treated as itself a full-fledged moral person. My work has focused on both that anchor and course.

This book has four associated, though distinct, parts. The first few chapters report and defend distinctions among collectivities to which those holding an individualist theory are conceptually blind. The next five chapters develop a theory of the corporation as a moral person and associate that theory with its distant theoretical cousins. There follows a short chapter that is intended to correct a common misconception about the use of the notion of collective responsibility among primitive tribes. The next four chapters provide applications of the theory to actual cases. In the process of working out these applications, principles of moral responsibility are uncovered and discussed. My purpose, however, has not been to write a book on moral philosophy. The discussions of what I call the Extended Principle of Accountability (EPA) and the Principle of Responsive Adjustment (PRA) are more suggestive than fully argued. That is left for another occasion. The use of the latter principle does, however, necessitate a slight modification in the theory of the corporation as a moral person. The twelfth chapter explores that modification and some of its happy consequences for the general theory. The final chapters carry the theory to the law, to corporate criminal liability. In those chapters I am not trying to work out all of the legal implications of the theory of the corporation as a moral person. Instead, I focus first on the legal history and then on what I regard as a creative, though still retributive, way to punish corporate criminality, a form of punishment that is consistent with the principles of moral responsibility I discuss in this book.

By way of a caution I think it should be made clear that I am not going to be claiming that my analysis throughout this book is an account of a speaker's meaning when ascriptions of collective (or corporate) responsibility are made. Indeed, it may well be that a majority of the people who use collective nouns and phrases understand them to be shorthand devices. I also do not claim that my account captures ordinary usage so that one can expect the average utterer of an ascription of collective responsibility to mean by it what would be entailed by my analysis. I would, however, like to think that once apprised of the sense my account would give to his utterance, the ordinary user would acknowledge that he could have had something of that sort in mind.

As with any book in philosophy and especially with one that has been in progress for so long a time, a number of people made significant contributions to its development. I mentioned earlier that H. D. Lewis shaped my first philosophical thoughts on these matters. I continue to regard his work as the locus classicus of the position I have ultimately come to reject. His work is extraordinarily clear and penetrating. Two other philosophers had much to do with the pivotal chapters of this book. Donald Davidson's influence cannot be overstated. His encouragement and suggestions regarding the theory of the corporation as a moral person had much to do with the final form of the argument. The late J. L. Mackie listened to my readings of the key chapters and gave some of the most useful and clever comments I have yet encountered in my academic life. I shall never forget the way John instantly brightened one depressingly gloomy day. Foul black clouds had engulfed my office building signaling the onslaught of yet another snowstorm when John decided, without prompting, that the only way to make me see an important point that I stubbornly refused to acknowledge was to sing for me relevant selections from Gilbert and Sullivan. John's death is an inestimable loss to all of us who knew him and to the broader philosophical community.

Others have also made contributions. My thanks to Norman Bowie and the staff at the Center for the Study of Values where I was able to write many of the chapters. I learned much from discussions with Eric VonMagness and David Cole while I was in Delaware. Others have helped by asking the right questions or publishing papers and books that offered criticisms or extensions of my work. Of particular note are John Danley, Deborah Johnson, Thomas Donaldson, Patricia Werhane, Lisa Newton, Rex Martin, and Richard DeGeorge. Kurt Baier gave continual encouragement and many suggestions. Legal theorists Christopher Stone and Brent Fisse have taken the trouble to provide me with extensive commentary on various chapters. They have opened my eyes to the legal implications of my theory.

My colleagues and students at the University of Minnesota and Trinity University have been helpful and supportive. Also, there are quite a large number of philosophers and philosophy students across the country who have listened to me talk on many of the topics in this book and have raised issues and questions that have ultimately, I hope, made this a better book than it would have been had they never voiced their opinions.

I owe a special debt of thanks to the secretaries who have struggled with my handwritten pages to produce the readable typescript. I am particularly grateful to Virginia Redford, my secretary at Trinity University. This book is better for the copy editing expertise of Lisa Moore.

I also acknowledge the support of the Exxon Education Foundation, Trinity University, the Center for the Study of Values, and the Graduate School of the University of Minnesota.

Collective and Corporate Responsibility

CHAPTER ONE

Types of Collectivities: A Preliminary Sorting

The idea of collective, let alone corporate, responsibility has been frequently and loudly decried as a vulgarism and red-lined from residency in the better moral neighborhoods. Some philosophers argue that all ascriptions of collective responsibility are only short-hand devices for the ascribing of responsibility to the individual human beings who happen to be involved in groups. It is said that all statements about collective responsibility ultimately can be completely reduced to ascriptions of individual responsibility. Despite a strong individualist tradition in Western philosophy, particularly evident in Kant's moral theory, the practice of making ascriptions of collective responsibility not only continues but has become more prevalent in ordinary discourse since the Second World War. As might be expected, given the institutional complexity of contemporary life, the preponderant ascriptions of collective and corporate responsibility occur when attention has been drawn to major social enterprises and especially to those that result in or include disasters or atrocities affecting human life or the environment of the planet.

History is often written as the acts of individuals, and social change is interpreted in terms of the choices of individuals. The historical, sociological, and anthropological literature is rife with sentences containing terms that refer to human collectives, groups, organizations, and institutions. What Durkheim has called "social facts"[1] are characteristically about such entities:

"The battalion attacked the enemy patrol."

"The police force restrained and then dispersed the crowd."

"The Jones family moved into an upper-middle-class neighbor-hood."

"The angry crowd trampled the rosebeds of the county park."

"Gulf Oil Corporation raised the price of gasoline by 5¢ per gal-lon."

No one would dispute that sentences like these are appropriately used to describe facts about our social life. For some time, how-ever, a heated debate has broiled over whether collective terms re-fer to unanalyzable social entities or whether they should be de-fined in terms of the behavior, psychological states, and identities of the individual human beings that comprise them.

The reductionist position has had many recent champions, in-cluding Sir Karl Popper, F. A. Hayek, and their followers.[2] The position these philosophers defend is a methodological principle. J. W. N. Watkins writes: "This principle states that social pro-cesses and events should be explained by being deduced from (a) principles governing the behavior of participating individuals and (b) descriptions of their situations."[3]

The principle is generally referred to as methodological individ-ualism (MI). Popper defends this principle in his famous attack on holistic theories of the state. He argues, in fact, that individualism is a part of the "old intuitive idea of justice." By that he means that justice has primarily to do with the treatment of individual persons and not with something like the Platonic harmony of the state. He further maintains that individualism conjoined with al-truism is the very basis of Western civilization, residing in the eth-ical doctrines of Christianity and Kant's humanitarian formulation of the categorical imperative: "Act so that you treat humanity, whether in your own person or in that of another, always as an end and never as a means only."[4]

The pedigree of individualism, of course, is not in question. Im-portant for present purposes are its methodological implications. Watkins offers reasons for adapting MI. He tells us that social things like prices, prime ministers, and ration books are created or formed only by individual attitudes.[5] The idea is that prices only exist because shopkeepers, manufacturers, consumers, and government officials have certain attitudes. Removal of or changes in those attitudes would bring an end to prices. As the phenomenon of prices is formed by such individual attitudes, its explanation must be given in individualistic terms. Perhaps that is true for the pricing system of the corner grocery, but is it also the case when the prices are set by cartels, or fixed by oil ministers, or imposed by corporate marketing divisions? In such cases it is not self-evident that the whole matter of prices reduces to individual attitudes. Even if prices were so reducible, it is not at all clear that such collective and organized units as multinational corporations are of the same variety of "social objects." Watkins does note that the fact that "social objects" are human creations does not logically entail that they "may not be governed by some overall law which is underivable from propositions about individuals" (p. 730). The reduction to individual attitudes is then no more than an intuitive appeal for support and not an argument in defense of MI.

Watkins offers a second appeal. He claims that the supposed fact that social scientists have no "direct access" to the "structure and behavior of a system of interacting individuals" (p. 730), though they do in the case of individuals, supports MI and defeats any type of collectivism. By direct access Watkins intends something akin to the access a chemist has to the essence of water by way of the explanatory model provided by H_2O. This appeal in behalf of MI is, however, flawed in a number of crucial ways.

If we interpret direct access to mean that what is wanted is the kind of transparency afforded by a detailed explanatory model, as in the physical sciences, then the MI social-science project will fail at the level of individual human beings. Hilary Putnam has persuasively argued that the partial opacity of human beings to themselves is a constitutive fact of present human nature. If we had a theory of our functional organization qua human beings or persons, and could use it to explain and predict behavior, attitudes, etc., would we continue to be the sort of creatures that collect and organize in the very ways we do? Putnam wonders, quite rightly, if we would be able to carry out any of the ordinary activities that characterize human social life, were we able to use such a theory across a significant class of cases of human behavior. "Would it be possible to *love* someone, if we could actually carry out *calculations* of the form: 'If I say X, the probability is 15 per cent she will react in manner Y'?"[6] Were we to possess such knowledge of ourselves, we would have natures radically different from what we now regard as the nature of a human being. A radical alteration of our nature, from partial opacity to general transparency, would, as MI enthusiasts must agree, change the "social objects" and institutions that social scientists investigate. Without the ability to understand ourselves in the way the chemist understands water, we do not have a direct access to individuals that is significantly any better than that which we have to organizations and institutions. We may, in fact, have better access to the macrostructural rather than the microstructural elements of our social system.

MI is not, however, utterly without value. It surely is an adequate rule of explanation for social organizations or groups that develop and function in ways analogous to the solar system. The behavior of the solar system, insofar as that system may be said to behave, can be fully explained by applying the inverse square law and the law of inertia to the system's components, if their relative positions, masses, and momenta are known.[7] In effect, understanding the behavior of the solar system involves reduction to component planets and the principles according to which they act and then deductively reconstructing the behavior of the system from that data. Were all social organizations and institutions planetary in nature, MI would have considerable explicative and explanatory utility and would serve as the principle of analysis even for ascriptions of collective responsibility. Typically, philosophers discussing statements blaming collectivities maintain that such statements always entail ascriptions of blame or responsibility to individual members of the collectivities. They certainly seem to have taken the planetary approach to all types of human collectives and organizations. To do so, however, is to ignore important distinctions. But that is not to say that MI reductionism is not true of most types of statements, including most causal responsibility ascriptions, made about some kinds of collectivities. If it is used as the principle of analysis of statements made about the other organizations, however, it will usually produce unjustifiable ascriptions of responsibility.

I shall call a group an "aggregate collectivity" if it is merely a collection of people.* A change in an aggregate's membership will always entail a change in the identity of the collection. In brief, a group or aggregate's existence as that particular aggregate is not compatible with a varying or frequently changing membership. The meaning of a sentence about an aggregate would be different if one of the individuals actually belonging to the aggregate had not, in fact, been a member of it. This feature, obviously, welcomes MI reductionism. By and large what is predicable of an aggregate collectivity is reducible to the assignment of like predication (allowing for some verbal leeway) to collectivity members.

There is, of course, a class of predicates that just cannot be true of individuals, that can only be true of collectives. Examples are abundant, and surely include "disbanded" (most uses of), "lost the football game," "elected a president," and "passed an amendment." Methodological individualism would be at a loss in responsibility contexts, if accountability ascriptions were of this sort. Clearly they are not, for although "John disbanded" is not sensible, "John is to blame" and "John is responsible" are very common and meaningful utterances. Insofar as our interest runs to such matters, it is to responsibility ascriptions that we need now turn.

For the sake of simplicity I propose to focus on expressions of blame rather than to open discussion to the whole panoply of predicates in our arsenal of responsibility ascriptions. Expressions of blame are paradigmatic of responsibility ascriptions such that where I use the term "blame" substitution of any of a large number of predicates in the "responsibility" family would not affect matters in any serious way.[8]

---

*I have borrowed the term "aggregate" from geology; I suspect that it is not used in just this way in that discipline, although the similarities are evident. I have not chosen the term from its logical use, i.e., as distinguished from sets. The notion of aggregate, as I use it, does presuppose a notion of the individual similar to the logical use of the term.

The sole function of blaming on many occasions is the identification of the cause of unhappy or untoward events (for example, "Blame the weather for ruining the vacation"). To blame is clearly to *fix* responsibility, to identify the cause or causes of an untoward or disvalued event; the weather is to blame for a ruined vacation or the dead battery is to blame for the flashlight's failure. To blame, however, is often to do much more than that, it is to *hold* responsible. That is where important distinctions must be drawn, for clearly we cannot in any sensible way *hold* the weather or the dead battery responsible for the unhappy events for which they are causally to blame. Within both our legal and moral practices some things and some people may be causally responsible for certain unhappy events, though they are not held responsible for them.

Blaming used no more than to identify the causal ancestry of an unwelcome or untoward event is not of an interesting moral sort. Such blame, of course, is the expression of displeasure at the cause of the focal event and expressions of disapprobation are clearly central to all blaming episodes. After all, the etymological roots of "to blame" lie in "to blaspheme" ("to speak evil of"). Clearly nonmoral blaming is appropriate even in cases of accident, mistake, and where the blamed party is not believed to be capable of helping what it does or of doing something other than what it did. A child, for example, is to blame for breaking his toy train, even though he is only four years old, and it was an accident. To resurrect one of Austin's famous illustrations, I am to blame for killing your donkey even though I shot it in the mistaken belief that it was my donkey.[9] Nonmoral blame and responsibility need not occasion evaluations of intelligence, states of mind, or intentions. There is no difference in kind between nonmorally blaming persons and blaming inanimate objects and such things as the weather. Occasions of nonmoral blaming are not directed at altering future behavior. This is most obvious in the example of blaming the weather. When used nonmorally "X is to blame for y" pins something on X: X was a cause of the event y, which the speaker would prefer had not happened. "The root system of the old oak tree is to blame for blocking the water line," simply identifies the cause or what is taken to be the cause of an unhappy event or occurrence. "X is to blame for y" is justified when X was a cause of y and y was an untoward event. Some types of nonmoral blaming are like scolding or rebuking or chiding, while others are merely expressions of attitude.

Ascriptions of moral responsibility and blame involve much more than identification of the causes of disapproved events, though they clearly are parasitic upon nonmoral responsibility. A moral responsibility or blaming ascription amounts to the assertion of a conjunctive proposition, the first conjunct of which identifies the subject's actions with or as the cause of an event and the second conjunct asserts that the action in question was intended by the subject or that the event was related, in ways to be discussed in later chapters, to the intentional acts of the subject. The primary focus of moral responsibility ascriptions is the subject's intentions rather than, though not to the exclusion of, occasions. Austin wrote: "In considering [moral] responsibility, few things are considered more important than to establish whether a man *intended* to do A, or whether he did A intentionally."[10]

If a basic (nonmoral) responsibility predicate is ascribed to an aggregate collectivity, using MI, it will be true that it is distributively ascribed to each of the collectivity's members. If "a" stands for an aggregate collectivity, then Pa entails Pm (where P is a nonmoral blame or other responsibility predicate and "m" is a member of "a"). Consider the famous case of Kitty Genovese's neighbors (more specifically, her neighbors who were home on the evening of March 13, 1964) who watched from their windows as Ms. Genovese was assaulted and murdered. They constitute an aggregate collectivity. As will be discussed in more detail in the next chapter, the identity we might want to assign to "Kitty Genovese's neighbors," must consist of no more or less than the identities of the people who lived in her neighborhood and were home that evening. Suppose it is said as it was in newspaper editorials: "Kitty Genovese's neighbors are to blame for her death." Our methodological individualistic understanding of aggregate collectivities licenses us to conclude that anyone who was a neighbor of Kitty

Genovese and was home on the evening in question, is nonmorally to blame for her death.

MI has drawn fire from some moral philosophers for requiring entailments such as this. In order to alleviate what might be an injustice to some members, especially when the collectivity's untoward action was not such that individuals are generally thought likely to be able to perform it alone, these philosophers have introduced the notion of degrees of blame and responsibility in a revision of MI. It then is argued that when the utterance "Kitty Genovese's neighbors are to blame for her death" is justified, it entails only that each member of that group of people shares some of the responsibility or that each is to some (perhaps undeterminable) degree to blame for her violent death. Haskell Fain, for example, talks of individuals who "share a 'collective' responsibility," and Kurt Baier writes of those who can be "said to bear a share . . . collectively a not inconsiderable share . . . of the responsibility."[11]

There is a fundamental reason, however, for rejecting revision of MI when it is applied to nonmoral responsibility ascriptions to aggregate collectivities. It need only be remembered that nonmoral responsibility ascriptions primarily identify what a speaker takes to be the cause or one of the causes of an untoward or undesired event. Just as many things, persons, and other events can be nonmorally to blame for some event as are causes of it. In effect, anything that has materially contributed to the event's occurrence can be blamed for it in this nonmoral sense. There simply is no reason to think of nonmoral responsibility as admitting of degrees except insofar as we would admit degrees to causal claims. There is not a set amount of blame for every event. And nonmoral responsibility is not like a pie that is divided and distributed; if X is a cause of y and y is untoward, then X is to blame for y. If Z was also a cause of y, then Z is to blame as well. If X and Z compose aggregate A and A is a cause of y, then, on the principles of MI, X and Z are causes and so to blame for y.

Questions of "more or less" are crucial in regard to moral responsibility, determining accountability and the relevance and acceptability of excuses. If an aggregate collectivity is nonmorally responsible for some untoward occurrence, each individual member of the aggregate may be said to be nonmorally responsible. The names of aggregate collectivities are only useful ways of referring to certain groups, what the collectivity or group does is done by its members, even if it is done in a concerted way. If the neighbors of Kitty Genovese did not go to her aid, then each and every one of her neighbors did not go to her aid, though obviously there was no concert of forebearance in this case. These matters merge into questions of aggregate structure and membership dispensibility that will be discussed in later chapters. It is important, however, that each member of a nonmorally responsible aggregate collectivity is or is not *morally* responsible (blameworthy or accountable) for the event in question only insofar as he is or is not capable of supporting some exculpatory or mitigatory excuse in his own behalf with respect to the event.

Suppose that a gang of teenagers, each of whom is high on hallucinogenic drugs, attacks and brutally murders an old woman. The gang is collectively *causally* responsible for the murder; therefore, each member of the gang is nonmorally responsible for it. But, supposing that each can support a plea of temporary insanity due to drug ingestion, none of them may be held morally responsible in the case of the old woman's death. (The fact that no one is blameworthy does not mean that in the course of judicial events no one should be held accountable or punished.) By way of summary we may say that if "a" is an aggregate collectivity and P is a nonmoral responsibility predicate and if "m" is a member of "a," then if Pa is justified, Pm is also justified.

It might be true that an aggregate collectivity did something that is untoward, undesirable, or in violation of some legal or moral code and that the act is of such a collective type that it cannot be predicated of the members individually. In such cases a nonmoral responsibility predicate may be justifiably ascribed to the collectivity and that will entail ascriptions of responsibility to the membership. "The mob rioted and destroyed the building" does not entail that "Mob member Jones rioted." But the riot was an untoward event; therefore, "The mob is to blame for the riot and its attendant destruction," is justifiable, and that entails "Mob member

Jones is to blame for the riot and its destruction." But, whether Jones should be held morally responsible, or partially so, for the riot and destruction will turn on the issue of whether or not an exculpatory or mitigatory excuse on his behalf is supportable.

Moral responsibility predicates cannot be legitimately ascribed to aggregate collectivities. Aggregates simply fail the tests for membership in the moral community. It is crucial that they are not intentional agents in and of themselves. Also, it makes no sense to say that an aggregate collectivity, in and of itself, could have done something different from what it did, except insofar as that amounts to saying individuals who constitute a critical mass of the membership could have altered their intentions and hence acted differently in the circumstances. Again consider Kitty Genovese's neighbors. To say that her neighbors could have gone to her aid is to say that a number, even one, of the persons in that collectivity could have intentionally behaved in a manner different from the way they actually did.

The fact that aggregate collectivities cannot legitimately be held responsible or hold persons responsible has an interesting upshot for those concerned with governmental accountability. We are told in the United States that our elected officials are responsible to their constituents, or to the people. In the case of the President of the United States the relationship is said to exist between the person in the office and "the American people." If "the American people" is the name of an aggregate collectivity, however, then the political rhetoric needs to be interpreted. If we ask how the American people as an entity, in and of itself, can hold the President morally responsible, we will no doubt be told of the election and impeachment processes. But the question is whether those processes are decision procedures through which the synthesized intentions of a collective entity are expressed in action or whether they are merely devices by which individual persons are able to express their individual actions. This matter is further complicated by the standard notion that the President's moral and political responsibility to the American people extends well into the past generations of Americans.

The terms "the American people" and "all Americans" may not

be equivalent. In "all Americans" "Americans" acts as a general term. What is true of all Americans is true of each and every American. If we were saying "All Americans were responsible for the Vietnam War," then we would have to justify blaming each American, a task which would be most difficult in the case of those Americans, for example, who refused to serve in the army or to pay taxes in support of the war effort. On the other hand "the American people" is not usually a general term. It seems to act like a singular term, naming or purporting to name an entity, albeit a collective one.

If we want to enforce MI and insist that responsibility is primarily an individual matter we could treat statements such as "The American people were responsible for the Vietnam War" as a shorthand version of "All American citizens who did not overtly behave in ways which manifested their nonmembership in the subcollectivity "American war supporters" are individually responsible for the Vietnam War."

But that is hardly an acceptable substitute, unless we are willing to admit that the membership of the collectivity named "the American people" can be defined, ad hoc, in terms of individual participation (overt or covert) in the untoward events that occasioned the speaker's utterance of the responsibility ascription. In other words, the referent of "The American people" varies depending on speaker intentions and understandings. If that is the case, then the collective entity referred to by "the American people" would only accidentally, if ever, satisfy the conditions for engaging in responsibility relationships. On the other hand, if "the American people" is taken to be a collectivity with an established decision and action procedure by which its membership concerts their intentions and actions, and if by "the American people" we mean an entity with an identity that is not merely a sum of the identities of all American people (whatever that might be), then the American people could be held morally responsible for certain events. "The American people" then would not be the name of an aggregate collectivity.

There are at least two types of aggregate collectivities defined by virtue of the light in which they are considered collectivities. One definitive consideration is the spatial and temporal contiguity of collectivity membership. The mob, Kitty Genovese's neighbors, and the people at the bus stop, are collectivities of this type. Although there may be exceptions, members usually are together in that place at that time because of each individual's pursuit of his own ends. There is no established decision procedure for determining group actions and often no strong bounds of solidarity.

This type of collectivity might be called a "random collective," and the classification of all aggregate collectivities as random is tempting. Something similar has been maintained by Virginia Held and David Cooper, but there is quite another type of aggregate collectivity that really is not random at all.[12]

Suppose someone were to blame white American racists for the plight of the various minorities in the United States. Clearly a collectivity like white American racists is not gathered at any one space nor at one time. Yet, commonly someone uttering a sentence of the sort, "White American racists are to blame for the plight of the blacks," intends that each and every white American racist be somehow covered by his utterance. However, "white American racists are to blame. . . . " clearly does not mean the same as "White American racists are blameworthy. . . ." In fact, the latter is meaningless. Instead, from the former one can derive like ascriptions of blame to individual white American racists and then justifiably ascribe blameworthiness to those individuals in cases where no exculpatory excuses are supportable.

An aggregate collectivity of this sort, it would seem, is defined by the very features of characteristics by virtue of which blaming or other responsibility predicates are ascribed to it. Such an aggregate, however, is not, in the usual sense of the term, random. If we were to settle the distinguishing of types of collectivities on the basis of randomness, we would obscure important similarites between two types of aggregate collectivities and deep dissimilarities between aggregate collectivities and what I shall call conglomerates and statistical collectivities.

To summarize: if A is an aggregate collectivity, whether of the sort whose definition explicitly involves spatial/temporal contiguity or of the sort defined in terms of a common characteristic or feature by virtue of which it is blamed or found to be responsible, then MI holds. Ascriptions of nonmoral responsibility are distributive. If responsibility or blame is justifiably ascribed to A, it has been also justifiably ascribed to each member of A, but ascriptions of *moral* responsibility can only be justified individually. MI, however, does not hold when the collectivity blamed is not of the aggregate sort.

A conglomerate collectivity is an organization of individuals such that its identity is not exhausted by the conjunction of the identities of the persons in the organization.* The existence of a conglomerate is compatible with a varying membership. A change in the specific persons associated in a conglomerate does not entail a corresponding change in the identity of the conglomerate. This identifying characteristic will be examined in detail in chapter 2. What can be said here is that the meaning of a statement made about a conglomerate will not change even if one of the individuals associated with the conglomerate had never been associated with the conglomerate. In other words, what is predicable of a conglomerate is not necessarily predicable of all of those or of any of those individuals associated with it, and this is also true of predictions of responsibility: only in rare instances does the name of a conglomerate refer to a determinate set of individual human beings. As examples consider: the Democratic Party, the Congress, the Rolling Green Country Club, the faculty of Yale University, the Gulf Oil Corporation, the Honeywell Corporation, the U.S. Army, and the Red Cross.

Statements ascribing responsibility to a conglomerate are not reducible to a conjunction of statements ascribing responsibility to the individuals associated with the conglomerate. There are at least three significant characteristics that conglomerates evidence and that are not found in the case of aggregates: (1) conglomerates have internal organizations and/or decision procedures by which courses of concerted actions can be, though not necessarily are, chosen; (2) generally, the enforced standards of conduct for individuals as-

---

*Again, the source of the term "conglomerate" is geological.

sociated in a conglomerate are different and more stringent than those usually thought to apply in the larger community of individuals; (3) members of a conglomerate fill differing defined roles or stations by virtue of which they exercise certain powers over other members, and it is important that a change in the identity of the persons filling those roles does not necessarily entail a change in the conglomerate's identity. Individuals become members of conglomerates in standardized ways, e.g., by becoming a stockholder, by enlisting, by being voted in, or by being employed. It is also of note that many conglomerates may be treated as persons under the law. Hence the General Motors Corporation can sue, be sued, and own property.

A misunderstanding would arise if one were to conclude that from statements predicating actions of conglomerates no statements predicating actions by at least some individual persons associated in the conglomerate ever follow. "The Red Cross supplied medicine at the scene of the disaster" does entail "Some member or members of the Red Cross did a number of things at the disaster site," though it does not necessarily entail that the actions predicated of the conglomerate are predicable of some member. Hence, "Texaco sold its holdings on Padre Island" does not entail "Some members of Texaco sold property (or their property) on Padre Island." This point will be pursued in more detail in a later chapter.

If a conglomerate is responsible for something, we cannot automatically conclude that "Some individuals associated with the conglomerate are responsible for it." For example, "The Democratic Party is to blame for the election of Richard Nixon in 1972" does not entail that "Some members of the Democratic Party are to blame for Nixon's election," but it does entail that "Some members of the Party acted in certain, though not necessarily blameable, ways in 1972." Also, "The Democratic Party nominated George McGovern" is not reducible to a series of statements about the votes cast by each member of the party. Each delegate at the national convention casting a vote for McGovern was, we may assume, behaving in a standard and acceptable fashion; that is, each voted for the candidate he favored and that is precisely what delegates are expected to do. The fact that McGovern was nominated, in a very real sense, was the result of the way the Democratic Party was then organized, e.g., the quota system, etc. The Democratic Party may be to blame for Nixon's election; but individual Democratic convention delegates may not be, since they behaved as they were expected to behave and the nominating proceeded according to accepted procedure.

If "c" is a conglomerate and P is a responsibility predicate, moral or nonmoral, and if "m" is a member of "c," then although Pc is justified, Pm may not be justified and can never be justified solely on the basis of Pc. To be sure many conglomerates are organized just so that they will shoulder responsibility for the failure of their projects without adversely reflecting on the individuals who are associated in them. The Honeywell Corporation, it may be remembered, was said by many to be responsible for the damage that was done by its antipersonnel bombs in North Vietnam. Most people, however, surely would condemn as unjust holding responsible, even in the nonmoral sense, every Honeywell employee, executive, and stockholder for that destruction. Perhaps this explains in part why we often recognize the exculpatory (or even justificatory) power of the "I was only doing my job" plea, despite its generally low rating among moral philosophers.

It may be the case that no member of a conglomerate in fact has performed in a specifically and individually substandard and hence blameable way, yet one still wants to blame the conglomerate for failing to meet an expected moral standard. "The Gulf Oil Corporation is responsible for financially ruining small, independent, gasoline station owners by pricing them out of the market," could, of course, be entailed by a series of statements predicating various sorts of behavior of individuals $(I^1, I^2 \ldots I^n)$ though none of I^1, $I^2 \ldots I^n$ needs to be an ascription of responsibility for Gulf's pricing practices or any morally substandard individual behavior.

If the ascriptions of responsibility to conglomerates cannot be distributed among the conglomerate's membership in the way required by MI, what reason do we have for making them? In the first place, one might blame a conglomerate because one has ideological reasons for not recognizing individuals as capable of

tainly does not mean that each and every American has the highest standard of living in the world. Nor does it mean that a conglomerate entity has the highest standard of living in the world (compare to "Exxon is the wealthiest oil corporation"). Also the statement "The American people grew tired of hearing about the Vietnam War" may be true when the statement "American John Doe grew tired of hearing about the Vietnam War" is false. These entailments do not hold because in uses of this sort the collective noun or noun phrase refers to a statistical collectivity. The name of the collectivity is, indeed, a shorthand for "most members of this group," hence "Most Americans grew tired of hearing about the Vietnam War" is the proper translation. The fact that some particular trait is predicated of a statistical collectivity provides only a likelihood of its justifiable predication in the case of any particular member of that type of collectivity. Ascriptions of responsibility predicates to statistical collectivities should be treated in much the same way as we treated such ascriptions in the case of aggregates. If "The American people are to blame for the Vietnam War" refers to a statistical collectivity (most Americans), then what we have is a disguised aggregate whose membership, if it is important to determine it, will be determined by the individual possession of those very features or characteristics in virtue of which blame is ascribed to the collectivity.

CHAPTER TWO
Crowds and Corporations

I have shown in chapter 1 that methodological individualism is blind to significant differences between types of human organizations. The individualist insist that only *individual human beings* can qualify as basic moral units and intentional agents. Hence, talk of group, collective, or corporate actions, intentions, goals, decisions, etc., is, when properly analyzed, reduced to or exposed as disguised talk about the actions, intentions, goals, or decisions of individual human beings. The MI program applied to theories of corporate economic behavior and corporate criminal liability tends to see corporations merely as market reactors and to be blind to their function as major elements in the broader social environment. For the present chapter I set aside the issue of what kinds of things can qualify as basic moral units in order to cast further doubt on the virtues of the individualist's unqualified assimilation of all human collective organizations to a single model. No appeal needs to be made to moral intuitions or arguments based on moral theory and principle about how responsibility or blame are to be properly assessed or punishment exacted if the individualist's program were not adopted. The distinctions exposed in the previous chapter between types of human collectivities and organizations can be deepened if we examine individuation and identity problems.

In Walter Van Tilburg Clark's *The Ox Bow Incident*, a motley group of people, after capturing what they are persuaded are cattle rustlers, summarily hangs three innocent men.[1] The name "The Ox Bow Mob" can be used to refer to that group of people in the

novel. The Ox Bow Mob is a certain collection of persons who bear
the names Gil, Osgood, Bartlett, Farnley, Moore, Ma Grier, Col-
onel Tetley, Mapes, Winder, Smith, Greene, Davies, Sparks, Hart,
Gerald Tetley, Amigo, and Croft.

Though I would like to focus on Clark's marvelous story, I have
learned that it is liable to raise difficulties for some sociologists that
can cloud the matters I want to pursue. Let us substitute a story
about the same people who comprised the Ox Bow lynch mob
gathered in Canby's Saloon in Bridger's Wells, Nevada, on a winter day in 1885. They get into a brawl and break furniture, mirrors, and windows. The brawl is a spontaneous event, not an organized protest against the high cost of a shot of red-eye. We will
refer to these people in the saloon as "The Canby Saloon Crowd."
Only those seventeen persons were in the saloon at the relevant
time, only those seventeen persons are the Canby Saloon Crowd.
There might have been a few other persons in the saloon or there
might have been an entirely different cast of characters. They might
all have been women. But there were not, and they were not. Those
and only those persons (that they are fictional is of no importance
here) designated by the above list of names constituted the crowd
in Canby's. We can wonder if the same group of persons would
have behaved as they did had someone else been in their company,
but no one else was in the crowd and somehow escaped our list.
We have them all. To catch the crowd and bring it to justice, the
sheriff must capture each and every person named on our list. If
Osgood and Farnley and Ma Grier escape his efforts, he has not
apprehended the Canby Saloon Crowd, even though he has locked
away the others. All of this seems intuitively corrrect. The Canby
Saloon Crowd is paradigmatic of that type of human collectivity I
have called an aggregate.

Suppose it is said:

The Canby Saloon Crowd dispersed after the brawl.

How are we to understand this statement? How ought the subject
be treated? An action, dispersing, is predicated of the crowd, and
it seems intuitively incorrect to say that the same action is neces-

sarily being predicated of everyone in the crowd. Osgood may certainly leave the scene, but his doing so would not normally be described as "dispersing." Crowds, mobs, and other sorts of collections disperse; individuals leave, vacate, move, etc. The dispersing in this statement is a collective action. "Dispersed" applies to the persons in the crowd regarded collectively. "Disbanded" is a similar predicate, said, for example, about the Ox Bow Mob after the lynching. It would not be true of an individual mob member that he disbanded.

"Canby Saloon Crowd" acts like a singular term in this sentence. It may be argued, however, that that is a function of the kind of predicate used. Following a convention of Gerald Massey, we may call such predicates "multigrade" insofar as they permit plural constructions at least at one of their argument places.[2] A unigrade predicate will not admit any plural constructions at any of its argument places. Some predicates not only admit plural constructions but accept nothing else. Perhaps "dispersed" is such a predicate. An argument might be made that such purely collective predicates disguise their subjects making it seem as if they were singular terms when they are only plural constructions utilized to save time. One could have said that each member of the crowd left the scene, naming each in turn, but in the interest of time "The Canby Saloon Crowd dispersed" does the trick. There is, then, no such thing as the Canby Saloon Crowd, there is just Gil, and Osgood, and the rest.

Although this approach has the virtue of not multiplying entities, it has its problems as well. The attempt to apply it necessitates major revisions that complicate the logic that underlies our semantic theory. Also there seems to be something counterintuitive in this for we may imagine that the sheriff of Bridger's Wells is terrified by the prospect of the Canby Saloon Crowd on the rampage again but not afraid of each person in that crowd when he meets each individually. More to the point, collective predicates comprise a relatively small percentage of the predicates of which plural constructions can be subjects. In the class of multigrades are such ordinary predicates as "lifts," "panics," and "runs," as in "The fraternity boys lifted the Volkswagen," "The passengers on TWA Flight 25 panicked when told the pilot would try to land without the use of the forward landing gear," and "Arsenal soccer fans ran screaming down the street." In these examples the expressions "lifted," "panicked," and "ran" would be represented in logic by the same predicates those expressions would receive in "Gil lifted the drink," "Osgood panicked at the sight of blood," and "Tetley ran for cover." Plurality would be handled in another way. In effect, ordinary logic is not very congenial to the view that plural constructions, like "The Canby Saloon Crowd," are not singular terms.

Suppose that "The Canby Saloon Crowd" is a singular term. What does it denote? Naturally one wants to say that it could only denote the people listed earlier. Strictly speaking, however, that cannot be the case. The Canby Saloon Crowd and the people who make up the Canby Saloon Crowd are not identical. Gil and Osgood et al. depart, return to their own daily affairs, outlive the crowd. If the people on the list outlive the crowd, then the crowd cannot be identical with them, they will have the property of having outlived it and that is a property the crowd cannot have.

What is the identity of the crowd? It seems correct to say the the Canby Saloon Crowd denotes a sum-individual that happens to be comprised of a specific collection of seventeen people (those on our list). The identity of the Canby Saloon Crowd is that of an aggregate. Its identity rests in the aggregation not in the mere compilation. "The individuals who make up the Canby Saloon Crowd" does not denote the crowd, but "The Canby Saloon Crowd" does denote the collection of individuals whose names appear on our list.* Rather than individuating sum-individuals, in terms of objects having common parts, it is less complicated and not coun-

---

*The adoption of this version of one of the precepts of the calculus of individuals does not violate Goodman's principles of regional nominalism. Nelson Goodman, "A World of Individuals," in *Problems and Projects* (Indianapolis: Bobbs-Merrill, 1972) pp. 155–172. I shall not adopt the Leonard and Goodman account of sum-individuals in terms of the fusion relationship defined by discreteness. H. Leonard and N. Goodman, "The Calculus of Individuals and Its Uses," *Journal of Symbolic Logic* (1940), 5:45–56. Their theory depends upon a primitive discreteness idea that is far too broad to satisfy our ordinary intuitions about the identities of groups. No two things can be discrete if that means they must not share any properties. If they meet the requirement of not sharing all but one property, they must both have the property of not being identical to a third entity.

terintuitive, as Tyler Burge has argued,[3] to hold that an aggregate collectivity is the same just in case the same relevant component members are present and component members will always be individual persons. Hence, it will not matter if parts of those persons are different so long as we regard each individual person to be the same. If Osgood were to have a heart transplant, that will not affect the reidentification of the Canby Saloon Crowd, though, depending upon the way personal identity puzzle cases are handled, it may be significant if he were to have a brain transplant. Simply, the member-components of an aggregate collectivity are parts of that aggregate, but not all things that are parts of an aggregate collectivity are its member-components.

Aggregate collectivities are identical if their member-component lists are identical. The Canby Saloon Crowd and the Ox Bow lynch mob are the same just in case the same persons are member components of each sum-individual. This further reinforces our intuitive view that any change in membership constitutes a change in the identity of the aggregate collectivity.

In the seventeenth century Leibniz and Arnauld argued over the essence of aggregates and the relationship between aggregates and substances. Arnauld wrote to Leibniz:

> I see no drawback to believing that in the whole of corporeal nature there are only "machines" and "aggregates" of substances, because of none of these parts can one say, accurately speaking, that it is a single substance.[4]

Arnauld made this claim to support his view that spiritual substance, because it has a true unity, is "more excellent" than corporeal substance.

Ignoring the business about excellence of substance, it is instructive to read parts of Leibniz's response.

> *What constitutes the essence of an entity through aggregation is only a state of being of its constituent entities;* for example, what constitutes the essence of an army is only a state of being of the constituent men . . . Every machine presupposes some substance in the constituent parts . . . the plural presupposes the singular and where there is no entity still less will there be

> many entities . . . I have therefore thought that *I should be permitted to differentiate between entities through aggregation and substances, since the unity of these entities exists only in our mind* . . . If a machine is a substance, a circle of men holding hands will be too, and then an army, and finally every multiplicity of substances. I do not say that there is nothing substantial or nothing except appearances in things devoid of true unity, for *I grant that they always have as much reality or substantiality as there is true unity in what goes into their composition.*[5]

I have used italics to call attention to some important points in Leibniz's position. In his view, the essence of an aggregate collectivity is a state of being of its component membership, the state of their having been associated in a particular fashion or of associating in a certain way. The essence of the Canby Saloon Crowd is just that of being seventeen specific persons gathered in Canby's Saloon in the town of Bridger's Wells in Nevada on a particular day in the winter of 1885. On Leibniz's account the *sense* that there is a metaphysical unity that attaches to the use of the name "The Canby Saloon Crowd" is only a by-product of our way of conceiving of that collection of seventeen persons. That is not to say that there is anything imaginary about the aggregate collectivity. The crowd exists because its component members do, and insofar as they are real, substantial, entities so is the crowd.

Let us pursue these matters. Suppose we adopt the principle that "Necessarily, for any objects X and Y, if there is a possible world in which X and Y are distinct, then there is no world in which X is identical with Y."[6] Let us call this the Plantingan Principle, after its formulator. It will be consistent with Leibniz's view and demanded by the Plantingan Principle to argue that in every possible world in which there exists the Canby Saloon Crowd, there must also exist all seventeen persons on our list and they must associate. If we imagine a world in which Ma Grier does not exist and in which the other sixteen meet at the saloon and get into a brawl, we have not imagined a world in which the Canby Saloon Crowd exists. If Ma Grier does not exist, is not present at the relevant time, we simply have a different crowd. Each member-component of the crowd in the actual world (or rather the world we have described) temporally indexed to the focal event is essential to the identity of the crowd. Suppose that X represents the seventeen-member Canby Saloon Crowd and that Y stands for those persons who reside in Bridger's Wells and are in Canby's Saloon and participate in the brawl. Y has fifteen members. Their names are those on our list minus the names of the drifters, Gil and Croft. X and Y in the world we are describing are distinct, hence, using the Plantingan Principle, there is no world in which they are identical. The inclusion of another person or the exclusion of any member will create a different crowd. That does not mean that Tetley and his son Gerald will commit suicide after the brawl (as in the Clark novel they did after the lynching) and thus change the identity of the Canby Saloon Crowd. The membership is fixed at the time of formation, which, depending on our interests, may be when a focal event occurs.

The actions of the crowd, i.e., that it got into a destructive brawl, do not determine its identity. The property of having gotten into a brawl in Canby's Saloon is not essential to the Canby Saloon Crowd, but that focal event establishes a time frame in which an aggregate selection-exclusion principle operates across potential collectivity members. In effect, we use a selection principle that incorporates the description of a focal event to fix the referent of the name of the aggregate. Imagine things went differently, imagine that Sheriff Risley and Judge Tyler of Bridger's Wells arrive before the brawl begins, have a calming effect on the crowd, and it disperses. We are still talking about the Canby Saloon Crowd, that very group of people who got into a brawl in Canby's Saloon, when we say that they would not have brawled had the sheriff arrived sooner. In this way a focal event is worked into a selection principle that we utilize in fixing the referent of the name of the aggregate. We want to talk about the crowd that got into a brawl in Canby's Saloon, whatever crowd that was, that is the Canby Saloon Crowd. We might have been interested in the crowd that was harangued by Judge Tyler, whatever crowd that was. We might discover that the crowd that got into the brawl and the crowd that was harangued are one and the same crowd. Of course, having been harangued and having gotten into a brawl are only contingent properties of the aggregate, which is just to say that it makes sense to wonder what the crowd would have done if it had not had such properties. Imagine a scenario in which the crowd, because it is harangued by the judge, does not get into a brawl, and another in which it gets into a brawl and is not harangued, etc.

The selection-exclusion aspect of the referent fixing of the names of aggregates captures something of Leibniz's idea that the unity of aggregates exists in our minds. Such selection principles are products of someone's decision to identify a number of discrete individuals as a particular group. There may be purely reportorial reasons for doing so, or there may be business reasons. The unity of the aggregate has no other basis.

The selection principle that fixes the referent of the name and hence the membership of an aggregate collectivity certainly need not be indexed to a specific event. Suppose it has been said that the passengers on TWA Flight 25 panicked during the landing of the airplane. (The plane had a malfunction in the landing gear assembly.) The event that has drawn attention to the aggregate may play no important role with respect to fixing the membership of that aggregate. The selection principle might be: all persons who purchased tickets for Flight 25, entered the aircraft, and occupied seats on the plane on the specified day. Only those persons are the passengers on TWA Flight 25 on that day. It might be argued that the difference between this selection principle and the one used for the Canby Saloon Crowd is that in this case we have used an essential property of the aggregate. "The passengers on Flight 25," it may be maintained, necessarily denotes those persons who entered that aircraft and occupied seats on the flight. I do not think that is true. Consider: "The passengers on TWA Flight 25 missed the plane," that is, imagine a world in which, owing to a mistake on the schedules, the plane departs with only its crew on board, and the passengers, who arrive at the airport one hour later, are left frantically waving their tickets at the airline counter. Although the selection-exclusion principle may describe a focal event or some contingent property shared in the actual world by the component members, unless it is a membership list, it can only be used to fix the referent of the name of the aggregate. It will not be stating an essential property of the aggregate.

We commonly hear or read sentences like:

"The Gulf Oil Corporation joined a uranium cartel."

How ought the subject term be treated? Should our treatment of it be assimilated to that of the subject term of "The Canby Saloon Crowd dispersed after the brawl"? Are we not dealing again with a collection of people, albeit one that is highly organized compared to the Canby Saloon Crowd? It may be thought reasonable to interpret the "Gulf Oil Corporation" in this sentence as a singular term that denotes an aggregation. To do so, however, is inconsistent with deeper intuitions about corporate identity.

If we try to specify the component membership of the Gulf Oil Corporation at any moment in time, major difficulties arise. It is not just that the Gulf Oil Corporation has a large number of stockholders, executives, and employees that makes compilation of a list comparable to the Canby Saloon Crowd list difficult. It is that the Gulf Oil list will always be in a state of flux. Stock is bought and sold during exchange hours. Employees are fired, die, are hired, promoted, resign, quit, etc. The list of persons who are associated in a relevant way with the Gulf Oil Corporation at 10:00 A.M. EDT on Friday, October 7, 1983, will probably not be identical to the list of associated persons at 10:05 A.M. on the same day. Certainly we can expect that some shares of Gulf Oil Corporation stock changed hands. And it is possible that at least one employee quit, resigned, retired, was hired, was fired, or died in those five minutes.

Suppose two lists have been compiled; Gulf Oil Corporation List A will be the list at 10:00 A.M. on Friday, October 7, 1983, and List B will be the list for 10:05 A.M. on the same day. The same names appear on both lists with one exception. On List A there appears the name "Bernard J. Ortcutt" followed by the job description "clerk," but that name is not to be found on List B. Are we inclined to say that when we use the name "The Gulf Oil Corporation" at 10:05 A.M. it does not denote the same thing that we used it to pick out at 10:00 A.M.? Have we two different entities, (1) the Gulf Oil Corporation (List A) and (2) the Gulf Oil Corporation (List B), two different nonidentical corporations? I think not. And if that is correct, the existence of the corporate identity through time is rather indifferent to the shifting of the identities of those persons associated with it.

Consider the following sentence:

"The Gulf Oil Corporation would not have joined the uranium cartel if Ortcutt had not left the company."

Though it may be wondered how a mere clerk could have such an effect on company actions, that is of no interest here. Our interest is in the denotation of the subject term. The counter-to-fact claim is made about the Gulf Oil Corporation, and it is said that had one of the persons formally associated with it remained in his corporate position, the firm would have acted differently than it actually did. That seems straightforward enough, but if the Gulf Oil Corporation were an aggregate, this statement would be very problematic. It may be read as saying that there is a possible world in which the Gulf Oil Corporation exists, and Ortcutt still holds his position with the company. But if the Gulf Oil Corporation is an aggregate collectivity, there cannot be such a world. That is, it would make no sense to ask what the Gulf Oil Corporation would be like or would have done if one of the persons not associated with it in the actual world were to hold a position with it in another world, by reason of nonidentity of subject terms. But that is nonsense.

Clearly it does make sense to talk of the Gulf Oil Corporation if Ortcutt holds his position or loses it. Gulf Oil before and after Ortcutt, no matter what changes in corporate life that might occasion, is the same entity picked out by "Gulf Oil Corporation" in the actual world. That a particular person holds a particular position with a firm is a contingent property of the corporation. This strikes me as a rather startling finding, so when I had occasion to participate in constructing a survey of major corporate executives of the largest American companies, I included the question: "Would your corporation be essentially the same if you worked elsewhere?" The response was overwhelming, often expressed with regrets at the admission. The wide majority stated the corporation's identity would not be altered if they and their colleagues worked elsewhere.

Gulf Oil Corporation's joining an international uranium cartel violates U.S. antitrust law. Suppose the Justice Department brings charges against the corporation. Who would accept the defense that because Ortcutt is no longer with the corporation it is not the firm named in the litigation (and it is only a coincidence that the names of the two corporations are the same)? Even if five minutes after the cartel is joined, all of the senior executives of Gulf Oil resign and are replaced by other people, the firm named in the litigation is the same entity that joined the cartel. Such a "not the same person" plea is no defense for the corporation and not because replacement employees and executives are understood to have assumed a moral obligation to treat the effects of the actions of their predecessors as if they were their own. No such understanding normally exists, nor would we want to encourage the practice of exacting from every new executive the pledge to morally stand by the actions of his predecessor. In fact, an argument might be made that such a practice would run counter to our basic tenets of accountability.[7] The lesson is that "Gulf Oil Corporation" does not name an aggregate collectivity in either sentence. What then does the subject term of "The Gulf Oil Corporation joined a uranium cartel" denote?

It denotes an entity that is itself an individual; in fact, I think that in the relevant moral senses, as will be discussed in the next chapter, it may be shown to be a person. Counterfactual talk about the Gulf Oil Corporation is talk about that very corporation, so when we counterfactualize the actual list of those associated with the corporation, we are still talking about the Gulf Oil Corporation (not some other corporation that is very like it, but not quite). "Gulf Oil Corporation" is what Saul Kripke calls a "rigid designator" that picks out the same object in every world in which that object exists.[8] The proper names of persons are rigid designators and their conjunction is a rigid designator chain. Every rigid designator chain refers to the same objects and no others in every possible world. If we say that the Gulf Oil Corporation and a certain rigid designator chain ("X") both rigidly designate the same thing, as is done in an identity claim made between Gulf Oil Corporation and the list of its executives, employees, stockholders, etc., there can be no possible world or imaginable situation in which Gulf Oil Corporation is not X. However, there certainly can be such a world. We have imagined one in "The Gulf Oil Corporation would not have joined the uranium cartel if Ortcutt had not left the company." In fact, there can be a world in which none of the persons designated by "X" exist, though the Gulf Oil Corporation exists.

Gulf Oil Corporation cannot be identified with the aggregation of the persons who are associated with it. This account does not violate Leibniz's Law, assuming we allow for indexing of properties to times and worlds (for any X and any Y, if X is identical to Y, then for any property P, any world W and any time t, X has P in W at t if and only if Y has P in W at t). If P is the property of having Ortcutt as a clerk in the actual world at 10:00 A.M. EDT on Friday, October 7, 1983, then it will be true that the Gulf Oil Corporation at both 10:00 A.M. and at 10:05 A.M. has P. Furthermore, we can imagine a world in which the Gulf Oil Corporation exists, and all of the persons picked out by X exist and are employed by Ralph Nader. Using the Plantingan Principle, there is no world in which the Gulf Oil Corporation is identical with X. The same may be said, of course, for any other rigid designator chain that picks out the people associated with the Gulf Oil Corporation at any other time.

CHAPTER THREE

The Corporation as a Moral Person

In his *New York Times* column, Tom Wicker expressed his aroused ire at a Gulf Oil Corporation advertisement that "pointed the finger of blame" for energy shortages and high prices at virtually every element of our society except the oil companies. Wicker, as might be expected, attacked Gulf Oil and the petroleum industry as the major, if not the sole, perpetrators of that crisis and most every other social ill, with the possible exception of venereal disease.

In a courtroom in Winamac, Indiana, in 1979–80, the Ford Motor Company was tried for reckless homicide in the deaths of Judy, Lyn, and Donna Ulrich. The three teenagers were incinerated when the Ford Pinto in which they were driving was hit in the rear at a speed differential of around thirty miles per hour. One of the law professors who worked as a consultant for the prosecution recently wrote: "What we were saying is that a corporation like all other persons must be forced at times to look at the very personal tragedies it causes."[1] The prosecution's case was directed at demonstrating the moral and criminal capacity for responsibility of the Ford Motor Company. No attempt was made to prosecute individual Ford executives or engineers. We need not concern ourselves with whether Wicker was serious or merely sarcastic when he made his charges against Gulf. Most certainly the prosecution in the Pinto case was serious and, although Ford Motor Company was acquitted of the charges, the concept of corporate moral and legal responsibility was not discredited. Indeed, it was provided with a landmark of courtroom precedent and popular acceptance. (The status of corporations under the criminal code is discussed in chapter

13.) I have shown in the previous chapters that corporations are not just organized crowds of people, that they have a metaphysical-logical identity that does not reduce to a mere sum of human-being members. In this chapter I will examine the sense ascriptions of moral responsibility make when their subjects are corporations. I hope to provide the foundation of a theory that allows treatment of corporations as full-fledged members of the moral community, of equal standing with the traditionally acknowledged residents: human beings. With such a theory in hand we should treat moral-responsibility ascriptions to corporations as unexceptionable instances of a perfectly proper sort and not have to paraphrase or reduce them. Corporations as moral persons will have whatever privileges, rights and duties as are, in the normal course of affairs, accorded to all members of the moral community.

It is important to distinguish three quite different notions of what is it to be a person that are frequently entangled throughout the various aspects of our tradition: the metaphysical, moral, and legal concepts of personhood. The entanglement is clearly evident in John Locke's account of personal identity. He writes that the term "person" is "a *forensic* term, appropriating actions and their merit; and so belongs only to *intelligent agents*, capable of law, and happiness, and misery." He goes on to say that by consciousness and memory persons are capable of extending themselves into the past and thereby become "concerned and *accountable*."[2] Locke is historically correct in citing the law as a primary origin of the term "person." But he is incorrect in maintaining that its legal usage entails its metaphysical sense, agency; and whether or not either sense, but especially the metaphysical, is interdependent on the moral sense, accountability, is surely controversial.

There are two distinct schools of thought regarding the relationship between metaphysical and moral persons. According to one, to be a metaphysical person is only to be a moral one; to understand what it is to be accountable, one must understand what it is to be an intentional or a rational agent and vice versa. According to the other, being an intentional agent is a necessary but not a sufficient condition of being a moral person. Locke appears to hold the interdependence view, with which I agree, but he roots both moral and metaphysical persons in the juristic person, which is, I think, wrongheaded. The preponderance of current thinking in moral and social theory, however, endorses some version of the necessary precondition view. Most of those holding such a position do exhibit the virtue of treating legal personhood as something apart from moral and metaphysical matters.

It is of note that many contemporary moral philosophers and economists both defend a precondition view of the relationship between the metaphysical and moral person and also adopt a view of the legal personhood of corporations that excludes corporations per se from the class of moral persons. Such philosophers and economists tend to champion the least defensible of a number of possible interpretations of the juristic personhood of corporations, but their doing so allows them to systematically sidestep the question of whether corporations can meet the conditions of metaphysical personhood.[3]

John Rawls is, to some extent, guilty of fortifying what I hope to show is an indefensible interpretation of the legal concept and of thereby encouraging an anthropocentric bias that has led to the general belief that corporations just cannot be moral persons. As is well known, Rawls defends his two principles of justice by the use of a thought experiment that incorporates the essential characteristics of what he takes to be a premoral, though metaphysical population and then derives the moral guidelines for social institutions that they would accept. The persons (or parties) in the "original position" are described by Rawls as being mutually self-interested, rational, as having similar wants, needs, interests, and capacities and as being, for all intents and purposes, equal in power (so that no one of them can dominate the others). Their choice of the principles of justice is, as Daniel Dennett has pointed out,[4] a rather dramatic rendering of one version of the compelling (though I think unnecessarily complex) philosophical thesis that only out of metaphysical persons can moral ones evolve.

But Rawls is remarkably ambiguous (and admittedly so) regarding who or what may qualify as a metaphysical person. He admits into the category, in one sentence, not only biological human beings but "nations, provinces, business firms, churches, teams, and so on," then, perhaps because he does not want to tackle the demonstration of the rationality of those institutions and organizations, or because he is a captive of the traditional prejudice in favor of biological persons, in the next sentence he withdraws entry. "There is, perhaps, a certain logical priority to the case of human individuals: it may be possible to analyze the actions of so-called artificial persons as logical constructions of the actions of human persons. . . ."[5] "Perhaps" is, of course, a rather large hedge behind which to hide; but it is, I suppose, of some significance that in *A Theory of Justice* when he is listing the nature of the parties in the "original position" he adds as item c "associations (states, churches, or other corporate bodies)."[6] He does not, unfortunately, discuss this entry on his list anywhere else in the book. Rawls had hold, I think, of an important intuition: that some associations of human beings should be treated as metaphysical persons capable, on his account, of becoming moral persons, in and of themselves. He shrunk, however, from the task of exploring the implications of that intuition and instead retreated to the comfortable bulwarks of the anthropocentric bias.

Many philosophers, including (I think) Rawls, have rather uncritically relied upon what they incorrectly perceive to be the most defensible juristic treatment of corporations as a paradigm for the treatment of corporations in their moral theories. The concept of corporate legal personhood under any of its popular interpretations is, I want to argue, virtually useless for moral purposes.

Following a number of writers on jurisprudence, a juristic person may be defined as any entity that is a subject of a right. There are good etymological grounds for such an inclusive neutral definition. The Latin *persona* originally referred to *dramatis personae*, but in Roman law the term was adopted to refer to anything that could act on either side of a legal dispute. (It was not until Boethius' definition of a person: *"Persona est naturae rationabilis individua substantia"* [a person is the individual subsistence of a rational nature] that metaphysical traits were ascribed to persons.)

In effect, in Roman legal tradition persons are creations or artifacts of the law itself, i.e., of the legislature that enacts the law,
and are not considered to have, or only have incidentally, existence of any kind outside of the legal sphere. The law, on the Roman interpretation, is systematically ignorant of the biological status of its subjects.

The Roman notion applied to corporations is popularly known
as the Fiction Theory. Frederick Hallis characterizes that theory
as maintaining that "the personality of a corporate body is a pure
fiction and owes its existence to a creative act of the state."[7] Rawls'
view of corporate persons, however, is not a version of the Fiction
Theory. The theory draws no dichotomy between real and artificial persons. All juristic persons, on the theory, are creations of
the law. The Fiction Theory does not view the law as recognizing
or verifying prelegally existing persons; it maintains that the law
creates all of its own subjects. Second, the theory, in its pure form
at least, does not regard any juristic persons as composites. All things
which are legislatively created as subjects of rights are nonreducible or, if you will, primitive individual legal persons. (It is of some
note that the Fiction Theory is enshrined in English law in regard
to corporate bodies by no less an authority than Sir Edward Coke,
who wrote that corporations "rest only in intendment and consideration of the law."[8]

The Fiction Theory's major rival in American jurisprudence and
the view that does seem to inform Rawls' account is what I shall
call the Legal Aggregate Theory of the Corporation. It holds that
the names of corporate organizations are only umbrellas that cover
(but do not shield) a specific aggregate of biological persons. The
Aggregate Theory allows that biological status has legal priority and
that a corporation is but a contrivance, the name of which is best
used for summary reference. (Aggregate Theorists tend to ignore
employees and identify corporations with directors, executives, and
stockholders. The model on which they stake their claim is no doubt
that of the primitive partnership.) As we have seen in the previous
chapter, to treat a corporation as an aggregate for any purpose is
to fail to recognize crucial logical and metaphysical differences between corporations and crowds.

It might prove of some value in clarifying the dispute between the Fiction and Aggregate theorists to mention a famous case in the English law. It is that of *Continental Tyre and Rubber Co., Ltd. v. Daimler Co. Ltd.* The Continental Tyre Company was incorporated in England. Its business was the selling in England of tires made in Germany, and all of its directors were German subjects in residence in Germany, and all but one of its shares were held by German subjects. The case arose during the First World War, and it turned on the issue of whether the company was an English subject by virtue of its being incorporated under the English law and independent of its directors and stockholders. Hence, it could bring suit in an English court against an English subject while a state of war existed. The majority opinion of the Court of Appeals (5-1) was that the corporation was an entity created by statute and hence was "a different person altogether from the subscribers to the memorandum or the shareholders on the register."[9] Hallis aptly summarizes the judgment of the court when he writes that "The Continental Tyre and Rubber Co., Ltd. was an English company with a personality at law distinct from the personalities of its members and could therefore sue in the English Courts as a British Subject."[10] The House of Lords, however, supporting the Aggregate Theory and no doubt motivated by the demands of the war, overturned the Court of Appeals. Lord Buckley wrote, "The artificial legal entity has no independent power of motion. It is moved by the corporator. . . . He is German in fact although British in form."[11] This view has seen many incarnations since on both sides of the Atlantic. I take Rawls' burying of his intuition in the logical priority of human beings as a recent echoing of the words of Lord Parker, who in the Continental Tyre case wrote for the majority in the House of Lords: ". . . the character in which the property is held and the character in which the capacity to act is enjoyed and acts are done are not *in pari materia*. The latter character is a quality of the company itself, and conditions its capacities and its acts and is attributable only to human beings. . . ."[12]

The third major rival interpretation of corporate juristic personhood resides in Germanic legal tradition. Primarily because of the advocacy of Otto von Gierke, the so-called Reality Theory recognizes corporations to be prelegal existing sociological persons. Underlying the theory is the view that law cannot create its subjects; it can only determine which societal facts are in conformity with its requirements. Law endorses the prelegal existence of persons for its own purposes. Gierke regards the corporation as an offspring of certain social actions and as having a de facto personality, which the law declares to be a juridical fact.[13] The Reality Theory's primary virtue is that it does not ignore the nonlegal roots of the corporation while it, as may the Fiction Theory, acknowledges the nonidentity of the corporation and the aggregate of its directors, stockholders, executives, and employees. The primary difference between the Fiction and Reality Theories, that one treats the corporate person as de jure and the other as de facto, turns out to be of no real importance, however, in regard to the issue of the moral personhood of a corporation. Admittedly the Reality Theory encapsulates a view at least superficially more amenable to arguing for discrete corporate moral personhood than does the Fiction Theory just because it does acknowledge de facto personhood, but theorists on both sides will admit that they are providing interpretations of only the formula "juristic person = the subject of rights," and as long as we stick to legal history, no interpretation of that formula need concern itself with metaphysical personhood or intentional agency. The de facto personhood of the Reality Theory is that of a sociological entity only, of which no claim is or need be made regarding agency, or rationality, or any of the traits of a metaphysical person. One could, without contradiction, hold the Reality Theory and deny the metaphysical or moral personhood of corporations. What is needed is a Reality Theory that identifies a de facto metaphysical person not just a sociological entity.

Underlying all of these interpretations of corporate legal personhood is a distinction, embedded in the law itself, that renders them unhelpful for our purposes. Being a subject of rights is often contrasted in the law with being an administrator of rights. Any number of entities and associations can and have been the subjects of legal rights. In earlier times, animals have been given legal rights; legislatures have given rights to unborn human beings; they have reserved rights for human beings long after their death; and in some recent cases they have invested rights in generations of the future. Of course such recipients of rights, though, strictly speaking, legal persons, cannot dispose of their rights. They also cannot administer them, because to administer a right one must be an intentional agent, i.e., able to *act* in certain ways. It may be only an historical accident that most legal cases are cases in which "the subject of right X" and "the administrator of right X" are coreferential. It is nowhere required by law, not under any of the three theories just discussed or elsewhere, that it be so. Yet, it is possession of the attributes of an administrator of rights and not those of a subject of rights that constitutes the generally accepted conditions of moral personhood. It is a fundamental mistake to regard the fact of juristic corporate personhood as having settled the question of the moral personhood of a corporation one way or the other.

Two helpful lessons are learned from the investigation of the legal personhood of corporations: (1) biological existence is not essentially associated with the concept of personhood (only the fallacious Aggregate Theory depends upon reduction to biological beings), and (2) a paradigm for the form of an inclusive neutral definition of a moral person is provided: a subject of a right. I shall define a moral person as the referent of any proper name or of any noneliminatable subject in an ascription of moral responsibility. The noneliminatable nature of the subject should be stressed because responsibility and other predicates of morality are neutral as regards person and person-sum predication.[14] I argued in the first chapter that ascriptions of moral responsibility involve the notions of accountability and being held liable for an answer. These notions presuppose the existence of responsibility relationships, and one of their primary foci is on the subject's intentions. To be the subject of an ascription of moral responsibility, to be a party in responsibility relationships, hence to be a moral person, the subject must be at minimum an intentional actor.[15] If corporations are moral persons they will evidence a noneliminatable intentionality with regard to the things they do.

For a corporation to be treated as a moral person, it must be the case that some events are describable in a way that makes certain sentences true: sentences that say that some of the things a corporation does were intended by the corporation itself. That is not accomplished if attributing intentions to a corporation is only a shorthand way of attributing intentions to the biological persons who comprise, e.g., its board of directors. If that were to turn out to be the case, then on metaphysical if not logical grounds, there would be no real way to distinguish between corporations and crowds. I shall argue, however, that a Corporation's Internal Decision Structure (its CID Structure) provides the requisite redescription device that licenses the predication of corporate intentionality.

Intentionality, though a causal notion, is an intensional one, and so it does not mark out a class of actions or events. Attributions of intentionality with regard to any event are referentially opaque with respect to other descriptions of that event. In other words, when described in one way an event is an intentional action, but that does not entail that on every other true description of the event it will be intentional. A great deal depends upon how the event is described. It is true, for example, that Hamlet intentionally killed the person hiding in Gertrude's room, but not true that Hamlet intentionally killed Polonius, although Polonius was the person hiding in Gertrude's room. The event may be properly described as "Hamlet killed Polonius" and also as "Hamlet intentionally killed the person hiding in Gertrude's room (behind the arras)," but it would be wrong to say "Hamlet intentionally killed Polonius." That was not Hamlet's intention. He thought he was killing the King. I shall presently argue that the referential opacity of attributions of intentionality drives a wedge between descriptions of certain events as individual intentional actions and as corporate intentional actions.

Certain events can be described simply as the bodily movements of human beings and sometimes those same events are redescribable in terms of their upshots, as bringing about something, e.g., (from Austin) feeding penguins *by* throwing them peanuts ("by" is the most common way we connect different descriptions of the same event),[16] and sometimes those same upshots can be redescribed as the effects of some prior cause; then they are described as done for reasons, done in order to bring about something, e.g., feeding the penguins peanuts in order to kill them. When we are interested in intentionality, what we single out as that prior cause is some desire combined with the belief that the object of the desire will be achieved by the action undertaken. (This, I think, is what Aristotle meant when he maintained that acting requires desire.) Saying "someone did *y* intentionally" is to describe an event as the upshot of that person's having had a reason for doing *y* which was the cause of his or her doing it.

The important point is that metaphysical personhood depends on the possibility of describing an event as an intentional action. Often a single event can be correctly described in a number of different and nonequivent ways. With respect to some events, there are layers of nonintersubstitutable true descriptions. Some layers merely describe the event as a movement or a piece of behavior. Other layers describe the same event as the effect of prior causes that are reasons or desires and beliefs. Significantly, a single event may be described as the effect of different sets of reasons, even of different kinds of reasons, so there may be more than one layer of true descriptions of an event at which it is appropriate to identify it as an intentional action. At every layer at which it is proper to describe an event as an intentional action, there is a metaphysical person, an actor.

Certainly a corporation's doing something involves or includes human beings doing things, and the human beings who occupy various positions in a corporation usually can be described as having reasons for *their* behavior. In fact, in virtue of those descriptions, they may be properly held responsible for their behavior, ceteris paribus. What needs to be shown if there is to be corporate responsibility is that there is sense in saying that corporations and not just the people who work in them have reasons for doing what they do. Typically, we will be told that corporate reasons are to be identified with the reasons and desires of the directors or of certain high-level managers and that, although corporate action may not be reducible without remainder, corporate intentions are always reducible to such executive intentions. Such a view is, in fact, captured in English legal precedent, specifically in the 1971 case of *Tesco Supermarkets Ltd. v. Nattcass*. The supermarket company was charged under a section of the Trade Descriptions Act of 1968. The case involved false price advertising. An assistant had replaced reduced-priced soap boxes with those marked at regular prices. The assistant did not notify the store manager who is responsible for seeing that sales items were properly priced. The manager failed to check the pricing on his own. The company argued that it had exercised due diligence and that the negligence was that of a person too far down in the corporate hierarchy to be identified with the intentions of the corporation itself. The House of Lords found in the company's favor, thereby endorsing the idea that corporate reasons are the reasons of senior executive staff members. Such a view, I shall argue, is not adequate to the understanding of corporate intentionality. It should, however, be strikingly plain that finding directorial negligence, for example, is not necessarily finding corporate negligence. If an underling can act for personal, self-serving reasons, so can a director, and his doing so may have nothing to do with the corporation's business practices. In fact those practices may make his self-serving possible by creating a climate of trust and honesty in which he can operate.

Every corporation has an internal decision structure. CID Structures have two elements of interest to us here: (1) an organizational or responsibility flowchart that delineates stations and levels within the corporate power structure and (2) corporate-decision recognition rule(s) (usually embedded in something called corporation policy). The CID Structure is the personnel organization for the exercise of the corporation's power with respect to its ventures, and as such its primary function is to draw experience from various levels of the corporation into a decision-making and ratification process. When operative and properly activated, the CID Structure accomplishes a subordination and synthesis of the intentions and acts of various biological persons into a corporate decision. When viewed in another way, as already suggested, the CID Structure licenses the descriptive transformation of events, seen under another aspect as the acts of biological persons (those who occupy various stations on the organizational chart), to corporate acts by exposing the corporate character of those events. A CID Structure *incorporates* acts of biological persons. For illustrative purposes, suppose we imagine that an event E has at least two aspects, that is, can be described in two nonidentical ways. One of those aspects is "Executive X's doing y" and one is "Corporation C's doing z." The corporate act and the individual act may have different properties; indeed they have different causal ancestors, though they are causally inseparable. (I hope to show that the causal inseparability of these acts is a product of the CID Structure: X's doing y is not the cause of C's doing z; nor is C's doing z the cause of X's doing y; although if X's doing y causes event F, then C's doing z causes F and vice versa.)

J. K. Galbraith rather neatly captures what I have in mind, although I doubt he is aware of the metaphysical reading that can be given to this process, when he writes in his recent popular book on the history of economics: "From [the] interpersonal exercise of power, the interaction . . . of the participants, comes the *personality* of the corporation." [17] I take Galbraith here to be quite literally correct, but it is important to spell out how a CID Structure works this miracle.

In philosophy in recent years we have grown accustomed to the use of games as models for understanding institutional behavior. We all have some understanding of how rules in games make certain descriptions of events possible, which would not be so if those rules were nonexistent. The CID Structure of a corporation is a kind of constitutive rule (or rules) analogous to the game rules with which we are familiar. The organization chart of a corporation distinguishes players and clarifies their rank and the interwoven lines of responsibility within the corporation. An organizational chart tells us, for example, that anyone holding the title "Executive vice-president for finance administration" stands in a certain relationship to anyone holding the title "director of internal audit" and to anyone holding the title "treasurer," etc. In effect it expresses, or maps, the interdependent and dependent relationships, line and staff, that are involved in determinations of corporate decisions and actions. The organizational chart provides what might be called the grammar of corporate decision-making. What I shall call internal recognition rules provide its logic.

By "recognition rule(s)" I mean what Hart, in another context, calls "conclusive affirmative indication," that a decision on an act has been made or performed for corporate reasons.[18] Recognition rules are of two sorts. Partially embedded in the organizational chart are procedural recognitors: We see that decisions are to be reached collectively at certain levels and that they are to be ratified at higher levels (or at inner circles, if one prefers that Galbraithean model). A corporate decision is recognized internally, however, not only by the procedure of its making, but by the policy it instantiates. Hence every corporation creates an image (not to be confused with its public image) or a general policy, what G. C. Buzby of the Chilton Company has called the "basic belief of the corporation," that must inform its decisions for them to be properly described as being those of that corporation. "The moment policy is side-stepped or violated, it is no longer the policy of that company."[19]

Peter Drucker has seen the importance of the basic policy recognitors in the CID Structure (though he treats matters rather differently from the way I am recommending). Drucker writes:

> Because the corporation is an institution it must have a basic policy. For it must subordinate individual ambitions and decisions to the *needs* of the corporation's welfare and survival. That means that it must have a set of principles and a rule of conduct which limit and direct individual actions and behavior.[20]

Suppose, for illustrative purposes, we activate a CID Structure in a corporation, Tom Wicker's whipping boy, the Gulf Oil Corporation. Imagine that three executives, Jones, Smith, and Jackson have the task of deciding whether or not Gulf Oil will join a world uranium cartel. They have before them an Everest of papers that have been prepared by lower-echelon executives. Some of the papers will be purely factual reports, some will be contingency plans, some will be formulations of positions developed by various departments, some will outline financial considerations, and some will be legal opinions. Insofar as these will all have been processed through Gulf's CID Structure system, the personal reasons, if any, individual executives may have had for writing their reports and recommendations in a specific way will likely have been diluted by the subordination of individual inputs to peer group input and higher level review and recommendation before Jones, Smith, and Jackson deal with the matter. A vote is taken, as is authorized procedure in the Gulf CID Structure, which is to say that under these circumstances the vote of Jones, Smith, and Jackson can be redescribed as the corporation's making a decision: that is, the event "Jones, Smith, and Jackson voting" may be redescribed to expose an aspect otherwise unrevealed, quite different from its other aspects, e.g., from Jones' (or Smith's or Jackson's) voting in the affirmative. Redescriptive exposure of a procedurally corporate aspect of an event is not to be confused with a description of an event that makes true a sentence that says that the corporation did something intentionally. But the CID Structure, as already suggested, also provides the grounds in its other type of recognitor for such an attribution of corporate intentionality. Simply, when the corporate act is consistent with an instantiation or an implementation of established corporate policy, then it is proper to describe it as having been done for corporate reasons, as having been caused by a corporate desire coupled with a corporate belief and so, in other words, as corporate intentional.

An event may, under one of its aspects, be described as the conjunctive act "Jones intentionally voted yes, and Smith intentionally voted yes, and Jackson did so as well" (where a "yes" vote was to vote in the affirmative on the question of Gulf Oil joining the cartel). Within the Gulf CID Structure we find the conjunction of rules that tell us that when the occupants of positions *A*, *B*, and *C* on the organizational chart unanimously vote to do something that is consistent with an instantiation or an implementation of general corporate policy and ceteris paribus, Gulf Oil Corporation has decided to do it for corporate reasons. The event of those executives voting is then redescribable as "the Gulf Oil Corporation decided to join the cartel for reasons consistent with basic policy of Gulf Oil, e.g., increasing profits," or simply as "Gulf

Oil Corporation intentionally decided to join the cartel." This is a rather technical way of saying that in these circumstances the executives voting is, given its CID Structure, also the corporation deciding to do something. Regardless of the personal reasons the executives have for voting as they do, and even if their reasons are inconsistent with established corporate policy or even if one of them has no reason at all for voting as he does, the corporation still has reasons for joining the cartel, that is, joining is consistent with the inviolate corporate general policies, as encrusted in the precedent of previous corporate actions, and its statements of purpose as recorded in its certificate of incorporation, annual reports, etc. The corporation's only method of achieving its desires or goals is the activation of the personnel who occupy its various positions. However, if Jones voted affirmatively purely for reasons of personal monetary gain (suppose she had been bribed to do so) that does not alter the fact that the corporate reason for joining the cartel was to minimize competition and hence pay higher dividends to its shareholders. Corporations have reasons because they have interests in doing those things that are likely to result in realization of their established corporate goals, regardless of the transient self-interest of directors or managers. If there is a difference between corporate goals and desires and those of human beings, it is probably that the corporate ones are relatively stable and not very wide ranging, but that is only because corporations can do relatively fewer things than human beings, being confined in action predominantly to a limited socioeconomic sphere. It is, of course, in a corporation's interest that its component membership views the corporate purposes as instrumental in the achievement of their own goals. (Financial reward is the most common way this is achieved.)

It will be objected that a corporation's policies reflect only the current goals of its directors. But that is certainly not logically necessary nor is it in practice true for most large corporations. Usually, of course, the original incorporators will have organized to further their individual interests and/or to meet goals which they shared. But even in infancy the melding of disparate interests and purposes gives rise to a corporate long-range point of view that is distinct from the interests and purposes of the incorporators viewed individually. Also, corporate basic purposes and policies, as already mentioned, tend to be relatively stable and are not generally couched in the kind of language appropriate to individual purposes. Furthermore, as histories of corporations will show, when policies are amended or altered, it is usually only peripheral issues that are involved. Radical policy alteration constitutes a new corporation, a point that is captured in the incorporation laws of such states as Delaware. ("Any power which is not enumerated in the charter and the general law or which cannot be inferred from these two sources is ultra vires of the corporation.") Obviously underlying the objection is an uneasiness about the fact that corporate intent is dependent upon policies and purposes that are products of the sociopsychology of a group of biological persons. Corporate intent seems somehow to be a tarnished illegitimate offspring of human intent. But this objection is another form of the anthropocentric bias. By concentrating on the layers of descriptions of events and by acknowledging only that the possibility of describing something as an agent depends upon whether or not it can be properly described as having done something (the description of some aspect of an event) for a reason, we avoid the temptation to look for extensional criteria. The world made at the layer of description relevant to corporate decision-making is populated by intentional actors that are not all of the same biological species. Indeed, a significant subset of the class of metaphysical persons has no biological entities as members.

The CID Structure licenses both redescriptions of events as corporate and attributions of corporate intentionality, while it does not obscure the private acts of executives, directors, etc. Although Jones voted to support the joining of the cartel because she was bribed to do so, Jones did not join the cartel, Gulf Oil Corporation joined the cartel. Consequently, we may say that Jones did something for which she should be held morally responsible, yet whether or not Gulf Oil Corporation should be held morally responsible for joining the cartel is a question that turns on issues that may be unrelated to Jones' having accepted a bribe.

Of course Gulf Oil Corporation cannot join the cartel unless Jones or somebody who occupies position A on the organizational chart votes in the affirmative. What that shows, however, is that corporations are organizations or associations including human beings. That should not, however, rule out the possibility of their having metaphysical status, as being intentional actors in their own right, and being thereby full-fledged moral persons.

This much I hope is clear: we can describe many events in terms of certain physical movements of human beings, and we also can sometimes describe those very events as done for reasons by those human beings, but further we can sometimes describe the same events as corporate and still further as done for corporate reasons that are qualitatively different from whatever personal reasons component members may have for doing what they do.

Corporate agency resides in the possibility of CID Structure licensed redescription of events as corporate intentional. That may still appear to be downright mysterious, although I do not think it is, for human agency as I have suggested, resides in the possibility of description as well.

CHAPTER FOUR

Corporate Internal Decision Structures

In chapter 3 I sketched an account of the primary aspects of Corporate Internal Decision Structures (CID Structures). I distinguished the three elements that constitute a CID Structure: an organizational or responsibility flowchart; and the two types of corporate decision recognition rules—procedural rules and policies.

Organizational, i.e., decision flowcharts identify stations and managerial levels and plot the lines of authority, subordination, and dependence among and between such stations within the corporation. An organizational grid sheet formalizes the grammar of corporate decision-making. My use of the term "grammar" here is not totally idiosyncratic. What I mean by it is not unlike what Wittgenstein seems to have had in mind when he said that grammatical propositions were "pieces of instruction" and that "Grammar tells what kind of object anything is." Grammatical propositions, as Wittgenstein saw them, are generally about two distinct though related things: (1) what it makes sense to say in what circumstances, what can sensibly be related or combined to what in certain kinds of circumstances, what kind of questions, exclamations, assertions, etc., can be sensibly made under what conditions; and (2) what things are called (the proper use of names, phrases, or descriptions.[1] That the pieces on the ends of the back row of the chess board at the start of the game are rooks is a part of the grammar of the game of chess or, another example from Wittgenstein, "The colour octahedron is grammar, since it says that you can speak of a reddish blue but not of a reddish green, etc."[2]

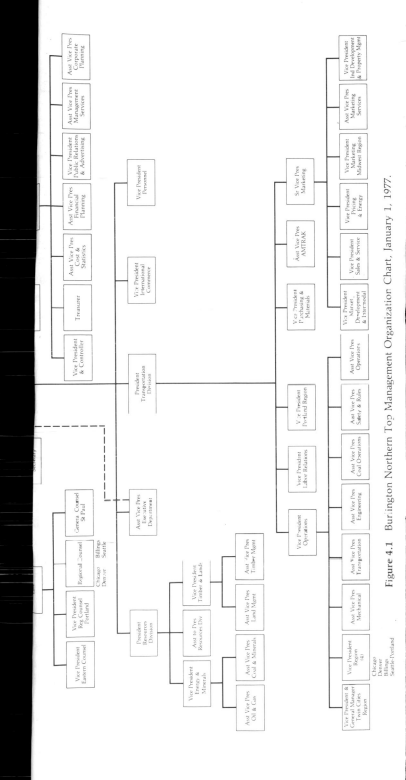

Figure 4.1 Burlington Northern Top Management Organization Chart, January 1, 1977.

In the standard
corporate organizati
in the literature of
mar of a corporatic
a fashion that is, ir
octahedron. One ca
ganizational chart (
number of significa
structure of that co
see that the general
presidents, one of
regional counsel fro
ident for law. Decis
that vice-president':
sponsible only to t
through him to the l
to the general operat
authority does not d
does he report to the
ident in conjunction
rector of internal au
nance and administr
beneath the chairmai

All of this is, of cc
able. Unfortunately,
large corporation will
large decentralized cc
charts. In order to ma
the facts, we should
of its grammar. Freq
organizations, and al
blessing of the organi
ways in decision-mak
structure runs along p
and plays at least as s
ments of the firm as d

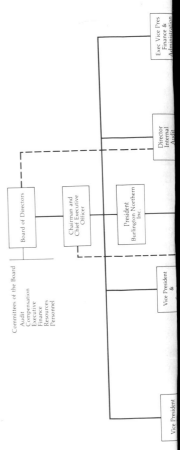

we cannot allow ourselves too much freedom with regard to organizational grammar. Even though meetings in the fifth-floor lavatory between the vice-president for public relations and advertising and the assistant vice-president for marketing services may be productive of a number of agreements about how promotional material ought to be distributed, until those agreements have withstood the scrutiny and received the endorsement of the vice-presidents for marketing, under the chair of the senior vice-president for marketing and, if required, been referred to the next level of management either for information or action, they are not decisions of that corporation.

The corporate officers within the scope of their discretion may vest decision-making powers in a particular officer with regard to certain kinds of actions. The assigned officer will then have a degree of discretion to proceed without further ratification. He may decide to pursue certain approaches or to act in certain ways because he has talked about the relevant issues with a friend who holds an office in quite a different department or level of management. That is to be expected. The key point is that the chart clarifies the authority of the actual decision-maker and, of course, identifies the levels and offices to which he must report, to whom or which he is responsible, and from whom or which he may expect the credit or the blame, the reward or the punishment after the actions have occurred. These responsibility entanglements as represented on the flowchart partially ensure the corporate character of actions taken, policies and procedures adopted. If, as some corporation watchers would have us believe, the published organizational chart in many corporations is an elaborate charade, and everyone who matters in the corporate decision structure is well aware of a phantom, i.e., unpublished, network, and decisions, and actions are carried out in accord with the phantom and not the published structure, then it is the phantom that is real and provides the grammar of that corporation's decision-making. The existence of an active nonformalized decision-making structure that operates in the stead of what may be an archaic formalized structure in no way affects the point of my analysis. The organizational chart that actually portrays the grammar of the organization's decision-making is all that is required. If such a chart is not to be found in the corporate literature but is rather a matter of common knowledge in the firm, anyone seeking to understand the corporate decision-making of that firm will have to construct the operative chart. Doing so would be rather easier than constructing a translation manual for a previously unknown language, such as Linear B, but some of the classic translation problems may crop up during the attempt to chart the process. The organizational chartographer, of course, has a great advantage over the radical translator: he is generally able to communicate in a common language with the managers who participate in actual decision-making in the corporation. Nonetheless, it may be instructive to think of his task along translation lines.

The recognition rules, however, are equally essential to the identification of a corporate act as the act of a particular corporation.

The idea of a rule of recognition is borrowed from H. L. A. Hart's version of legal positivism.[3] For Hart, a recognition rule is a fundamental secondary rule in a legal system that ultimately determines what laws are valid in that system. In other words, a demonstration of the validity of any law is incomplete if it does not terminate in the citation of a rule of recognition. To show that a law is valid one may need to uncover a chain of validity back to the basic recognition rule of the system. Ronald Dworkin provides a clear account of what Hart has in mind. Dworkin writes:

> A parking ordinance of the city of New Haven is valid because it is adopted by a city council, pursuant to the procedures and within the competence specified by the municipal law adopted by the state of Connecticut, in conformity with the procedures and within the competence specified by the state of Connecticut, which was in turn adopted consistently with the requirements of the United States Constitution.[4]

Rules of recognition or at least the ultimate rules of recognition are not valid because they cannot pass the test of conformity contained in a more fundamental rule. Their role in the system depends, for Hart, on their general acceptance by those who fall under the legal system. I am not here interested in whether Dworkin's criticisms of Hart's account of recognition rules are cogent. Rather, what Hart has said about the role of recognition rules translates rather neatly to the corporate scene. By my account, recognition rules within the Corporate Internal Decision Structure determine and justify the corporate intentional character of corporate actions. They warrant the identification of particular decisions as corporate, but they cannot be justified. That a rule is a recognition rule of a CID Structure is a factual matter. We find out what rules of recognition are in place within its CID Structure by consulting the basic operational documents and written policies of a corporation.

A positivistic account of rules of recognition creates no major difficulties for our account. In fact, we could hardly expect anything else. Corporations, like legal systems, are inventions, artifacts. Their basic recognition rules will necessarily be constructed by those who create those corporations just as the Constitution of the United States was the creation of the delegates to the Constitutional Convention of 1787. Acceptance within the corporation can be determined both by a dispositional study of managerial personnel and an analysis of the operational principles and policies that are contained in such published sources as annual statements, codes and policies for employees, and business principles memoranda.

I do not think that much needs to be said regarding procedural recognitors. Corporations have established specific procedural rules for the making of corporate decisions. Unless those rules have been satisfied, actions taken cannot be regarded as corporate actions of that firm. (I leave ambiguous whether the actions in question must always be done as a following of the rules or only as according to the rules. An action's according with a rule is, of course, not necessarily the same as its having been the upshot of following that rule.) In this regard the situation is almost perfectly analogous to the way procedural rules function in games, e.g., the rule of alternating play in chess or the rule that a rook or a bishop or a queen or a king cannot be moved from the back line if in doing so it must jump over a pawn (or any other piece) that blocks its path.

In some corporations procedural rules may be at a minimum,

and a common understanding among managers may exist to the effect that, although superiors generally need to be kept informed of decisions made at lower levels and veto power resides in the superior office, inferior-level decisions that are consistent with official (assigned) duties are implementable. In effect, though, in such arrangements, official or station duties are usually clearly defined, and the appearance of wide discretion is only a disguise for implicit procedural structure. The notions "within one's authority" and "exceeding one's authority" are almost always clearly defined, at least in daily operation, even in what may appear to be very open or free-formed corporate decision structures.

Policy recognitors are quite another matter. Before discussing them, however, there is a point of interpretation regarding the organizational chart and the procedural recognitors that ought to be clarified.

My account would seem to imply that decisions made by managerial officers that are not consistent with organizational structure or established procedure are not decisions of the corporation. It is argued by some that I must loosen this requirement or I will be faced with the unhappy circumstances of having a neat theory that does not fit the facts because few corporations would ever act if such a criterion were imposed.[5] What is needed, I am told, is a more positivistic interpretation of organizational charting and decision procedures. In effect, it is argued, verisimilitude demands that a corporate act be identified with whatever an appropriately powerful person in the corporation gets underlings in the corporation to do or gets those outside, especially those in government, to accept as a corporate act. Remember the illegal gifts made by some corporate executives to the Nixon reelection campaign in 1972. The funds used were, in many cases, corporate funds, but the proper corporate channels in some celebrated cases were not taken. Executives, whether thinking they were acting for the greater benefit of the corporation or not, deposited corporate funds in the reelection committee's coffers. When the cases were adjudicated, a curious situation occurred. Sometimes the executives themselves were convicted of illegal use of company funds and sometimes the corporations were fined for violation of laws governing campaign gifts.

And in some cases both executives and corporations were penalized. One good reason to be clear about a positivistic interpretation of the organizational chart and procedural elements of a CID Structure would be to bring some degree of consistency to the law.

CID Structures, on my account, have a normative job to do. Their ability to perform that job is hamstrung, however, if we must press a positivistic interpretation on their organizational and procedural elements. My account is certainly not, even as modified above, positivistic. An action is not that of a corporation just because its chief executive officer (CEO) says that it is. No CEO has that authority for, if he did, anything he did for his own aggrandizement with, for example, corporate funds or corporate employee time, by his merely saying so, would be a corporate act. He could never be wrong about it, and he could always evade responsibility by pinning the act on the corporation. Individualists, no doubt, would find such an outcome much to their liking because they have in hand what they rightly perceive to be a remedy for such a use of the corporate shield. Destroy the shield altogether! Declare it to be a fiction and reduce all collective or corporate actions to those of individuals! The CEO's proclamations about the corporateness of his act are thereby rendered empty. Such a strategy, however, as we have seen, simply ignores too many important facts about corporate life even if it has the virtue of preventing managerial misuse of the corporate shield.

The individualist, simply, throws out the baby with the bath water. As long as we insist on a strict, nonpositivistic interpretation of the CID Structure's organizational and procedural elements, the CEO will be exposed to individual censure, and the corporate actor will remain to perform another day. If the act is genuinely the result of individual actions taken by the appropriate people in accord with the established procedures in the company, then the culprit will truly be said to be the corporation, and it will be the corporation not because the CEO says it is, but because the criteria for the incorporation of individual actions have been satisfied.

A repository of some of the policy recognitors of any corporation, as suggested in chapter 3, may be the corporate charter, though that need not be the case and often little if anything in the way of policy can be found written in a charter. Some charters, to be sure, do not even specify the purpose of the incorporation. Nonetheless, the charter should not be overlooked in the attempt to identify or understand the policies of a corporation.

The interpretation placed on the function of the charter with regard to the determination of the corporate character of actions is, however, rather problematic, again owing to the vagueries and lack of information written into most charters. Most charters made in the United States simply allow the newly formed corporation to engage in business for "any lawful purpose." All nonlawful activities undertaken by corporate officers or employees, even if established procedures have been followed, are taken on a strict interpretation to be ultra vires of the corporation. Given such a strict interpretation, corporations can never properly be said to break the law. When the law is broken by what appears to be a corporate act, the individual who performed the offending deed is really culpable and the corporation must be legally absolved. Corporations, by definition, are always absolutely perfect law-abiding citizens. Law-breaking can only be accomplished by individual natural persons. The old legal maxim is *societas delinquere non potest*. Ultra vires understood as captured in the charter and interpreted in this fashion would not only set the boundary on corporate legality but on corporate intentionality as well. If such an interpretation of ultra vires were allowed to stand, corporate actions would be rendered trivially moral (or legal) and totally uninteresting from the moral point of view or from the legal point of view. Having found the corporation to be a moral person, we would also have found it to be necessarily angelic. And that would neither correspond to the facts of contemporary life nor be consistent with our intuitions. An ultra vires defense by the corporation has an empty ring especially when the matter in question is the crash of a DC-10 or a Ford Pinto. Such a defense, however, is no longer accepted in most jurisdictions.

Ultra vires in corporate law has been superceded by or reinterpreted into an implied powers doctrine that allows holdings of corporate liability in a vastly broader sense than would have been continenced by the old rule of the strict liability of natural persons for ultra vires acts. This more liberal view of corporate responsibility has also found its way into the *(Second) Restatement of Agency*, which reads: "If the agent knows that action of this sort has been customary in his principal's business, he has reason to infer his principal's consent thereto, and hence he incurs no liability."[6]

Courts have consistently used the business judgment rule rather than the old ultra vires doctrine, e.g., *Marsili v. Pacific Gas & Electric Co.*,[7] as the ambit of corporate intentionality. The supplanting of the traditional ultra vires doctrine, that is, the voiding of the strict ultra vires plea, legitimately opens the court to the consideration of corporate crime and, we should add, immorality as arising not only *intra vires* but in pursuit of legitimate corporate ends by the exercise of business judgment. What, however, is a legitimate corporate end, a legitimate corporate endeavor? The outside boundaries, of course, are not going to be set by the definition of the "lawful activities" clause of the charter. If that were the case, we would be back where we started in strict ultra vires. What is wanted is an understanding of the enterprise of a corporation, indeed, of the nature of the corporate raison d'être, from which ends and endeavors legitimacy can be gauged. The law, rightfully, is brought in as a constraining factor, but not as a defining one.

Let us take the case of Ford Pinto engineering. Surely, given an understanding of the enterprise in which Ford Motor Company is engaged, it must be agreed that a legitimate corporate endeavor is the design and manufacture of a compact, fuel-efficient, low-cost automobile at the lowest possible production costs. The law does not make it legitimate. "Legitimate" in this sense of the term has to do with according with general expectations, patterns, and standards for the activity. There are good lexical grounds for this interpretation. Also there is a sense of "legitimate" that is defined as "being reasonable" as in "a legitimate solution to a mystery." Neither sense depends upon the law. In fact, the sense of "legitimate" conveyed in "legitimate corporate endeavor" is probably a combination of "reasonable" and "according with established patterns." Hence, it is a legitimate endeavor of Ford to develop the Pinto in the way it did (including its having an inadequate [from

the point of view of safety] fuel tank design) even if Ford might
have been found liable for deaths resulting from poor designs, as
Toyota was in a somewhat similar case. A corporate endeavor is
not illegitimate just because the actions performed by corporate
personnel in carrying out the endeavor produce or amount to a
corporate criminal act. It is just because the endeavor was reasonable and fitting within the framework of the corporate enterprise,
a matter of corporate business judgment, that the law, especially
enterprise and product liability law, is a constraint and a remedy.
Hence, a legitimate (sense one) endeavor or action of the corporation may be adjudicated illegitimate (sense two) and the offending
corporation penalized. The business judgment rule simply shifts
the definition of "legitimacy," as applied to corporate acts to determine ultra vires, from "legal" to "reasonable within the standards of the enterprise" and that is, both on lexical grounds and
with regard to the facts of contemporary life, a legitimate shift.
The upshot is that with regard to policy recognitors the charter is
not usually a particularly helpful document. If we need to know
what set of policies are operative in a corporation, some subset of
which must be instantiated in its decisions and actions, we need to
look beyond the charter.

Most major corporations, and almost every corporation that has
passed from the hands and direction of a founding entrepreneur
(whose own personality and personal policies were writ large in all
corporate actions) into technological management, have developed, over a period of time, a set of operating policies. By "policies" what is meant are rather broad, general principles that describe what the corporation believes about its enterprise and the
way it intends to operate. Policies contain basic belief and goal
statements regarding both the what and the how of corporate life,
but they are not detailed statements of appropriate methods. G. C.
Buzby, president of the Chilton Corporation, in a very perceptive
address to the conference board of the Business Round Table, at-
tempted to clarify what he understood corporate policies to comprise. He wrote:

In order to be effective as guides to innumerable day-to-day decisions and actions, policies must be stated in broad terms, yet they must be sufficiently precise and clear to have real meanings for the people involved.

He continued:

Policies must also be formulated with a long-range point of view in order to achieve the advantages that derive from consistency of purpose and to avoid the disadvantages that inevitably result from decisions based on short-sightedness and expediency.[8]

Buzby correctly saw that for policies to really play the regulative, normative role necessary for them to be fundamental in corporate decision-making and acting, they would have to be accepted as inviolate. This feature of corporate policies, however, brings clearly into focus real differences between the corporate sense of "policy" and that of individual human beings, a point not seen by Buzby (p. 5). Suppose it is true that Richard Nixon had adopted a policy of honesty in all matters. We should say of Nixon then that he had decided to be or try to be honest in his dealings with other persons. He was not an honest man just because he adopted such a policy, but if we knew he had done so sincerely, we would have some good reasons to expect him to behave in certain ways when, for example, making promises or giving reports. In no important sense, however, was his policy of honesty inviolate. That is, Nixon could regularly violate his policy of honesty, and still the things he says or does are utterances and actions of Richard Nixon. That is exactly what is not supposed to happen in the case of corporate policies.

Recall that in the previous chapter, Buzby was quoted as saying that, "the moment a policy is sidestepped or violated, it is no longer the policy of that company" (p. 5). This is rather ambiguous. Does Buzby intend that an act arising from an instantiation of violated policy is not a corporate act, or that if such an act is performed in the procedurally correct manner that the violated policy was in fact not a policy of the corporation and that some other phantom policy actually was corporate policy? If he intends the latter, then stated corporate policies would lose their normative value, or at least we would always have to acknowledge that some policy or other exists and was followed, but we may not be able to identify which one or which subset was involved in particular decision-making or acting. It would make little sense to talk of recognition rules under such an account. That is clearly not Buzby's intent, in fact, his argument is designed to expose and enhance the normative aspect of corporate policy-writing. He intends his claim to be understood as the stronger or clearly normative one: an act or decision that is in violation of corporate policy is not an act of that corporation. In this way established corporate policy fills the gap that may have been perceived to have been created by the liberalization of the ultra vires doctrine. Nonetheless, it is important to recognize that "policy" here is used in a somewhat special sense.

There are definitely going to be some difficulties with adopting this view of corporate policies. Foremost among them will be the concern that a corporation will be able to shirk responsibility for violated policy actions of officials even if those actions were performed by persons in appropriate authority positions and in appropriate ways. Suppose we test this outcome against our intuitions by reference to an example of a specific class of cases: foreign bribery.

Let us imagine that Vice-President Jones of the Transnational Aircraft Corporation is in charge of foreign sales. Transnational needs foreign sales to maintain a viable share of the market in the industry. Transnational has a clearly written, properly ratified, and well-distributed policy statement against the use of corporate funds to influence buyers, especially in foreign markets where such practices may not be discouraged by law. We may imagine that Transnational's statement is similar to that of GAF Corporation:

> Honesty isn't merely the best policy. It's the only policy. Dishonest, immoral, illegal, or unethical conduct is unacceptable in GAF's way of doing business. Illegal conduct includes price-fixing, giving or taking bribes or kickbacks, reciprocity, allocating markets, giving improper political contributions, pilferage, and misuse of company funds[9]

and Proctor and Gamble's statement on antitrust and legal constraints in foreign countries:

> The Company offers its products for sale to its customers at a price which it unilaterally determines to be appropriate. All competing customers are offered our products on the same price basis . . . The Company will not permit competitive information to be obtained through bribery, fraud, theft or coercion.[10]

Jones is in Indonesia trying to sell a number of planes to that country's national airline. He realizes that he will be unsuccessful, indeed Transnational's major competitor will make the deal, unless he pays the foreign company buyer a rather healthy sum of money. He decides to do so and makes the sale. He does not report the bribe as such, but includes it in the discount he has authority to allow. Hence, he, in effect, merely reduces the sale price of the airplanes on the ledger. Has Mr. Jones violated company policy? Clearly he has. But is his act not an act of Transnational Aircraft Corporation?

I do not think we can answer that question on the basis of the information given. What is needed is further information about the reaction of Transnational when it becomes fully cognizant of the Jones–Indonesian Air transaction. Let us suppose that Transnational's board or Jones' superior decide that Jones acted properly despite the stated policy. Doing so could identify the corporation with quite a different policy than the one written in the company literature, revealing that true policy and written policy are quite different. It also would identify Jones' action as corporate. Should Transnational respond by firing Jones or taking steps to recover the bribe funds, then we would have confirmation of the fact that Jones overstepped his corporate authority, that his actions were not corporate, and indeed, grounds might be uncovered to support the claim that Transnational had not actually sold its airplanes to Indonesian Air. (Matters similar to these will be of focal concern in chapter 11.) If we were to try to apply the law to such a case as this, we would surely find it most complicated, but the existing law of agency should prove salutary.

If it is agreed that matters may go either way dependent upon the response of the corporation to the revelation, then we should have to conclude that Buzby's inviolatability condition is overstated. What Buzby should have said is something rather more moderate, but still normative: that every corporation has a certain set of policies, some remain more central or fixed than others, that policies can and do change, but the central policies of a corporation are inviolate or their corporately endorsed violation constitutes a different corporation. The identity of the central policies of any particular corporation could only be revealed through a careful study of actual corporate behavior over a period of time. Written statements may be indicative or they may only be window dressing. Acceptance among the corporate personnel or the higher managerial officers determines the content of the policy recognitors.

It may be believed that where the formal organization of a corporation is unconventional or extremely loose, the CID Structure analysis is unworkable. In fact, some unconventionally organized firms claim that they are structured in the way they are in order to enforce individual personal responsibility in corporate decision-making, to actualize a rule of reduction for corporate decisions. These corporations tend to be realtively small and professional in nature. One such company is Gore Associates, a multinational that was originally organized to manufacture polytetrafluoroethylene products, and has diversified into computer electronics, filtration membranes, textile fibers, and other polymer products. By and large, the company is a chemical engineering development firm. Gore Associates began as a basement business of William Gore; under his direction it has grown in only three decades into a multinational operation with plants in five states and a number of foreign locations.

What is apparently different about Gore Associates (unique, if one reads the corporate literature) is the organizational structure of the firm. Gore, himself, insists that it is the organizational structure adopted by the firm that is responsible for its great success. It is claimed that the Gore Associates model of corporate organization is based on primary principles of human nature. Those principles, according to Gore, are: (1) all people are aggressive, (2) all feel friendship and love, (3) all are dreamers, and (4) all people have a hierarchy of needs: survival, security, belonging, status, and self-actuation.[11]

There is no point in this context to questioning, discussing, or disputing Gore's analysis of human nature. (It may come as some surprise to philosophers to find a successful businessman who has taken a good deal of time to try to think systematically about human nature without their assistance or that of academic psychologists.) Gore treats his human nature analysis in conjunction with some principles of group productivity that are more articles of faith then of demonstration, as the cornerstone of his organizational-model theory. His argument is that given his assumptions about human nature and statistical conclusions about group productivity, what he calls a lattice model of organization is recommended for a corporation in search of success. By "lattice model" he means that all persons in the organization interact "directly with every other person with no intermediary. Lines of communication are direct—person to person" (p. 8). His organizational chart is radically different, of course, from the standard variety. The name "lattice" is derived from the way the chart looks. (See figure 4.2.)

	A	B	C	D	E
A					
B					
C					
D					
E					

Figure 4.2.   A, B, C, D, E, etc., are associates of the corporation. They are the proper names of people, never offices.

Gore identifies the following as attributes of his lattice structure:

There are no fixed or assigned authority lines;

Sponsors rather than bosses operate in the system;

Natural leadership defined by "followership" naturally emerges;

Communication is person to person;

Tasks and functions are organized through commitments;

Objectives are set by those who must carry them into actions;

Discipline is group-imposed. (p. 8)

It is, of course, obvious and not only recognized but a precept of Gore's theory that lattice organizations need to be kept relatively small. The corporation, however, can operate, Gore believes, as an aggregate of a number of latticed groups. Be that as it may, even Gore admits that there are some serious difficulties with the adoption of a lattice approach throughout the corporate world. Most important of these are the facts that: (1) policy virtually dictated by "a firm hand at the helm" (p. 10) must be rather extensively developed and adhered to throughout the organization to prevent too much diversification as latticed groups pursue their own projects; (2) complete consensus in a group is seldom reached, and the historical process necessary for the emergence of a natural group leader can often be delayed by group dynamics; hence, misdirection, misconceptions, and miscalculations may not be checked; (3) reward systems are harder to develop and incentives are often inappropriately administered because they are dependent upon the determination of a lattice group or the group's perception of its members.

The lattice model, despite certain appealing aspects, does not seem to be a feasible alternative to standard authoritarian structures for most corporations. Gore Associates itself is, despite its founder's denials, very much under the direction of its president and his family. Nonetheless, alternate, nonauthoritarian structures in the organization of corporate decision-making do exist in many corporations, are implemented, and certainly affect the way those corporations act. Hence, as such they must be subsumable in my basic account of CID Structures or that account would be deficient. Subsumption, however, is no problem. As we have seen, CID Structures need not be organizationally homogeneous. Mine is not a structural theory, but a functional one. What matters is not that a corporation has a box-and-line organization, but that it has some operative decision procedure in place that functions as an incorporator of the decisions of corporate managers or associates. It needs to have a grammar. That many large firms are organized in the standard box-and-line authoritarian way is an historical fact that management textbook writers have recognized for many years. The fact that many such writers think that is the best way to organize a firm is incidental and irrelevant to my account.

It is of note that in corporations that purportedly operate within nonauthoritarian systems what I have called "policy recognitors" are highly developed and extensive. As a general rule we should expect that where structures are authoritarian and strictly enforced, policies will be less fully developed or more general in nature. But this is purely a practical matter and ought not to be regarded as anything more than that. Structure cannot replace policy; grammar is not logic. As corporations become even more diversified and decentralized and as the fear of government intervention and adverse public opinion continue to play prominent roles in corporate decision-making, we should expect more policy writing and policy enforcement even in the most authoritarian firms. That, of course, is because it will be in the corporation's interests to spell out as fully as possible the range of its activities and what constitutes its legitimate business judgment and interests.

The Gore lattice model is, of course, intended to reduce the corporation to responsible individual researcher/entrepreneurs who just happen to be associated in their endeavors. There may exist some such groups carrying on their activities, or their aggregated activities, in this fashion. Gore Associates, however, does not appear to be one of them. In its case, the authoritarian structure, or at least the salient aspects of that structure, are not only present but focal with respect to planning and development. The lattice model may operate at certain levels of corporate decision-making at Gore as it certainly does in all major corporations, but its enshrinement at

Gore is more a matter of the rhetoric of the company than a true or complete picture of the grammatical structure of that corporation's decision-making and acting.

It is probably the case that in most functioning corporate units both lattice and standard textbook organizations operate. It is also likely that they do not run on parallel circuits within the organization. In other words, to some degree (if not fully) the two models are compatible. My suspicion is that investigation of actual practices will reveal that the Gore lattice model, at least in the case of Gore Associates (and probably anywhere else it appears) is a very effective and efficient productivity tool, but that it is not a rich enough conceptual paramorph for its articulation to have an acceptably high positive analogy to the corporate world it purports to model. It is important that my account of CID Structures can, without modification, accommodate unconventional ways within a particular corporation of defining the grammar and the procedural recognitors of that corporation.

CHAPTER FIVE

The Power of the People in Groups and Corporations

When a crowd or a mob or a relatively random group of people (like the passengers on today's TWA Flight 25 to Los Angeles) did something, it is reasonable to say that its component membership did it. Further, if the group in question has the power to do something, then we would normally allow that each of the persons who constituted the group, at least to some degree, has the power to do it. Attributions of group power usually are distributive, although the basis for determining proper distribution may not be evident.

When organizations such as multinational decentralized business corporations have the power to act in some decisive fashion in an international business or political affair, the determination of the power of any natural person with respect to the same affair appears to be quite a different matter from the group-power cases. It is not at all clear that even those persons who occupy superior managerial-level positions in such corporations may properly be said to have much power with respect to the events over which the corporation has power. There seems to be a block to distribution that needs to be exposed, and there are strong moral and legal reasons for trying to do so. Determinations of moral and legal accountability are usually thought to be dependent upon resolutions of questions regarding what someone could have done in a situation. In other words, it is important to know what a person's power was with respect to some event for which he is being held to account.

I shall uncover some of the grounds for the distribution of power in aggregative cases such as crowds and then use what is therein revealed to further widen the distinction between aggregate collectivities and conglomerates.

As a starting point I draw on an important paper by Alvin Goldman that has not received the attention it deserves.[1] Goldman provides a series of analyses of individual and collective power that will serve as a touchstone. In order to avoid contentiousness about Goldman's theory of basic actions, however, I will reformulate his account in a way that is neutral as regards the issue of what constitutes a basic act. Let us say that

> [P] A person (X) has power at a certain time (tl) with respect to (w.r.t.) an issue or occurrence (E) (at tn) if and only if the following two conditions hold: (1) There is some intentional action or actions that if X wanted E to come out in one way (yX), X would perform that action (or actions) at the appropriate times between tl an tn and if X did perform that action at those times, y would occur at tn; (2) There is some intentional action or actions that if X wanted E to come out not −y, X would perform that action at the appropriate times between tl and tn and if X did perform that action at those times, not −y would occur at tn.

As Goldman points out, the conditionals involved in this account of individual power are subjunctive conditionals, not casual subjunctive conditionals (p. 227). The truth values of these conditionals, when the proper substitution for variables has been made, may be assessed by utilization of the apparatus of possible-worlds semantics. Consider again our Canby Saloon Crowd story: fifteen persons are gathered in the only saloon in a small Nevada town on a winter's night in 1885. Included in the crowd is a woman named Ma Grier. She is a rather gristly sort of person, who is far more at home on the range than in the drawing room. For no apparent reason, a brawl erupts in the saloon. Empty glasses, whiskey bottles, chairs, etc., fly around, reducing the place to shambles. Down by the end of the bar a stranger in town is being battered by four or five of the locals. It is a full-scale donneybrook.

We want to know whether Ma Grier has power with respect to the continuation of the brawl or its escalation into wanton destruction. Suppose that she does want the brawl to continue. She finds it exhilarating! The brawl continues. We need to counterfactualize Ma Grier's desire about the continuation of the brawl, while holding constant her physical abilities, her beliefs, and the resources at her command. It will not do, for example, to imagine a world different from the one of our story regarding Ma Grier, in which not only is her desire with respect to the continuation of the brawl different but she possesses a Thompson submachine gun rather than a Colt 45 or a half-empty whiskey bottle. The only change we are to allow in the possible world is the change in Ma Grier's wants so that Ma Grier does *not* want the brawl to continue (and any nomologically necessary changes in her neurological events that change occasions). In every other way the relevant possible world resembles the world of our story. The question is whether Ma Grier's desire that the brawl stop (nomologically) implies that she perform certain actions that (nomologically) imply that the brawl stops.

The matter would be very simple if the brawl were a solo performance, which unfortunately it is not. The entire crowd in the saloon is involved in bringing it off, even the bartender is throwing bottles around the room. Ma Grier is but a member of the crowd. When we have to take the crowd into consideration, it is difficult to determine whether or not she has power with regard to the brawl.

A reasonable way to deal with such group performances is to collectivize the analysis of power. We can modify [P] to read:

[Pa] An aggregate of persons has power (at tl) w.r.t. E (at tn) if and only if (1) there is some intentional action (or actions) such that if each member-component of the aggregate wanted E to come out one way (y), each would perform his respective action (or actions) at the appropriate time between tl and tn and if each member-component did so, y would occur at tn and (2) there is some intentional action (or actions) such that if each member-component of the aggregate wanted not −y, each would perform his respective action (or actions) at the appropriate time and if each did so, not −y would occur at tn.

Implicit in this account of aggregate collective power is a coordination allowance. The actions of any one member, in spite of his desire to bring about y (or not −y), will have to be coordinated with the actions of other member-components in order to determine if the aggregate has power in the situation. For the aggregate actually to do what it has the power to do, members must have rather reliable information about what others are about to do, or they are likely not to contribute in an appropriate way. (The coordination problem here is much like that confronting players of Prisoner's Dilemma.) Minimal coordination probably sets the parameters on the lower end of the actualization of collective power.

It seems clear from [Pa] that the crowd in the saloon has power with respect to the continuation of the brawl, but [Pa] does not entail that any member (or each of the members) of the crowd has any power with respect to the continuation of the brawl. It is probably the case that none of the members of the crowd can satisfy the conditions of [P] with respect to stopping the brawl. That, however, is counterintuitive. As mentioned earlier, our expectations are that a crowd's power with respect to some event should distribute in some way over its component membership. What, after all, is a crowd, but a group of people? It has no other identity, as was argued in chapter 2. Cannot the identity of the crowd with its members be used to generate the desired distribution principle? Although from the point of view of identity each member-component is essential to an aggregate collectivity, it is not the case that each member-component is not dispensable with regard to some particular activity of the aggregation or with regard to some matter whose outcome is within the power of the collectivity. Our interest lies in whether or not a particular person who is a member of an aggregation has some individual power in a matter about which we have determined that the aggregation has collective power. If we had simply said that when a group has collective power every member has some individual power, we would be open to the obvious objection that we could always form a second group by adding a randomly selected person to the first group, and because it would be true that the new group has power with respect to the matter in question (by virtue of the old group having had power with respect to that matter), this randomly selected person will also have some power in the matter. Suppose the randomly selected person is a five-month-old baby who is placed on TWA Flight 25. We need to find a way to determine whether a person is dispensable with respect to specific matters about which the group or crowd of which he is a member has power.

Goldman suggests an explication of the desired notion of dispensability (p. 239). Following his lead, we may say that someone (S) is a dispensable component-member of an aggregate collectivity with respect to a certain matter, E, over which the aggregate has collective power. If there is an outcome of E such that if all component-members except S wanted that outcome to occur, it would occur even if S opposes its occurrence. Conversely, S is nondispensable with respect to E, if his opposition would alter the outcome even though the other members of the group still want it to occur. The power distribution principle (after Goldman) for groups will be:

> A person S has some power w.r.t. issue E if there is some group G such that S is a nondispensable member of G w.r.t. E and the members of G have collective power w.r.t. E.

It is rather easy to give examples of nondispensability in groups with respect to specific tasks. Suppose a group of three elementary school girls, walking in the woods, discover a seriously injured man trapped under a fallen tree. The group of girls has collective power to move the tree, but none of the girls could move it on her own. Also, if any one of the girls refuses to help in moving the tree, the tree will not be moved by the others, no matter how hard they try. Each girl in this situation is a nondispensable member of the aggregate.

We may suppose that with respect to stopping the brawl in the saloon there were both dispensable and nondispensable members of the crowd, though it will be very difficult to uncover nomological grounds for drawing the dispensability distinction in this case. A plethora of psychological and sociological factors is involved. Suppose we stipulate that no matter what one of the characters in the saloon wants with respect to the brawl, because he is regarded by the others as a coward or a fool, the outcome will be unaffected. He (call him "Gerald Tetley" after the character in *The Ox Bow Incident*) will be a dispensable member of the crowd in the saloon, on any account, with respect to the brawl. But what of the others? Would not the brawl go on even if each, in turn, wants it to stop? Assume that none of the people in the saloon has individual power, for the brawl will continue no matter which one of them individually appeals for an end to the fighting. But is each, in turn, dispensable with respect to the continuation of the brawl? Does each person in the crowd really satisfy the conditions of dispensability (satisfied by Gerald Tetley) in this case? Even though there are no individually powerful members of the crowd in the saloon with respect to the continuation of the brawl, and no individual members could have stopped the brawl unless more than one of them wanted to stop it, that does not mean that there were no nondispensable members of the crowd. Collective power in this case is not necessarily nondistributive.

There is at least one way to show that there are nondispensable members of the crowd in the saloon when the crowd has collective power with respect to the brawl. It is reasonable to suppose that if some of the persons in the crowd had wanted to stop the brawl, the brawl would have stopped. The others would have stopped even if each personally wanted to continue. Obviously there is no formula with respect to this business, but it is reasonable to expect that after a certain number of people in the crowd decide to stop brawling, the others will quit as well, if only out of a sense of foolishness or a lack of opponents. Exactly who is in that critical mass, in the absence of sociological information, probably is not determinable. On a purely quantitative, it may be that five or as many as thirteen members are necessary to achieve critical mass. If the right three persons were to change their minds, the rest of the crowd might disperse. But which three? There is a possible world in which Ma Grier and two other persons in the crowd (a wealthy rancher and the hardware store owner) do not want to continue the brawl, and the others, even if reluctantly, stop brawling. In such a scenario we counterfactualized what those three members want, make certain assumptions (supported by sociological data) about their collective power over the remaining members and how they would make their desires known to the rest, and hold constant the desires of the rest. This would get very complicated and would depend upon a way of analyzing the power of one person or a subgroup over others in a group. The task of providing such an analysis may be shirked for the purposes of this chapter, but it remains an important aspect of the determination of the power of persons in groups. All that is needed for present purposes is the stipulation that some critical mass of members of any aggregate collectivity has collective power with respect to most outcomes of the matters in which the collectivity has collective power. We can also, then, show that each member of that critical mass subgroup has *some* individual power as well with respect to those matters. As already suggested, in actual cases group dynamics and the personal power over others of individual members may serve to exclude certain members from ever being in the critical mass. Nonetheless, in many aggregate cases the critical mass may be composed of any of the aggregate's component members. This will, of course, be especially true of very random groups rather than of groups that regularly collect: a difference between the passengers on the TWA airplane and the saloon crowd. Allowing that we may have to exclude certain members who are notably weak or under the influence of others, we may say that if an aggregate collectivity has collective power with respect to some matter, each member of the aggregate has some individual power with respect to that matter; that is, none is powerless. Each could be a nondispensable member of the subgroup that can alter the outcome of the matter.

Suppose it would take only any ten persons in the saloon crowd to stop the brawl. Each person in the crowd is to be regarded as a potential part of that critical mass and so will have some power with respect to the outcome. Suppose that nine people in the crowd want the brawl to stop and a tenth, Ma Grier, is confronted with the choice of joining them. The attitudes of the other four are held constant. (We have excluded Gerald Tetley.) If Ma Grier joins, critical mass will be achieved, and the brawl will stop. If she doesn't, the brawl will continue unless one of the other four changes his mind. With respect to the continuation of the brawl, Ma Grier has some individual power. She and the other nine will be nondispensable members of the crowd with respect to the brawl because for each person in the critical mass it will be true that if all ten want the brawl to stop it will stop, and if only nine want it to stop, and she does not want it to stop, the brawl will continue. In this case, however, any four of the members of the critical mass may be replaced by any of the four outside the critical mass who are in the crowd. What is true of the power of any one member of the crowd (excluding Gerald Tetley) then is true of the power of each with respect to the continuation of the brawl. Substitutivity of any person in the crowd for a person in the critical mass allows distribution of some power to each person in the crowd who survives the exclusion test. Where substitutivity is severely restricted by sociological conditions, the critical mass may itself constitute a separate group with collective power over the crowd. Its nondispensable membership will have been determined on the basis of something other than a simple weight of numbers principle, e.g., social status.

This analysis of the power of individuals in aggregations provides the structure for our common accountability assessments of individuals in group actions. Persons who can be shown to have been impotent with respect to an outcome caused by a group of which they just happen to be members are usually excused from bearing responsibility for the outcome, though they may bear the blemish of guilt by association. On the other hand, insofar as most aggregate-collectivity members will not be able to support an impotency excuse, it will be true that each has some power with respect to the outcomes of the group's action. This kind of analysis, of course, identifies the basis for attributions of causal responsibility to members for group actions. Questions of whether a member of a group knew he had some power to bring about a different outcome or whether he should have known that he did, must be settled before ascriptions of legal or moral responsibility are justly laid upon him. The analysis provides a ground for the factual claim that he *could have* done something significant, but it leaves open the matter of whether it is reasonable to claim that he *should have* been aware of his power with respect to the outcome in question. Interesting questions may also be raised about whether an individual should have or even could have known he was a member of the relevant aggregate collectivity with respect to some event. Such questions may, however, be left aside for now. Assuming that no exculpating excuse can be supported on behalf of a nondispensable member of the group, he ought to be held accountable for the event in question. Common intuitions about the moral responsibilities of persons in crowds are buttressed by the analysis. Moral blame in such cases is not assessed because of mere association or because of power per se, but with a view toward the intentional action or inaction of a person. A framework for evaluating the "there was nothing I could have done" plea is also provided. Such a plea should not be confused with the "I would have been just one against so many" plea.

Although, as suggested, many more complications need to be added to the analysis to make it more fully adequate even to handle cases like the saloon brawl, enough has been said to contrast the power of individual human beings in aggregate collectivities with that of individual persons in large decentralized business corporations. It is important that such a contrast is, technically speaking, a nonstarter because corporations cannot be described in terms of collective power. They can, of course, join collectives, as the Gulf Oil Corporation did when it illegally joined the international uranium cartel. They also are to be found in such aggregate collectivities as "U.S. taxpayers," "owners of real estate in Pittsburg, Pennsylvania," etc.

Such a simple dismissal of the contrast, however, will be, and rightly so, regarded with suspicion. Clearly we do talk of some individual person's power, a chief executive officer's (CEO's), power (for example), when a corporation joins a cartel. (We should keep in mind, of course, that no matter what the CEO does, *he* cannot join the cartel.) We should be able to apply [P] to the CEO's situation, supposing that the crucial act of joining involves the CEO's signature. The CEO has power with respect to the joinging of the cartel if and only if a change in what the CEO wants with respect to the joining will change the outcome of the matter. If the CEO wants the corporation to join the cartel, he will sign, and it will join. If he does not want it to join the cartel, he will refuse to sign, but will that result in the cartel not being joined by the corporation? Does the CEO have such power?

Practically speaking, it may be the case that he does have power with respect to the joining of the cartel. His opinions may be held in the highest of esteem and so he may override the wants of the members of the board of directors, etc., or it may be the case that the board members so highly regard the CEO's managerial talents that they will not challenge his decision, even if they do not approve of it. On the other hand, it might be the case that if the CEO does not want to sign, because he does not want the corporation to join the cartel, that he will be replaced by someone who will sign, and the cartel will be joined by the corporation. The CEO's job, as it were, might depend upon his signing the papers. If that is the case, and certainly we may imagine any number of examples of a similar nature, the CEO cannot be said to have power with respect to the corporation's joining the cartel. His power really is with respect to *his* signing of the relevant documents. Of course, the corporation's joining might be delayed if the CEO refuses to sign and that may warrant our allotment of some power to him with respect to the matter, but the outcome of the matter may not be altered. The person occupying the position of CEO is dispensable with respect to this matter, which may be another way of saying that the power of the CEO rests in the office not in the individual.

Important for the contrast, the power of the office that can be ascribed to the officeholder in the decentralized business corporation is not exposed in any critical mass or nondispensability analysis of the sort that works in the case of aggregate collectivities. Analyses of that sort could be used to talk of the power of individual stockholders or of individual board members with respect to certain corporate matters: those matters in which the corporation responds to the commands of an aggregate. But the officeholder's, even the CEO's, power with respect to most matters is not really a function of his group memberships. The power that attaches to

the executive or managerial office, by and large, is not purely derivative, if at all, of an agency transfer from the aggregate stockholders or aggregate board of directors or from any other collectivity.[2] The stockholders, for example, do not transfer, via an agency
agreement, their collective power with respect to certain issues to
the CEO. They have little or no collective power with respect to
most of the relevant matters handled in his office in the first place,
and what collective power they have, they collectively retain as a
control over management. The CEO is not simply the agent of the
board nor of the stockholders, though he is accountable on many
matters to the board. Fully explicating this point, however, would
lead us far afield into the concept of agency, representation, etc.,
within corporate structures. That may be left for another time.

It is closer to actual corporate practices and to the proponder-
ance of legal opinion to say that the corporation itself has power
with respect to certain matters, and in some cases, that may be
redescribed by saying that a person holding a certain position in
the corporate structure has some power, in virtue of his holding
this position, with respect to the matters in question.[3] In other
words, a state of affairs in which a corporation has power with respect to a certain matter may be redescribed as a situation in which
a CEO has some power with respect to that matter. The requisite
redescription device in this case, as in cases of corporate intentional action, is a Corporation's Internal Decision Structure (its CID
Structure). For the purposes of this chapter, reiteration of the
constituent aspects of CID Structures is superfluous. I want only
to suggest in the present context that the tripartite nature of a CID
Structure licenses the redescription of facts about corporate power,
in some cases, as statements about the power of corporate personnel. That is surely not to say that the power of a corporation with
respect to any issue is a function of the aggregate power of those
persons who occupy managerial places on its organizational chart
or sit on its board of directors or hold stock in the corporation.

CHAPTER SIX
Kinds and Persons

As noted in chapter 3, on August 10, 1978, a Ford Pinto was hit in the rear by a van and burst into fire, incinerating its three passengers. On September 13, 1978, the Ford Motor Company was indicted in Elkhart Indiana Superior Court on three counts of reckless homicide. Ford Motor Company filed a Memorandum in support of Dismissal of the Indictment in which they argued that homicide statutes cannot be applied to corporations. In part, their argument went as follows:

> It is the prosecutor who thinks "that the legislature should have made '[the reckless homicide statute] more comprehensive." [But], the homicide provisions of the new Criminal Code are clearly designed to keep people from killing other people. To construe [it] as applicable to corporations would mean that it must be read: "A *corporation* who recklessly kills *another human being* commits reckless homicide. . . ." This simple substitution shows that the statute is not designed to apply to corporate conduct.

The state responded in opposition to Ford's reading of the statute that the legislative intent was captured most clearly in Ford's own statement that the law was designed "to keep people from killing people." The state cited the *Indiana Code* (35-41-1-2 that states: " 'person' means a human being, corporation, partnership, unincorporated association or government," and " 'Human being' means an individual who is born and is alive." It further cited the *Code* as saying: "A corporation . . . may be prosecuted for any offense . . ." (35-41-2-3[a]). The reading to the effect that the legislature intended that a corporation, as a person, could be prosecuted for the crime, but that it could not be a victim of such a crime is supported by similar statutes in twenty-two states by the relevant section of the *Model Penal Code,* and by the Supreme Court ruling in *United States v. Union Supply Co.,* 215 U.S. 50, 30 S. Ct. 15 (1909).

Ford countered that to be a metaphysical and hence a moral person, an entity must be at least a human being. Only members of the class of human beings, they maintained, can be persons in the sense relevant to criminal prosecution. The judge, however, ruled in favor of the state and denied Ford's dismissal motion, finding that corporations are, themselves, subjects of the criminal law and as such that they are properly treated as members of the class of intentional actors. The judge's ruling, of course, is quite consistent with the theory of the corporation as a moral person put forth in chapter 3. Nonetheless, there is a considerable amount of concern that the basis of Ford's motion is fundamental to our notion of what constitutes a "full-blooded" person. Corporations are, after all, artifacts.

If they are to be treated as citizens of the moral world and the subjects of homicide prosecutions, then one of two things must be the case: (1) the term "person" names a natural kind or a concept that is necessarily, if in part, defined in terms of natural kinds, but "moral person" does not name a concept that depends on the concept of person; or (2) "person" does not name either a natural kind or a concept according to which it is possible to classify what is partially defined in terms of natural kinds, and "moral person" is (as in [1]) independent of the concept of person, or interdependent with the term "person," or, alternatively, personhood is a necessary precondition of moral personhood. If corporations are moral persons, "person" cannot both be the name of a natural kind and interdependent with or a necessary precondition of being a moral person. The argument that should be made, the one that is consistent with the Ford ruling is that "person" is not a natural-kind term, nor does it name a concept that classifies what is necessarily defined in terms of natural kinds. It is to such an argument that I now direct attention.

A natural kind is a class of individuals gathered according to a sameness criteria that is rooted in a comprehensive scientific the-

ory.[1] Hilary Putnam writes, "What *really* distinguishes the classes
we count as natural kinds is itself a matter of (high-level and very
abstract) scientific investigation."[2] In other words, the essential
nature of a thing, by virtue of which it is included in the extension
of a natural-kind term, that which it shares with other members
of the kind, is, at base, a matter of physical theory construction.

Natural-kind terms are, in the currently popular parlance, rigid
designators, like proper names that pick out the same thing in every
possible world.[3] Although stereotypical characteristics are usually
associated with natural kinds, these do not determine the extension of natural-kind terms. The referent of natural-kind terms is
fixed by using exemplars of the kind rather than by listing stereotypical characterization. John Locke told a marvelous story about
Adam confronted by one of his children bearing a glittering substance. Adam names the substance *Zahab* (gold). Locke says, with
respect to the sameness criteria for gold,

> He (Adam) has a standard made by nature. . . . He takes care that his
> idea be conformable to this Archetype, and intends the name should stand
> for an idea so conformable. This piece of matter, thus denominated *Zahab*
> by Adam, being quite different from any he had seen before, nobody, I
> think, will deny to be a distinct species, and to have its peculiar essence;
> and that the name *Zahab* is the mark of the species, and a name belonging
> to all things partaking in that essence.[4]

When Adam names the glittering substance *Zahab*, we may say
that he intends to pick out *that* stuff, whatever it is, and any other
stuff that is the same as it. Adam performed a kind of baptism.
The exemplar stands in for the kind that includes it. The most
comprehensive true scientific theory will reveal the essential properties of the kind. In the *Zahab* case that theory would expose the
atomic structure of that glittering stuff.

(A number of objections have been raised against this way of
assimilating the treatment of natural-kind terms to that of proper
names, to treating them as rigid designators. Some of the objections, especially those recently developed by Moravcsik and by
Dupre, raise severe difficulties.[5] For present purposes, however,
such criticisms may be overlooked.)

Our philosophical tradition certainly has *not* identified "person" as a natural-kind term. Against that tradition, what would motivate the treatment of "person" as a natural-kind term? David Wiggins has noted that if "person" were a natural-kind term, the puzzling and currently fashionable science fiction fission-and-fusion examples (where people split in half and continue separate lives or where two previously different people are described as fusing into one ongoing person), concocted to throw doubt on various traditional personal-identity criteria, could be conveniently handled by appeals to natural laws and scientific theory.[6] Possible worlds in which the laws of nature that are actually involved in fixing the referent of "person" do not hold, are worlds without persons. Wiggins writes:

> If person is a natural kind, then when we consider the problem of the identity of persons through change, the whole logic of the situation must exempt us from taking into account any but the class of situations which conforms to the actual laws of the actual world. For these serve, and nothing but these can serve, to define the class of persons. And this seems to excuse us from allowing the spontaneous occurrences of delta formations in the consciousness of persons. (p. 158)

If "person" were the name of a natural kind, and we could show that these science fiction inventions violate the laws of nature that actually hold with respect to persons, we would be showing that a world in which people split into two separate conscious persons or in which two persons join together to become one has laws governing what it is to be a person that are radically different from those in our world. And that would mean that, in such a world "person" would not mean what we mean by that term. There is a corollary to this in Putnam's celebrated Twin Earth story about water. The story goes that despite the stereotypical similarities of Earth water with what is called "water" on an imagined Twin Earth, there is found to be a distinct difference in the molecular construction of the two liquids. When the chemical formula of Twin Earth water is found to be other than H_2O, it is, *eo ipso*, learned that Twin Earth water is not the same as water.[7]

This approach, though it may appear to be promising with respect to settling long-standing personal identity puzzles, is, however, as Wiggins himself allows, fatally flawed. "Person" simply is not a natural-kind term in the way "water," "tiger," and "human being" are. If "person" were a natural-kind term, then its extension, like that of *Zahab,* could be fixed by use of a sameness relation to any exemplar. Suppose we are all willing to grant that Carl Sagan and Ronald Reagan are persons, the class determined by this method to Sagan or Reagan, given existing comprehensive scientific theory, would not, however, be the class of persons but the class of human beings or Homo sapiens. "Person" and "Homo sapien" may usually be used to pick out the same thing, say Ronald Reagan, but "person" is neither a translation nor a variant of "Homo sapien." It will not do to say that a person is, whatever that, pointing to Sagan, is and whatever *that* is will be known after empirical investigation has revealed its microstructure. "Person is not manifestly equivalent to the real essence Homo sapiens."[8]

It may well be the case that providing the explanatory scientific model for the natural-kind "human being" is much more complicated than it is for water, but within the framework of a zoological taxonomical theory, it should be possible to provide what is wanted. Putnam, however, in his *Locke Lectures* balks at this. He tells us that "we are not, realistically, going to get a detailed explanatory model for the natural kind 'human being.' "[9] His reason for thinking that rests on his mistaken equation of "being a person" with "being a human being." He argues that the partial opacity of each of us to each other is a constitutive fact of what it is to be a person.

> Would it be possible to *love* someone, if we could actually carry out calculations of the form: "If I say X, the possibility is 15 percent she will react in manner Y?" . . . Would it be possible even to think of *oneself* as a person? (p. 63)

Putnam, I think, is quite right about the partial opacity of each of us to each other, though his example surely does not show what transparency would be like. Is opacity, however, a constitutive fact about persons? If we treat what it is to be a person as solely a matter of convention, we could make opacity a part of the functional descriptions we agree to use to pick out members of the class. That, of course, is surely not what Putnam has in mind. At best we would have formulated a stereotypical feature without providing anything like the "scientifically palpable real essences" that make Putnam's natural-kind theory persuasive, e.g., water is H_2O.[10] I think we do have a rather straightforward way of accounting for the partial opacity between persons, which will become clear presently. The point of interest here is that Putnam's shift from human beings to persons and his sighting of a fact about persons to establish the claim that the required scientific explanatory model of human being is not to be forthcoming, fails his own enterprise. We should echo with the tradition; "person" is not, though "human being" is, the name of a natural kind.

Had Carl Sagan been presented to Locke's Adam in the way the hunk of glittering substance was, Adam might have used a term to stand for this specimen before him (and any of its kind) whatever essential kind properties it turned out to have. He may or may not have been later delighted to learn that he was also in the extension of that term, that he and Carl Sagan were members of the same natural kind. Alternatively, Adam could have done something quite different when confronted with Carl Sagan. He might have invented a term (e.g., "person") intending it name the aggregation of a certain collection of properties or characteristics, those he had associated to form a sortal concept (one used to classify things), and believing those properties to be present in the specimen, he calls Carl Sagan a person, that is, he includes Sagan in the extension of "person." On this version Adam decides that Carl Sagan is one of that kind he has called "person" because Sagan has or evidences certain properties. (Adam, of course, could be wrong about whether Sagan actually has the required properties, but he cannot be wrong about what those properties are. This sortal concept is, after all, his creation.)

In the earlier case, Adam believes that Carl Sagan is of a kind of species even if Adam has no idea or only a very bad idea of what the essential kind properties are. Suppose he names his exemplar of that kind, "human being." After intensive examination is conducted, it may turn out that Carl Sagan has, despite outward appearances, a radically different physiology from every other individual who has been regarded as a member of the human-being kind that Adam has named by using Carl Sagan as his ostending exemplar. Suppose it is learned that Sagan landed in Adam's vicinity in a spaceship that had been launched from a destructing planet in a distant galaxy. Technically speaking, "human being" would have been annexed by Adam to Carl Sagan's kind, and the rest of us would not be entitled to it by reason of not being in its extension. Practically, of course, if these circumstances had occurred, we would initiate a new random-exemplar test, declare a previous misuse that would exclude Carl Sagan from the class of human beings and operate within the parameters of accepted scientific theory. None of this, however, need affect Carl Sagan's status under the other kind classification. He still, we assume, behaves and evidences the characteristics that led Adam to earlier identify him in the extension of "person." This man from deepest space may not be a human being, but he is a person. The purely operational definition account of the membership criteria for the extension of "person" (here attributed to Adam), may offend the general conviction that whether or not something is a person ought to be more than a matter of legislation or of social practice or convenience.

There is a long tradition of dispute over whether intelligent extraterrestrial beings, computers, and even some nonhuman animals (remember Locke's rational parrot) belong in the class of persons. There also has been reasonable dispute over whether certain human beings are persons. Wiggins certainly realizes that "person," despite important advantages if it did, does not name a natural kind. He offers the modification that something is a person if it is an animal of a natural kind whose members perceive, feel, imagine, and desire. Person then is "a nonbiological qualification of animal."[11] It is an animal classification that cuts across the grain of the usual zoological taxonomy, and so efficiently excludes artifacts such as computers and corporations.

The motivation for insisting that to be a person is to be an animal is rather weak. It would appear to be the strongest claim that can be made that is consistent with scientific evidence and natural-kind theory. Wiggins supports the inclusion of a natural-kind element on little more than an appeal to what he takes to be widely held convictions or intuitions regarding the way robot cases should be handled. Certainly most of us would be reluctant to issue civil rights to robots, and we would probably say that we do not want to do so because such artifacts ought not to be given the kind of consideration owed to living or natural things. Wiggins writes, "To have feelings or purposes or concerns a thing must, I think we still think, be (at least) *an animal*" (p. 162). Wiggins qualifies this claim by saying that he does not believe that an animal could not be artificially synthesized. And by that he means that we might build something that has feelings, purposes, and concerns programmed in. Such a creation, however, Wiggins insists "would not be an automation" (p. 162). Visions of Hal of *2001: A Space Odyssey* spring to mind. Wiggins, of course, could say that physical laws would be violated by the actual creation of a Hal or he might allow that Hal is capable of feelings, purposes, and concerns and deny that Hal is an automation. But whatever he does with *2001*, he cannot deny that Hal has no place in a zoological taxonomy. Hal simply is not, nor would it make sense to say that he could become, a member of a natural kind.

The cold fact is that it is not that something is natural or living (in a biological sense) that stimulates our convictions about rights or considerations. The possession of certain kinds of capacities is crucial. Undoubtedly, we have a species bias that inclines us to root for the human being against Hal, but that ought not to be confused with our reflective consideration of the sort of treatment owed to and expected of feeling, purposive, concerned, desiring, self-motivated, project-making things that can "conceive of themselves as having, a past accessible in experience—memory and a future accessible in intention" (p. 161). The class of persons seems to be formed around just such a series of functional descriptions. On reflection, we may root for the human being against Hal just because Hal is guilty of intentionally killing a number of persons and because he has manifested the intention to continue his murderous behavior against the remaining astronaut. Hal has committed reckless homicide and should be punished accordingly.

Wiggins concludes his argument for an animal element, in the concept of person with the curious remark: "By *person* we mean a sort of animal, and for purposes of morality that (I maintain) is the best thing for us to mean. . . . It is on pain of madness that we shall try to see ourselves as both *Homo sapiens* and something with a different principle of individuation" (p. 167). The argument here is remarkably underdeveloped. Of course it would be madness if the two kinds in which we see ourselves were incompatible biological taxa. But that is exactly what the Lockean distinction between "same man" and "same person" is not. Furthermore, it is not unintelligible for me to imagine there may come a day when, though I will still be a human being, I will not be a person. It may now be my desire that when and if that day arrives, my life will be ended by the intervention of some person. Alternatively, I may now have altogether different wishes regarding my biological existence should I cease to be a person. I may now desire that extraordinary means be used to maintain the physiological functions of my body even if I have forever lost the capabilities to feel, to have purposes and concerns, or to remember.

In accounts of personhood like that of Wiggins the natural-kind element seems, for the most part, to be idle. In order for it to really have a significant role, it should function as the glue that holds together the collection of various capabilities, etc., that are listed in the functional descriptions that gather the kind. Wiggins expressly rejects such a view when he suggests the possibility that species or natural kinds "who come near enough to us" (p. 161) ought also to be regarded as persons. "Near enough" is notoriously slippery. Wiggins, in fact, though perhaps with some chagrin, analyzes this nearness condition in terms of the functional descriptions. Hence, an animal of another species is a person if its species' typical members are thinking, intelligent beings capable of having purposes, desires, etc., and of considering "themselves as themselves the same thinking things, in different times and places" (p. 161). It appears as if the animal element is but a nod to our convictions about the value of living organisms and a rather suspicious, ad hoc way of solving fission and fusion puzzle cases by ruling them impossible. The natural laws that govern animal kinds do not permit deviant delta formations in the lifelines of animals in the actual world.

The real difficulty with an approach like the one proposed by Wiggins is that it is unable to offer a way of avoiding conventionalism when it comes to the inclusion criteria for the class of persons. The natural-kind gambit fails to produce a real essence of person that will serve as an effective constraint on the conditions to be counted essential in the operational definitions. Hence, the position collapses into the descriptivist conventionalism it was created to destroy. Wiggins, however, does raise the right issues with respect to any conventionalist account of person. The key question ought to be, "Are we free, conceptually speaking, to shorten or lengthen the list of capacities included in the functional definition of person?" If we are unconstrained in this, we could declare an open-door policy that admits all manner of living things and as many artifacts to the club as suits our social, legal, or moral tastes. But such a policy would render the concept of person about as useful as that of stuff or thing.

The control on membership in the class of persons that is wanted might be provided in two rather different ways. The first is to adopt the view that the class of persons is determined by a purely nominal essence of person that is an invention of our conceptual history. In effect "person" would be treated as an artifact kind. For example, a pencil is a tool for writing and a clock a device for keeping track of time; actual mechanisms and construction of materials may vary as long as certain functions are performed. Performance of the function is what matters.

Suppose we call any group of things collected according to a set of purely conventional, functional descriptions a custom-governed kind. There may be social or semantic laws of association involved, but nothing like laws of nature will determine the crucial membership criteria for custom-governed kinds. The test of general use and practice is the only check on the adequacy of such criteria in the functional descriptions incorporated in the nominal essences of custom-governed kinds. Family resemblances, like those to which Wiggins seems to have final resort, should be expected to play a dominant role in determining the extensions of terms of a custom-governed kind. Hence, kind membership may be extended despite radical structural differences among members.

The second alternative captures the notion that although natural laws cannot be used to govern membership in the class of persons, total abandonment of a structural account is neither wise nor required. A body of empirically verifiable generalizations, such as, for example, those identified with common-sense psychology, can function, with respect to the determination of the membership in the class of persons, in much the same way as natural laws govern natural-kind membership.[12] Persons, on this account, are those things that behave in those ways that, by and large, are explainable by appeal to a coherent set of true empirical generalizations. The empirical generalizations that govern what is a person cluster around such states, primary of which is intentionality, that can be ascribed to entities by us on the basis of observed outward manifestations or behavioral evidence and which explain the molar behavior of those entities.

This account incorporates, it should be noted, a well-grounded doctrine in the law of contracts: the identification of intent with outward expression within the framework of ordinary meaning. Hence, Learned Hand wrote: "A contract is an obligation attached by the mere force of law to certain acts by the parties, usually words, which ordinarily represent a known intent."[13] And in the decision in *Brant v. California Dairies* (4 Cal. 2d 128, 133–34, 48 P. 2d 13, 16, 1935), we read: "it is now a settled principle of the law of contract that the outward manifestation or expression of assent is controlling."

There are, we may say, at least three types of kinds: custom-governed kinds, natural law-governed kinds, and empirical generalizations-governed kinds. (There certainly are other useful ways to draw these distinctions. One particularly fruitful way may be to do so in terms of what Moravcsik calls aitiational frames.)[14] To avoid the pure conventionalism of custom-governed kinds, we should require that membership in the class of persons be governed by a coherent set of true empirical generalizations, as are to be found in common-sense psychology. Such generalizations will be laced with probabilities and approximations, but inexactness of that sort is no stumbling block. The test of the set of generalizations, actually accepted, of course, will lie in its explanatory power with respect to the behavior of exemplars of the kind.

Consider the following example of such a generalization: someone who desires an object and believes that acting in a certain way will obtain the object, ceteris paribus, will act in that way. The coherent set of like generalizations, in fact, provides a behavioral elucidation of the concept of intentional action and actors. If something is a person, some of its molar behavior will be explainable by subsuming that behavior under those generalizations that express the concept of intentional action. This then captures our common belief that to be a person is, at least, to be an intentional actor.[15]

It is important that the account of person as an empirical generalizations-governed kind does not relegate the proper use of "person" to a matter of convention or politics. There are entry requirements that are not merely a matter of our legislation.

Recall that Putnam had offered as a constitutive fact of persons that they are partially opaque to each other. We are now in a position to explain how such a fact might be taken to be constitutive of the class of persons. The empirical generalizations that explicate the sameness relation for the kind are just that, generalizations. They should be expected to be laced with ceteris paribus and other qualification clauses, though with regard to much of the behavior of any random exemplar, they need to be projectable and universal, to support counterfactuals, and to ground explanations of past phenomena and predictions of future behavior. In other words, they must satisfy the conditions generally applied to laws of nature, though lacking assurance of application (the ceteris paribus nature of these generalizations) is the constitutive fact of partial opacity noted by Putnam. If I know from his expressions of desire that my neighbor wants a Triumph sports car and believes that if he takes a certain job he will make enough money to purchase the car, I should predict that he will take that job. But if he does not, I will not regard his not doing so as sufficient grounds to remove his name from the roster of persons. I will, of course, ask him if he really wants the Triumph and if he really believed that taking the job would make it possible for him to buy the car. I should want to check that I have the facts right. But, even if I do have all of the information, his choice to refuse the job may be based on psychological or other states about which I have, or even he has, no available knowledge. What we look for when we identify something as a person is that much of its behavior accords with the coherent set of generalizations we have identified. If in the case of a particular entity we find consistent departure from expectation, we should decide that the thing in question is not a person. If our generalizations were often undependable, we would have to frame a better set that would collect Carl Sagan and Ronald Reagan and Jane Fonda and me. Putnam's theory maintains that the extension of a natural-kind term is exposed by means of a theoretical sameness relation given in terms of natural laws to a suitable exemplar. On my account membership in the class named by "person," is also exposed by means of a sameness relation to a suitable exemplar. The sameness relation in the case of "person," however, is explicated in terms of a coherent set of empirical generalizations rather than natural laws. That, coincidentally, accounts for the fact that persons are partially opaque to each other, and hence why we are not realistically going to succeed in the enterprise of constructing a scientifically detailed explanatory model for "person."

To decide that something is a person is at least to have determined that it makes sense to redescribe some of its behavior in a way that makes true sentences that say that it acted intentionally. The empirical generalizations of common-sense psychological theory provide the theoretic superstructure for such redescriptions. In chapter 3 we located grounds for the redescriptions of corporate behavior by isolating the corporate intentionality aspect of corporate behavior. Business corporations, at least some of them, belong in the class of persons by virtue of standing in the appropriate sameness relation to Ronald Reagan, Carl Sagan, Jane Fonda, and me. What makes us all persons is not that we are made of the same stuff or have the same microstructure, but that our behavior can, by and large, be explained (and often predicted) by subsuming it under a certain specific set of empirical generalizations.

Corporations are to be counted as persons, but, some may argue, that provides only a prima facie reason to admit them to moral citizenry and that, on the basis of a number of other considerations, they should be excluded from the class of moral persons. "Moral person" on this account may name a kind that is gathered by some set of conventions or is gathered by an extended set of empirical generalizations beyond those that define the membership criteria for being a person. Some philosophers tell us, that for a person to be morally responsible, it must possess or evidence a set of properties over and above those of persons per se. In order to be held responsible, for example, it is sometimes argued that a person must be capable of expressing regret or remorse (or both) and of suffering punishment.[16] Intentionality and the empirical generalizations that explicate it, it may be argued, are not rich enough to include the functional descriptions thought necessary for moral accountability. Being a moral person would then be determined solely by our conceptual agreement about what properties we think an entity must have for it not to offend our sense of justice if we were to blame it or punish it for its deeds. This would, of course, render "moral person" the name of a custom-governed kind, and hence whether or not something is a moral person would be nothing but a matter of convention. Even if it is granted that corporations are persons, because they do not or cannot evidence the identified capacities, they cannot be moral persons.

"Moral person," would, on this account, be a sortal term used for cataloging some persons. Its extension over persons is determined by an intension that relates directly to our conception of justice or accountability. Dispute over the proper list of functional descriptions no doubt will be long and contentious. With respect to those descriptions, I do not think corporations will fare as badly as may be usually supposed.

We need not, however, discuss specific capacity issues. I suggest that the capacities and capabilities usually wanted for "moral persons" can be unpacked from the set of empirical generalizations that elucidate the intentional agency and that we have already identified as defining the sameness relation for "person." For example, consider regret. Imagine someone incapable of regret.

What are we imagining? There seem to be two kinds of answers, one draws attention to an individual who acts in a hardhearted, self-centered, antisocial, nasty manner. But what of the matter of incapacity? Someone may commonly manifest all of those traits, and it may also be true of him that he possesses the capacity for regret. The second answer provides a technical analysis that supports predictions of someone's future behavior. When it is said that a person is incapable of regret in this sense, something is being said about his capacity to view himself as the someone who did certain things, to think of himself as the person who did x (where x is an untoward action) and to feel or wish that he had not done x or that x had not had certain upshots. Regret, understood along lines such as this and when it has to do with the personal behavior of someone rather than with the feeling of disappointment or sorrow one might have about something that is out of one's control (e.g., "I regret that I have but one life to give for my country"), is subsumable in the standard elucidation of intentional agency. We may formulate an empirical generalization of common-sense psychological theory as: A person that has intentionally done something, x, and knows or remembers that he did x, and knows or believes that doing x by him (in the circumstances) was wrong or evil, ceteris paribus will manifest some distress or sorrow or even grief when he thinks about or remembers his having done x. Saying of someone that he is not a moral person because he cannot feel regret, then, amounts to saying that he is not a person.

There is one response to this general program that should be mentioned. It is the gambit that claims that "moral person" is really the name of the *compleat person,* the fully equipped and operational model. An incapacity of the relevant moral variety will illegitimize ascriptions of moral responsibility, while not affecting the integrity of the person in matters of personal identity. It is even fashionable in some circles to refer to such morally incapacitated individuals as dysfunctional persons. Yet the notion of a dysfunctional person is as slippery as any imaginable. If it means that an individual is technically in the extension of person by satisfying the sameness relation to Carl Sagan but is sadly impaired in such a way as to lack some crucial ability of *complete persons,* the concept of person has been knocked out of joint. All manner of things might have to be treated as dysfunctional persons. Remember the story of the prince who was turned into a frog? Imagine that it wasn't a talking, distressed, unhappy frog that knew it was really a prince, but just a frog, croaking away its little life on a lily pad, eating flies rapaciously, utterly oblivious to the fact that if a beautiful princess were, for God knows what reason, to kiss it, it would turn into a handsome prince. Would *that* frog qualify as a dysfunctional person, or is it not a person at all, or what? If "dysfunctional person" only means that something once upon a time was a person, but now is crucially disordered so that the empirical generalizations that are true of persons are no longer true of it, then we might just as well call it a former person. If there is a reasonable use for "dysfunctional person," it could be in cases where we believe, on good grounds, that the disorder or impairment is repairable or curable. The term would then serve as a protection device against the loss of personal identity during a gap, as, for example, in near-complete amnesia cases and perhaps in the frog-prince case. On the other hand, if the disorder is irreversible or irreparable, there are just no good reasons to cling to "person" at all. Hardhearted though it may sound, the popular expressions, "He's just an animal!" and (in other contexts) "He's just a vegetable!" have appropriate uses in cases of some former persons who are human beings.

We are, I think, best advised to hold that if something is a person, it is a moral person and reject the idea that a moral person is some special kind of variety of person, or a person with a difference, or a fully developed person, or whatever. If, as I have argued, intentional agency is the conceptual nexus elucidated by a set of empirical generalizations that define the sameness relation to a suitable exemplar that determines the class of things that are persons, and no more or less is needed to determine membership in the class of moral persons, then, if corporations are intentional agents (as I argued in chapter 3), they are persons cum moral persons. And, of course, that will also be true for Carl Sagan, Ronald Reagan, Jane Fonda, and me.

CHAPTER SEVEN

Plato, Bradley, Rousseau, and the Corporate Personality

The theory of the corporation as a moral person, it may be noted, has certain clear affinities to what is often called "the organic theory of the state."[1] The organic state theory boasts many famous proponents, including Plato, Hegel, and Bradley. Characteristically, organic state theorists maintain that an independent community with an established government constitutes an organic person or an individual. States are not created by contracts among members, they arise naturally. States literally are persons. In fact, they are, for some theorists, much more complete or total persons than are their flesh and blood brethren.

Early in the *Republic*, when discussing the formation of states, Plato maintains that "a state comes into existence because no individual is self-sufficing." He defends a principle of division of labor based on the proposition that "no two people are born exactly alike. There are innate differences which fit them for different occupations."[2] The picture Plato draws in Book II is that of a state naturally emerging because of the shortcomings of individual persons in providing for their own needs on an independent basis. The economic dependence of human beings, however, certainly does not make the state an organic person. The fact that people need to form interdependent communities in order to prosper, if not to survive, does not entail that the resulting social entity is itself an individual. And, it certainly does not entail that the social entity is an individual person in the same sense that the butcher Lazar Wolf, the tailor Motel Kamzoil, and the dairyman Tevye, are persons. Plato, however, is convinced that the state not only is a person in just the same sense that Tevye is, he thinks the state is more a person or a better specimen of a person than is Tevye, or Lazar, or indeed any individual member of the community. T. D. Weldon claims that such extravagant claims for the state are common in organic theories.[3]

That Plato believed the state literally is a person seems clear from his comments in Book II and elsewhere in the *Republic*. In one place he first convinces his listeners that a shortsighted person told to read an inscription in small letters would be most pleased to discover the same inscription written on a bigger scale. The analogy for Plato is obvious:

> We think of justice as a quality that may exist in a whole community as well as in an individual, and the community is the bigger of the two. . . . So I suggest that we should begin by inquiring what justice means in a state. Then we can go on to look for its counterpart on a small scale in the individual.[4]

Integral to this argument with regard to the organic state theory would seem to be the dubious assumption that justice is a quality or a property that can only be exhibited or had by persons. Plato, as is well known, has other arguments to show that the state bears properties usually identified only with people, and that it has those properties is more than a metaphoric or a purely aggregative or statistical sense. Two examples are worth mentioning: happiness and interests. They are obviously related.

Adeimantus asks Socrates to respond to the objection that the rigorous lifestyle prescribed for the Guardians will not make them particularly happy. The response is: "Our aim . . . was not to make any one class specially happy, but to secure the greatest possible happiness for the community as a whole." On first reading it might be believed that Plato is a utilitarian. On that reading, the happiness of the few must give way to that of the majority, which is identified with "happiness for the community." Plato, however, is not a utilitarian. The happiness of the community, for him, is not

dependent upon a utilitarian calculation. Plato carefully argues that
even if one took pains to insure that the Guardians, the farmers,
and all of the other members of the other classes of society were
individually happy, if one could "spread this well-being through
the whole community," the state would be destroyed. No class of
workers should be endowed with a happiness that will make them
anything "rather than that class of workers." Plato, as is his fashion, provides an analogy: the coloring of a statue. Suppose someone claimed that because the eyes were very important parts of the
body, they ought to be painted crimson rather than black. Plato's
reply: "You must not expect us to paint eyes so handsome as not
to look like eyes at all. This applies to all parts: the question is
whether, by giving each its proper color, we make the whole beautiful."[5]

For Plato then, the state's happiness is not identical to or even
derived from the sum of the happinesses of its members. On Plato's theory, as Weldon has aptly written:

> The State is happy when a particular type of political organization is real-
> ized in it, and if we want to know whether a particular state is a happy
> State, we must inquire into the extent to which that condition is satisfied.
> We should get absolutely nowhere by discovering that the individual citi-
> zens were happy.

Weldon also rightly points out that Plato's understanding of the
state's interests in no way depends upon what the joint or several
interests of its people may be. The interests of the state in a particular matter, or the interests of the state generally, is not determined by adding the interests of its members and it may be very
different from such a sum of individual interests.[6]

Some critics have pointed out that the Platonic conception of the
organic state actually amounts to a denial of the full personhood
of isolated individual citizens. I do not think that was Plato's intent, nor is it implied by his view. His theory does amount to a
defense of the view that justice need not be equated with the equal
treatment of all persons in the state. For the organic state to be

just, its members must successfully carry out a variety of tasks. Some of those tasks are, by their nature, more important to the well-being of the state than others. Hence, those who are naturally suited to perform those tasks ought to receive rather better treatment, indeed preferential treatment, than those who are only suited to less important tasks. Again, Weldon has clearly (if unenthusiastically) presented the position:

> The equality of man is not a self-evident fact but a dangerous delusion . . . within the State men are equal to precisely the extent to which the interest of the State requires that they should be equal and no more.[7]

In effect, in Plato's republic, status, determined by natural talents rather than contractual arrangements between theoretical equals, determines the structure of human social relations. In this respect the modern decentralized multinational corporation very nearly mirrors Plato's conception. In the corporation there may be a pretense of equality among all employees and indeed, in some ways, all are equal. The law has seen to that. But, as regards the development and furtherance of the corporation's interests and the corporate well-being, equality is not even paid lip service. Upper-level management receives higher salaries, has more benefits, more perquisites, better working conditions, etc., than do assembly-line workers or janitors. Only the most diehard of corporate democracy reformers would argue long for the equality within the corporation of those at all corporate levels. Without meaning to diminish the importance of the janitor's work, the corporate interests are certainly more dependent upon the decision-making of the vice-presidents. Hence, unequal treatment in recognition of corporate importance is totally consistent with the corporate interest. If, with Plato, one were to believe that the larger unit or person is requisite for the happiness and well-being of the smaller unit or the human being, then it is clear why every one, seeking his own happiness or wishing to further the ends of justice, should discourage the imposition of equal treatment. Justice is not giving to all equally, it is giving to each that which strikes the proper balance for the whole.

What is due to each is determined by status within the corporate body, and what is due is, generally, merit resulting from natural talents that determine status.

The popular rhetoric of many corporations, particularly in the 1950s and 1960s, echoed the dictum "what is good for the company is good for its employees." (The converse of the slogan was seldom heard in the corridors of corporate power!) The slogan has obvious Platonic overtones insofar as it puts forth the position that only when the employee is induced (or compelled) to achieve what amounts to the good of the firm will the employee realize personal good. The employees' good is not independent of the company good. In fact, on some readings, it may be that an employee cannot be said to have any good that is not derivative of the company's good.

All of this sloganing, of course, is just rhetoric (in the worst sense). Most everyone will recognize that what is unequivocally good for an employee often directly impedes the progress of the company towards the realization of its goals. Certainly some of the employee's good is derivative or dependent on the achievement by the firm of what is good for it, but it would not take too much imagination to list a number of employee goods that are quite independent and some that are even incompatible with the good of the corporation. It is for that reason that employees form unions and corporate boards issue codes of conduct forbidding bribery and other kids of self-serving among employees.

It is important, however, that the converse of that popular slogan also is conceptually erroneous. The converse expresses the proposition that the firm's good is but the sum of the goods of those associated with it. The good of the firm, on such an account, is additive or cumulative and, of course, dependent. The firm is supposed to exist only to further the aggregate goods of those associated with it. The converse of the slogan, in fact, improperly represents a corporation as an aggregate collectivity.

Talk of the good of an aggregate is, indeed, to talk in cumulative, or additive, or sometimes statistical terms. What, for example, is good for the passengers on TWA Flight 25? The arrival of the plane as scheduled? An uneventful flight? Suppose that 80 per-

cent of the passengers on Flight 25 are being flown to a prison camp
where they will undergo severe torture and risk of death. The fact
that Flight 25 will arrive at its destination as scheduled would hardly
seem a good for them. It would have been better for 80 percent of
the passengers had Flight 25 been delayed or, better yet, had it
been forced by weather or mechanical failure to land in some re-
mote spot, injuring none of the passengers or injuring only the crew
or guards assigned to the flight. The good of an aggregate, if aggregates can be said to have a good, seems generally to be reducible to at least the good of the majority of the component membership. An analysis of what is bad for an aggregate can be provided
along similar lines. To use an example from an earlier chapter,
suppose it is said that it would be bad for the Canby Saloon Crowd
if it were caught by the sheriff and punished for destroying the
saloon. All that seems to be meant is that it would be bad for each
member of the crowd were he or she to be caught and punished.

As Plato might not, however, have allowed, corporations (just
as states) can often correctly be said to have goods in a noneliminatable or reductive sense that do not trickle down to employees.
What is good for General Motors, in some cases, not only may not
be good for the country, it may not be good for the employees of
General Motors. We have recently seen in the Chrysler case, that
what seems to be good for the company, staying in existence, may
cost its employees in terms of salary and earning power. Employees in such cases, of course, have to decide whether they will bear
the costs of the firm's continued existence. If the company insists
that employees receive no wage increases in a time of double-digit
inflation, employees may soon learn that they cannot afford to work
for the good of the company. It is of some note to Platonists that
Chrysler tried to convince the union to cooperate with the firm's
recovery scheme by using the slogan, "What is good for Chrysler
is good for its employees!"

Parts of the *Republic* may leave one unconvinced that Plato was
fully committed to an organic state theory. No one, at least in the
history of English philosophy, however, was a more thorough-going
organic theorist than F. H. Bradley. In the fifth essay of *Ethical*

Studies, Bradley attacks the individualists, such as Kant, as propagators of a delusion: that individuals exist, in an objective sense, before civil association, that "individuals are real by themselves.[8] Bradley argues that the facts "refute" the individualist. No individual man exists in the way required by the individualist's theory. "What we call an individual man is what he is because of and by virtue of community, and that communities are thus not mere names but something real" (p. 166).

Bradley asks us to examine an Englishman and try to point out what he is that is himself alone and not a product of his society with other Englishmen. "Apart from his sameness with others, he is not an Englishman—nor a man at all; . . . if you take him as something by himself, he is not what he is" (p. 166). To be sure, Bradley does not mean that if our Englishman were the last of the race, as Chingachgook was the last of the Mohicans, that he would cease to exist. What he means is that the Englishman stripped of the network of relation that comprise the community into which he was born is an abstraction without a real essence. For Bradley, a human being "is what he is so far as he is what others also are" (p. 167).

No child, Bradley tells us, is flung into this world from heaven. All are born of parents who have certain ancestries. "But the child is not merely the member of a family; he is born into other spheres" (p. 169), including the English nation. Bradley continues to develop this theme by adopting a kind of Darwinian view of man and society. He writes:

> If Mr. Darwin's conjecture as to the development of man from a social animal be received, we must say that man has never been anything but social, and society was never made by individual men. . . . Thus the child at birth; and he is born not into a desert, but into a living world, a whole which has *a true individuality of its own,* and into a system and order which it is difficult to look at as anything else than an organism. (p. 170)

The theory of the corporation as a moral person is *not,* despite certain obvious analogies, a version of, or a modification of, an organic-state theory. The state for both Bradley and Plato (and the other organic theorists) is a natural entity, a thing in nature, and in some ways more real than its citizens. For Bradley, the very essence of a citizen is dependent upon the existence of the organic state. That which an individual citizen is essentially, is derivative of his place in the structure and history of his state. "State" on the different version of the organic theory names a natural kind, an organism that has its own "true individuality." Corporations are clearly not natural organisms. They are artifacts, creations of entrepreneurs, or of technocratic managers and lawyers. They could be thought of as inventions of economic necessity, but they are not natural entities. Corporations are more like machines than organisms and as such they have certain affinities to the invented contractual states of Hobbes and Locke, products of human ingenuity.

Setting aside the connotations of the title of his book, Hobbes's *Leviathan* is not a natural monster. It is an artifact. (Perhaps, if Hobbes had known of the Mary Shelley novel, he might have preferred the title *Frankenstein* for his treatise.) Weldon, in fact, prefers to characterize political theories such as those of Locke and Hobbes as "machine theories."[9] It is, however, hard to ignore the many similarities between the operating decentralized multinational business corporation and the picture of the organic state drawn by either Plato or Bradley. The corporation may be described as self-identical through time, possessing interests, having goods, etc. Its functions can be viewed as organismal, its personnel seen as occupants of stations in the organism or elements of the natural system, "many spheres subordinated to one sphere," organs working for the whole, some but as a "heartbeat in its system." Bradley writes, "The organs are always at work for the whole, the whole is at work in the organs. And I am one of the organs."[10] A cursory reading of much of the official literature that is distributed to employees in large corporations has an unmistakable Bradley-sounding tone. The employees are GFers at General Foods, P & G people at Proctor & Gamble, Duponters, or IBMers. For example:

All employees must keep constantly in mind that P & G people, wherever they are located and whatever they do, are expected to conduct themselves as Company representatives in accordance with the highest possible integ-

rity . . . try to do the right thing—is a principal facet of the total character
of Proctor & Gamble. And it is P & G's character that is the underlying
asset which holds the company together.[11]

The corporate personality is a key factor in corporate success.
That is the message of much of the recent literature. Large corporations that do not develop and display a clear corporate image,
both internally and externally, tend to fare badly in the economic
world. Corporate image is, of course, much more than logos and
letterhead designs. It involves style, expectations, a thoroughgoing
sense of unity and direction that permeates the corporation. Dif-
fusion and disarray, even in the matter of symbolism, can spell the
financial demise of the firm. Perhaps nothing is more important to
the corporate personality than the recognition of the fact that corporations are not founded, do not come into existence, to make
money or to make a reasonable profit for investors. Economists and
other business analysts most frequently forget this fact, and when
their hands dominate in the shaping of a corporation, as for example, in a merger, the resulting corporation is more likely than
not to experience unnecessarily difficult times. Too often we are
told that the business of business is to make money. That simply
is not true, and it is especially not true for the hundreds, if not
thousands or tens of thousands of people who work for major corporations. Corporations make automobiles, airplanes, breakfast
cereal, dog food, etc. They provide utility services, transportation,
health care, etc. Obviously, they do so in order to make a profit,
but with respect to the corporate personality and image, the factors that unify the corporate enterprise, the making of money especially for shareholders, is secondary. If the primary object of
corporate enterprise were to make a profit, then there would be
precious little to distinguish one corporation from another. Economists and lawyers who work on mergers and takeovers have a
woeful record of ignoring corporate personalities and their ramifi-
cations in the corporate enterprise. Corporate lawyers tend to work
out financial arrangements, tend to treat mergers as matters of sale
and acquisition, and ignore the personality, structure, and the at-

tendant loyalties of the managerial, professional, and other staff of the firms involved.

It is common after a corporation has passed out of the almost total control of an entrepreneur, the founding father, it needs to mold, even contrive, an identity that relates to the corporation's objectives. In a particularly engrossing study of company identities, Wally Olins has written:

> Cultivated corporate identity becomes the substitute for the personality of the entrepreneur. . . . Many mature organizations manage to develop an ethos, a way of doing business, that is so characteristic and so much a part of them that they seem to pursue it relentlessly . . . regardless of who runs the company . . . the corporate identity expresses itself in their every action.[12]

Olins goes on to say that when the "soul of the company" is not dominant in the ongoing activities of its personnel or when corporate interests are very broad and complex, as for example, they are with such diversified giants as Unilever and Swift, then those corporations "need the formal disciplines, structures, and assistance that a specially prepared corporate-identity program can provide" (pp. 83 and 87). The echoes of Plato's *Republic*, particularly the discussion of the myth of the metals, are unmistakable.

As an example of failure to develop, promulgate, and cultivate a clear and concise corporate personality, the VFW Fokker merger is classic. Without going into too many details, Olins has provided a very complete account (ch. 5), a few facts will suffice to make the point. After the war the German aircraft industry was virtually destroyed. A number of companies in the Breman area, Focke-Wulf, Weserflug, ENRO, Heinkel, Henschel, Sportavia Putzer, and Rheinflugzeugbau, merged to form Vereinigte Flugtechnische Werke (United Aircraft Works) or VFW. Its first project was the development of the VFW 614. The merger was, however, not totally an integrated success. Little cooperation developed or was encouraged among the formerly independent companies by the new executive officers. In fact, the old company names were, by and large, retained.

In 1970, a few years after the creation of VFW, another merger was engineered. This one involved VFW and Fokker. Fokker was a Dutch, not a German, company in the civil aircraft business. In many ways, analysts agreed, Fokker and VFW should have been an ideal merger. As Olins describes it:

> Fokker had a first-class marketing and sales organization, a history of sound, practical aircraft manufacturing and an excellent, clear image. VFW had brilliant, unconventional engineering, a very widespread selection of products, no real commercial know-how, virtually no image at all, and the implicit backing of Germany, Europe's richest state. (p. 56)

Apparently, much time was expended in the development of the organizational structure and the financing of the new company. Little if any thought was given to the matters of image, either as it would affect internal affairs or as it would affect external affairs. Identity problems almost immediately emerged. What would the new company be called? In almost laughable fashion it was decided by the merger engineers to call the company VFW-Fokker in Germany and Fokker-VFW in the Netherlands. No one would feel in his home base that his company was taking a back seat. The Dutch half of the company continued to call its products Fokkers, while the German company used VFW-Fokker for some of its products and retained the older company names for other products. Not only did this jumble confuse outsiders who dealt with VFW-Fokker (or Fokker-VFW), it created a factionalism in the company that can be best characterized as involving internal bickering, the maintenance of old loyalties, redundant research and development in an intracorporate competitive climate, and not surprisingly, cut-throat competition in sales campaigns by some factions of the company against others.

The consultants hired by VFW-Fokker to identity the causes of its problems and to recommend solutions made what would seem to be obvious suggestions: change the name of the company, neither "VFW" nor "Fokker"; develop programs to foster new loyalties to the new name and develop a new "visual system," a style, corporate colors, logo, etc., that insiders as well as outsiders would immediately associate with the new corporation. Old names should only be retained as product or brand names if they were spread through the organization and not allowed to singly be retained by their former companies for their products. In short, a new entity would have to emerge or be created from the union of the two companies, an entity with its own image and personality if the problems encountered by VFW-Fokker were to be solved. The commercial, financial paperwork on the merger was only a first step, and VFW-Fokker failed to complete the work necessary to foster a new corporation that could have proved a highly successful entity. The lesson is "that putting companies together on paper is not the same as putting them together in reality. It demands the creation of a common culture." Olins, in fact, maintains the new corporation must go so far that offices, signs, systems, and furniture should all be familiar to employees if they were to travel from one factory or research plant to the next (p. 61). A successful corporate merger is one that creates an harmonious, synergistic, if complex, entity that can then endure through time. The corporate personality in such cases is, of course, an invention, but its growth and development, its integration into the lives of the employees, and its perpetuation may be recognized as resembling most of the central features of the Platonic or Bradleyian organic state.

There is, in fact, a classical theory of the state that, though rejecting any natural origin account of the state, nonetheless characterizes the invented state in what may be regarded as organic terms. The theory is Rousseau's. In chapter 5 of Book I of *The Social Contract*, Rousseau compares a subjugated multitude to a true state. He says of the former that it is "an aggregation, perhaps, but certainly not an association for they would neither have a common good nor be a body politic."[11] In the famous passages of the next chapter, Rousseau describes how an aggregation of individual people can use a mechanical device, a contract, to create an association that, at least, resembles the organic state in important particulars.

Leaving aside the specifics of the contract in which each individual person in the aggregation unconditionally agrees to the total alienation of "himself and all his rights to the whole community"

(p. 60), the contract itself becomes the instrument of the genesis of a new being. Rousseau writes:

> Immediately, in place of the individual person of each contracting party, this act of association creates an artificial and collective body composed of as many members as there are voters in the assembly, and by this same act that body acquires its unity, its common *ego*, its life and its will. The public person thus formed by the union of all other persons . . . is now known as . . . the body politic. (p. 61)

Rousseau continues by arguing that after a multitude of people is so united, any injury to the state is felt by each member (p. 63). Further, when discussing the limits of sovereign power, he maintains that, "Just as nature gives each man an absolute power over all of his own limbs, the social pact gives the body politic an absolute power over all its members. . . ."[14]

This is not the place to discuss Rousseau's political theory in any detail, though it is of comparative interest to note the fact that Rousseau regards civil union as essential for not only civil liberty and property rights, but for moral freedom "which alone makes man the master of himself" (p. 65). This regard for civil union would seem to place him among the self-realizationists like Bradley who view the organic state as necessary to true individual human worth. If individuals can exist totally outside of the state for Rousseau, they cannot achieve what it really is to be a complete human person in the absence of true civil union. Such a high-minded, moral goal, in fact, justifies constraining individual persons from disobeying the general will of the state. But then that amounts, for Rousseau, to nothing more than forcing them to be free. The "political machine" is required for moral freedom, and so it is required for the realization of true humanity. As such, the civil state brings about a significant change in each of its citizens, converting them from animals of nature to ennobled rational beings.

> His mind is so enlarged, his sentiments so ennobled, and his whole spirit so elevated that, if the abuse of his new condition did not in many cases lower him to something worse than what he had left, he should constantly bless the happy hour that lifted him forever from the state of nature and from a narrow, stupid animal made a creature of intelligence and a man. (p. 65)

My point here is not, of course, to investigate such extravagant claims. It is only to identify what may be regarded as a distant relative of the theory of the corporation as a moral person. Mechanical creation, at least in the eyes of Rousseau, is not a hindrance to an organic-like conception of the created entity.

Rousseau's theory of the state has another aspect that is to be found in the theory of the corporation as a moral person. In Rousseau, the individual human being for moral purposes is not totally absorbed into the state, but instead may be individually treated with regard to responsibility. Although the state is necessary for the individual human being's realization of moral personhood, the state is not more real or morally more significant than the citizen. In fact, insofar as the general will cannot be in error, there may be a sense in which the state, for Rousseau, because it is by definition always morally correct, cannot be a moral person in any interesting sense. There seems to be a kind of narrow ultra vires doctrine involved. At any rate, Rousseau never describes the state as having moral freedom, at least not in the way citizens have such freedom. In my theory of the corporation as a moral person, both corporation (under certain conditions) and individual human beings associated with or employed by corporations may be held morally accountable and even for the same untoward outcome. It does, however, seem to me that without doing a great deal of damage to Rousseau's (or even Bradley's) theory an instructive analog may be exposed.

Suppose we ask "when does the state act?" For Rousseau, the state acts when the general will is carried out. But what does that mean? Putting aside the odd mathematics of Book II, chapter 3, we might say that an event is properly described as a state action if the actions of citizens can be redescribed in such a way that makes true the statement that the occurrence in question was an exercise of the general will of the civil association. Rousseau provides, if not explicitly or fully, redescription devices that allow or give license to the making of a descriptive transition from individual citizen acts to state or sovereign acts. The focus of those redescription devices is Rousseau's conception of the general will and, especially, of how that will is revealed. Redescriptions of certain actions of certain citizens (individually or in concert)—those actions motivated by the general will, hence those that are sovereign actions—expose the existence of an acting entity that at other levels of description is unrevealable. Indeed, that entity wills actions that are not reducible at another level of description merely to the actions or the wills of individual human beings acting individually or aggregatively. Sovereignty, Rousseau tells us, is inalienable and individual human beings acting individually or aggregatively. Sovereignty, Rousseau tells us, is inalienable and indivisible. "Either it is the will of the body of the people, or merely that of a part" (p. 70).

In a memorable passage Rousseau attacks other theorists who try to perform the reduction of state or sovereign acts to those of individual citizens. He writes:

> Sometimes our theorists confuse all the parts and sometimes they separate them. They make the sovereign a creature of fantasy, a patchwork of separate pieces, rather as if they were to construct a man of several bodies— one with eyes, one with legs, and the other with feet and nothing else. . . . This is more or less the trick that our political theorists perform—after dismembering the social body with a sleight of hand worthy of the fairground, they put the pieces together again anyhow . . . we should find that whenever we thought that sovereignty was divided, we had been mistaken. . . . (pp. 70–71)

For Bradley, of course, the level of description at which the state emerges is, in regard to the personal identity, moral worth, responsibility, etc., of human beings, paramount to levels at which only human beings are to be found. As earlier indicated, for Bradley, those human beings who might be said to exist at levels of description lower than that at which the state acts, are of somewhat dubious reality and surely ill and incompletely formed creatures. They would seem to be more shadow than substance. Rousseau clearly does not take so drastic a position with regard to citizens. I think that without doing him a great injustice we may characterize him as holding a middle position between the poles of Bradleyianism and methodological individualism. In this regard the theory of the corporation as a moral person has a distant ancestor in Rousseau's theory.

Moral agents or persons are to be counted at levels of description at which the intentional actions of entities are not divisible or reducible to other intentional actions. That does not mean that incorporated acts might not involve quite a number of intentional actions by human beings that are adequately and even fully describable at a level of description that does not allow for corporate acts. What it means is that redescription devices, such as CID Structures, do not necessarily preserve intentionality, in part because intentionality is an intensional and not an extensional notion. Also, the specific act in question, the one that is the object of the ascription of responsibility, depends for its existence, not only upon the acts or movements of things and persons that can be adequately described at some other descriptive level, that is prior to the introduction of the redescription device, but upon the redescription device itself. Casual inseparability does not entail the reducibility of moral responsibility.

Causation is a relation between events. In the case of corporate actions and the actions of persons associated with the acting corporation there is, in the relevant sense, only one event, albeit one that takes different nonequivalent descriptions. Some of those descriptions are intensional, including those that describe the event as the intentional act of a corporation. The casual context, of course, is extensional. If there is only one event in question, then whatever it causes will be caused by that event no matter how it is truthfully described.

If it is true that Hamlet's killing Polonius, the father of Ophelia, causes Ophelia to be an orphan, then Hamlet's killing the person hiding behind the arras in Gertrude's room also causes Ophelia to be an orphan. What surely cannot be true is that Hamlet's killing the person hiding behind the arras causes Hamlet's killing Polonius. An event described in one way cannot cause itself as described in another way. There is only one event. It is not that there is some basic event, one whose description is privileged vis a vis all other possible true descriptions, that has aspects that can be variously described as individual and corporate (or individual and sovereign for Rousseau). It is that there is an event in a certain casual sequence of things, however it is described, and it may, if certain conditions for description hold, be described as a corporate intentional act. If other conditions hold, it may also be described as the intentional act, or acts of a human being, or a group of human beings.

This is not an epiphenomenal theory nor is it a casual generation theory. I do not believe that corporate acts depend upon individual acts, if that is supposed to mean that the descriptions of the events in question that says they are individual human intentional acts are regarded as privileged.

The fact that descriptions of intentional acts are intensional explains why changes in descriptions of the same event, while preserving reference, do not preserve the truth or falsity of the description, its truth value. For example, both the sentences "Reserve Mining Company decided to deposit its taconite tailings in Lake Superior" and "Director Sly (or Reserve Mining), along with the majority of other directors, voted yes on the question" refer to the same event and could be substituted for each other, if reference to the event is the only concern, as in casual contests. Substitutivity of terms that refer to the same event in other kinds of contexts, as for example in explanations and in ascriptions of moral responsibility, does not carry a guarantee of the preservation of truth values.

The explanation of Director Sly's vote, suppose he voted that way because he had accepted a bribe to do so, may be no explanation for the fact that Reserve Mining decided to dispose of its tailings in the lake. That is because explanations relate facts, not events, and the same event may be redescribed in terms of the many different facts about it. Causal inseparability and referential substitutivity, with regard to these matters, are idle. Although I do not claim to be providing the interpretation Rousseau intended for his confusing account of the general will as "the sum of the difference" ("the pluses and minuses which cancel each other out"),[15] I think Rousseau's idea is not unlike the view I have defended. Regardless of the reason Director Sly may have for voting yes or even regardless of the personal reason another director may have for voting no, the corporate reason for disposing of the tailings in Lake Superior can be quite unrelated to the personal reasons the members of the board of directors or the senior managerial staff have for voting or acting in a certain way. Rousseau writes: "There is often a great difference between the will of all (what all individuals want) and the general will." The will of all is nothing but "the sum of individual desires" (p. 72). The general will is the will that expresses the common interest. In corporate terms the analog to Rousseau's conception bears out: there is often a great difference between what all persons in the corporation (or all persons in corporate managerial positions) want and what is in the corporate interest. As previously argued, corporate-policy recognitors are independent of and not reducible to the wants, beliefs, and desires of those persons associated with the corporation.

It is left to others to pursue the analogy between Rousseau's political theory and the theory of the corporation as a moral person, though it is worth mention that the usurpation of corporate power to personal ends can be fruitfully conceived of in terms strikingly similar to those Rousseau uses to talk of the abuse and degeneration of government in Book III of *The Social Contract*.

CHAPTER EIGHT

Tribes

In his justly famous article on collective responsibility, H. D. Lewis writes:

> Primitive peoples pay little heed to the individual; the unit is for them the tribe or the family. But reflection upon the affinity between the doctrine of collective responsibility and the undiscriminating "ethic of the tribe" should go a long way to discredit the former.[1]

Lewis makes two serious mistakes when he tries to assimilate collective and corporate responsibility to his conception of the ethic of the tribe. One is a factual error concerning the ways in which the individual natural person is treated in tribes that operate systems of collective or corporate accountability. The other is a type of logical error: unwarranted exclusion of a middle ground in an ordinary disjunction, one to which the clause "but not both" has not been appended. Hence, ordinary or non-exclusive disjunctions are true even when both disjoints are true. Lewis is certainly not alone in committing this error or in trying to point those who hold collective or corporate responsibility theories as advocates of an either/or exclusiveism. Professors Miller and Ahrens recently claimed in a paper commenting on my theory of the corporation as a moral person applied to a pollution case that the "central issue raised" when my theory is confronted with such cases of corporate misbehavior is whether the responsibility for the harm caused is to be ascribed to the corporation or to some individual member of the corporate body. Miller and Ahrens maintain that adoption of my theory forces one to conceive of these matters only in exclusive disjunctive terms. Either one may side with "corporationists" and lose the individual natural person *or* one must abandon the idea that the corporation can be nondistributively held morally accountable for events. One can capture either the corporation or the individual natural person, but (echoing Lewis) they argue, one cannot capture both.[2]

Lewis implies, and Miller and Ahrens argue, that only an exclusive disjunction will represent the issue as between individualism on the one side and any collective, corporate, or tribalist theory on the other. But surely there is a third disjunct that is being overlooked, or, rather, there is another and, in fact, preferred reading of the disjunction. Both the corporation and some person or persons associated with it (in some cases) may be held accountable for the same event. The disjunction is nonexclusive. It is true if one or the other or both of the disjuncts is true; otherwise, false. An event may support a number of different ascriptions of moral responsibility as it supports a number of different descriptions of causal responsibility. This is never thought to be a problem when responsibility for the same event is ascribed to two or three or more natural persons, for example in a gang-mugging case. In fact, it is to just such multiple individual responsibility ascriptions for the same event, that individualists like Lewis, want to distribute collective accountability claims. The real crux of the difficulty lies not in multiple accountability ascriptions, but in the fact that Lewis, Miller and Ahrens, and others are committed to doing the metaphysics of moral personhood with only a very restricted number of count nouns, with those that pick out individual human beings exclusively. If the metaphysics of moral personhood is done in terms of intentional actors, the temptation to see the disjunction as an exclusive one can be easily overcome.

My theory of the corporation as a moral person surely is misrepresented if it is thought to endorse an exclusive disjunction that sets the corporation over and against individual natural persons. I am not committed to the view that if a corporation is blamed or held morally accountable for an event, then the natural persons associated in that corporation are, eo ipso, exculpated from moral blame or responsibility. It may also surprise Lewis to learn that the primitives he is so fond of citing do not interpret their views of collective and corporate responsibility as excluding individual responsibility. Their views are usually inclusive, or rather, they entertain more than one descriptive position from which to conceive of the responsibility for events. We certainly can agree with Lewis that our intuitions would be offended if the adoption of a collective- or corporate-responsibility theory is used only as a way of getting natural persons off the moral hook. My theory does not do that, nor, as I hope to show, do the accountability systems of many preindustrial societies.

Rawls, it will be recalled, maintains that, with regard to organizations, "there is, perhaps, a certain logical priority to the case of human individuals."[3] By "logical priority" Rawls may mean that if individual natural persons did not exist, the groups and organizations could not exist. That is, of course, unexceptionable, but it is neither a significant point for our interests, nor one upon which confirmed individualists, like Lewis, rest their positions. Lewis, for example, appeals to what he takes to be basic intuitions about what Joel Feinberg has called "clutchability."[4] Corporations, however, if my arguments are cogent, also satisfy clutchability conditions, and it should not be forgotten that Rawls includes organizations and corporations in the class of persons in the "original position."[5]

The real difference between Lewis' and my view is to be located in the definition of what a moral person is or, in other words, of what is the basic moral unit. On my account, basic moral units are intentional actors, for Lewis they are human beings. Lewis would also have us believe that tribalists (by his definition) regard the tribal unit as morally basic. There would, it would seem, be little or no dispute among us, about how responsibility ascriptions function when they are about basic moral units. Reduction, for moral purposes, of a basic moral unit to its constituent parts simply is incoherent. For example, if natural persons are morally basic, then it would be nonsensical to talk of holding a person's right hand or index finger morally to account for having moved in a certain way when the person fired a gun killing another person. If the tribe is morally basic, then holding members responsible for their actions would be incoherent.

Lewis' version of the tribalist's position is best understood as the view that the collective unit or the tribe is morally the basic unit. Lewis, however, does not impute to the tribalist any theory that amounts to making the claim that tribes are intentional agents. Actually, on his account the tribe is an aggregate that happens, given the "barbaric" attitudes toward morality that are to be found in preindustrialized societies, to bear all responsibility for component member behavior. Lewis is, no doubt, right about one element of his "understanding" of the tribalist position: tribes are not generally, I would suppose, thought of by their members in conglomerate terms, as having intentions. That may, of course, be more a matter of lacking the notion of intentionality than anything else. At the very least, tribal members often do talk of tribal interests, goods, and policies.

If we were to classify Lewis' position, my theory, and Lewis' version of tribalism, we should say that with regard to what constitutes a basic moral unit, we have at least three alternatives: mature (or competent) natural persons, intentional agents, and collective units. Setting aside the fact that there may actually exist some societies in which Lewis' tribalist theory governs the ascribing of moral accountability, the preponderance of anthropological evidence regarding primitive peoples who do operate collective-responsibility systems strongly indicates no exclusive tribalist position of the sort Lewis suggests. The evidence is unclear, however, with regard to whether or not an inclusive position, such as my own, would properly describe the practices. The stumbling block is clearly the lack of information about the way certain tribal units function as decision-makers and actors. Much is still to be learned from the primitive practices that have been the object of research by Sally F. Moore.[6] It will be useful to outline some of her findings before drawing some useful lessons.

Moore catalogs four basic types of tribal collective arrangements for the handling of economic responsibilities: noncorporate stock-associate groups, egocentric networks, lineage-corporate groups, and tribal corporations (p. 83). (For Moore, collective responsibility is understood primarily in economic terms as when a group of people are together held to account for the actions of one or more of their component members.) The Jie and Turkana tribes operate stock-associate systems in which each individual, in effect, creates an association for himself, assembles an aggregate of persons that collectively will make good his debts or the damages done to him by an opponent. Moore explains:

> Stock associates are all those individuals with whom a man maintains reciprocal rights to claim gifts of domestic animals on the more important occasions of social life. A man's stock associates include his close agnates, close maternal kin, close affines and bond friends. Each man has his own assortment. . . . Disputes are settled by payments of stock solicited from the stock associates who in turn expect a share of any payments received. (p. 80)

Interestingly, responsibilities fall on stock associates because each has a relationship to a certain person, not because of the relationships that exist among the members of a stock-associates group. There are clear affinities between such an arrangement and that which exists between a corporation and its stockholders. The group that is held collectively liable is an aggregate assembled by an individual even though the disputes, debts, etc., in which that individual is embroiled are individual matters, not collective ones. The individual, it seems, does not usually consult his stock associates before entering into a dispute or fight that puts at risk some of the assets of his associates. It is important, though, that if he makes a habit of engaging in costly adventures, he is likely to find the aggregate of his stock associates to have dwindled down to only his most loyal kith and kin.

A variant of the stock-associate scheme is practices in the Kipsigis and the Lango tribes. In those tribes, however, a concentric circles model is operative. Each member of the tribe is understood to be surrounded by concentric circles of kin to whom, working from the center out, he may appeal for aid in meeting his debts, for example in raising a blood payment for a homicide. Contributions are made to the individual debtor, as an individual, and outer-circle occupants are only approached after inner-circle members have either refused or failed to produce the needed funds. In these schemes, the debtor is expected to make the major contribution from his own sources. It is important that in both this egocentric network scheme and in the stock-associates scheme, responsibilities as between tribes or as viewed from the outside are treated as if they fall on the collective units, when, in fact, they fall on individuals.

The Suku tribe, Moore tells us, organizes its economic responsibilities in a totally collective way.

> The lineage is a corporate group with assets regarded as allocated to individuals but circulating freely and treated as a common resource for virtually all purposes, everyone chipping in to make payments whenever necessary. (p. 83)

Members of the Arusha Masai tribe, in a somewhat similar fashion, raise blood payments, etc., by "contributions" from all member-components of the tribe. The size of each member's contribution in any particular case is determined at an assembly of lineage counselors. Here again the practice is deceptively collective. When viewed from an external vantage point the basic moral unit for the Arusha Masai, the bearer of accountability, that which is responsible for untoward extratribal behavior, appears only to be the tribe itself, taken as a unit. But that is an allusion of point of view, even in the case of extratribal affairs.

In the Arusha Masai as well as in the other tribes, the right to expel any member is crucial to the workings of the responsibility- and obligation-incurring systems. Expulsion sets the parameters on tribal liability for the behavior of its members. Kinsmen or other tribal associates, in all of the above cases, "can limit their liability simply by refusing to support an individual who has imposed too much or too often on their assets" (p. 84). Insofar as expulsion is the primary regulatory tool, it must be the case that the tribe is *not* the basic moral unit for these peoples. The tribe or other collective structure, however, is treated as if it were basic and non-reducible at the intertribal or extratribal level. This suggests that these preindustrial societies have developed an internal/external dichotomy that operates in responsibility matters. One helpful way to conceive of the functioning of such a dichotomy in the tribe is to understand the set of rules that are operative (among tribal members) in the determination of the proper subjects of account-ability ascriptions as containing, in part, description or redescrip-tion licenses. To think of the rules along those lines is to treat the set of such rules rather as if they work the way CID Structures work in cases of corporate intentionality. Clearly, of course, in the tribal cases intentionality is not at issue for the tribes, and I do not mean to suggest that tribal members regard the collective units in their accountability schemes as persons. I have no reliable data that indicates how they conceive of the tribal or kinship units. That is a job for an anthropologist. My only interest here is to show that tribalists, that is those who, for certain purposes, treat tribes or other kinship units as sometimes morally basic, need not be com-mitted to the position Lewis has foisted on them. If they have a sufficiently high set of rules for describing and redescribing inter-nal and external issues, they may regard both the tribe and its in-dividual members as morally basic or nonreducible units that bear full moral as well as economic responsibility for misdeeds.

The tribal accountability schemes discussed above have appar-ently proved efficient in handling intertribal difficulties. Punish-ments and compensations are exacted at the collective level when injuries have been perpetrated on the member or members of one tribe by a member or members or another. No attempt is made in such cases by the offended to identify and punish the individual offender. Satisfaction, as between tribes or when individuals deal with those of tribes other than their own, is a tribal business. The tribe is held corporately responsible, and it meets its obligations and debts in whatever way it sees fit. Once the external matter has been settled, internal matters may be addressed.

Internal allocations are worked out in a variety of ways, but in no case, to my knowledge, is the offender treated as if he has no individual responsibility for the debt. In some tribes, self-help (as in the stock-associates scheme) is only a mechanism whereby the offender amasses the goods necessary to meet the obligation. Strikingly, the process has the effect of more firmly cementing tribal relations. In fact, moral responsibility for the offense is not distributed to tribe members, even if from the external point of view the tribe shoulders the moral responsibility for the untoward event. Lewis' precept that no one can bear the moral responsibility for another's actions is not violated, as he thinks it is, by the collective and corporate responsibility schemes of those tribes discussed above.

Moore offers the following hypothesis:

> Where every member of a corporate group has the power to commit it . . . to a collective liability, a corollary rule always exists whereby the corporation may discipline, expel or yield up to enemies members who abuse this power or whom the corporation does not choose to support in the situation in which he has placed them. (p. 89)

Her hypothesis appears to be borne out by the anthropological data, but again, that is a matter for anthropologists and not a philosopher. Obviously the hypothesis has an analog in contemporary corporate life. Although the corporation may be morally responsible for an untoward event caused by a corporate decision, if particular individual executives made poor decisions, or failed to gather the appropriate data, or ignored relevant information, they may be disciplined or even fired. Corporate internal discipline is not terribly different from tribal internal discipline.

CHAPTER NINE
The Medical Profession

I am concerned in this chapter to deal with sentences such as the following:

1. "The medical profession is responsible for the inequitable delivery of health care in the United States." (Meaning that, let us stipulate, the medical profession has pursued and is pursuing a profit-motivated course of action that directs service primarily to the wealthy.)

2. "The emergency medical team at Fair Hope Hospital must be given the full credit for saving the life of Mr. Tulkinghorn after he was critically wounded by a gunshot." (Meaning that the team performed certain tasks in the emergency room, removal of the bullet, stoppage of the bleeding, etc., such that had the team not acted as they did the patient would have died.)

3. "Fair Hope Hospital is to blame for understaffing the nursing surveillance stations in the Intensive Care Ward." (Meaning that the hospital is using less than full nursing shifts in that ward.)

4. "Dr. Allan Woodcourt is responsible for missetting Mr. Gridley's broken arm, thereby causing him further pain and suffering." (Meaning that Dr. Woodcourt failed to perform the task for which he had been engaged and the result was further agony for Mr. Gridley.)

All four sentences ascribe responsibility for occurrences. None of the four is idiosyncratic. Sentences of these varieties are in common usage. Reference to medical issues is not particularly important. Other professional groups and organizations could have been substituted for those I have selected from the practice of medicine. I shall argue that no single analytical tool will allow us to properly interpret the responsibility ascriptions contained in each of these four sentences.

My concern in this chapter is with the way the theoretical apparatus and distinctions drawn earlier in this book are to be applied to these four sentences. Recall sentence 1: "The medical profession is responsible for the inequitable delivery of health care in the United States."

First, this is a rather sweeping condemnation. The speaker no doubt intends to paint with the broadest of brushes. But what has he said? It is of primary importance to learn whether "the medical profession" is the name of a conglomerate or of an aggregate collectivity. There is surprisingly little written to help us answer that question, though the same issue does arise with respect to the legal profession, the teaching profession, engineering professions, etc. Is "the medical profession" a shorthand way of referring to all of those who legitimately (legally?) practice medicine at any one time (the time of utterance of that name in a sentence?). Or, is the medical profession something more than or other than the simple sum of medical practitioners, something about which one may, e.g., talk of intentions, decisions, and actions? Does the medical profession, as we understand it, have internal decision structures by which courses of action can be chosen? Does it have ways of acting, as a profession? That is, is there a standard way by which to identify the legitimate redescription of the acts of individuals as the acts of the profession? Do individual medical practitioners fill specifiably differing roles and exercise different levels of power and accept different kinds of duties by virtue of their being associated in the medical profession? To answer these questions we must first overcome the inclination to identify the medical profession with the AMA. The AMA is *not* the medical profession nor does it speak for the profession, regardless of what the AMA may claim. It is, to be sure, a professional organization that includes and represents approximately 50 percent, by its claims, of the members of the profession. The existence of the AMA or any similar organization is surely not a necessary condition for the existence of the profession.

The medical profession is a certain class of persons whose members have a special kind of education and/or training and have demonstrated competency to the satisfaction of some governmental body or some body empowered by government to confer licensure. For the licensure step to be accomplished with as much uniformity as possible, an organization like the AMA may provide governmental bodies with a list of criteria for deciding who qualifies for membership in the profession, what Kenneth Kipnis has called "gatekeeping procedures."[1] But the professional organization is not the profession, even if it purports to speak for the profession. The profession is just that collectivity of persons who have been certified and actually practice medicine in some capacity.

The list of identifying characteristics of profession members must, as mentioned, include certifiable possession of a special competence in medicine, but whether or not what Kipnis calls a "public commitment to devote (oneself) to the realization of some significant social value" is also such a characteristic seems to me dubious. I suppose attesting to the Hippocratic oath would satisfy Kipnis' condition. But it is likely we would not want to identify the members of the medical profession simply as that group of persons who have taken the oath. Hence it surely is not a sufficient condition.

The idea that a profession has (or should) made (make) a collective commitment to work for the realization of some social value is, however, of importance in providing the background for our sentence (1). If we identify the medical profession as the class of certified medical practitioners, we may further say that it is desirable that that class of persons accepts a special social obligation: the health care of the members of the society.

We need not identify professional membership in virtue of shared commitment, but having established the identity of the collective, we may impose certain duties upon its members, and perhaps we may even set the price of continued certified membership as the continued competent attempt to carry out those duties. Hence, flagrant malpractice may constitute grounds for loss of membership. But the profession does not exist because of the duty; the duty is socially imposed upon the profession and is distributively accepted by individual members as the continual cost of membership.

This constitutes the outline of an argument with the conclusion that "the medical profession" names an aggregate. It is of interest that the duties assigned to the profession are rather general and broadly based. It would seem to make little sense to say that the medical profession is responsible for the proper setting of Mr. Gridley's broken arm, but it makes good sense to say that Dr. Woodcourt's responsibility to properly attend to Mr. Gridley is, in part, a distribution of Dr. Woodcourt's profession's general duty to proper health care. Assuming that he has been engaged by Gridley, however, Woodcourt, perhaps in a more primary sense, has accepted an obligation to properly treat his patient-customer. Regardless of what we may be idealistically inclined to say about the commitment of the aggregate profession, we must not forget that medicine is also a business based on contract!

Sentence 1 should be read as an ascription of responsibility to an aggregate. In other words, it should be translated to read that the component membership of the aggregate is causally responsible for the fact that health care in the United States is not delivered in what the speaker regards as an equitable manner. That translates to saying that each of the individual members of the aggregate bears responsibility for that condition and, of course, one may further say that each member is morally responsible if there are no mitigating or exculpating reasons for not holding him accountable. One might turn up excuses of the sort, "What could one doctor do?" or "I've done my part with the free clinic on Saturday mornings when I could have been on the golf course," or "I only just finished interning last month," etc. Each of these types of excuses would need to be carefully examined in specific cases. That is not of concern here. To the point, however, is the fact that excuses of these sorts are all too commonly offered when someone utters sentence 1, and that fact, at least, endorses the analysis given of sentence 1. It should not be forgotten that excuses of these types, even disassociative ones, are indicative of the readiness to acknowledge that something with which one is associated has been at least causally involved in an occurrence that has gone wrong or been untoward. The individual defense against accountability, to paraphrase Austin, is to admit that what happened was not a good thing, but not to accept the full, if any, moral responsibility for it.[2]

Sentences 2 and 3 do not admit to the same sort of analysis as does sentence 1 because they are about entities different in kind from that which was the subject of sentence 1. Sentence 2 praises the emergency team at Fair Hope Hospital for saving a gunshot victim's life. Sentence 3 condemns Fair Hope Hospital for understaffing nursing stations. It is rather easier, given our theoretical apparatus, to deal with sentence 3 than number 2. Fair Hope Hospital is, we may presume, an organization of the conglomerate type. It is a business corporation, the paradigm of a conglomerate, with, we may presume, a CID Structure, allowing it to satisfy the conditions necessary for it to be treated as an intentional actor. If Fair Hope is to blame for an untoward situation then we, as it were, have the culprit straightaway. It does not follow, however, that some particular administrator at Fair Hope Hospital has acted in a substandard or morally unacceptable fashion and thereby caused the untoward situation for which blame is being properly assessed. Generally, of course, it will be true that some executive of Fair Hope Hospital has made a bad decision, even one for which he ought to be held morally, if not legally, accountable. But that determination is quite another matter from determining whether or not sentence 3 is in order as it stands or whether it is but a shorthand device in need of reductive or distributive translation over individual human beings. "Fair Hope Hospital" is not a shorthand way of referring to a large number of persons who work at the hospital. Of course, individual human beings at the various levels of administration at Fair Hope Hospital do not necessarily escape moral accountability simply because the hospital is blamed for understaffing nursing stations. The moral accountability of administrators is a matter of what they actually, intentionally, did or were willing to do or did not do. The fact that their actions are redescribable as corporate actions and that corporate actions can be morally assessed is no shield from individual responsibility.

My inclination is to treat the emergency team as a conglomerate, but I have reservations. If the team is structured in such a way that decisions and actions are reached and performed according to an established decision structure and if positions of authority have been created that function in the team-action process irrespective of the particular practitioner filling the position, then I think it proper to regard the identity of the team as not merely constituted by the particular doctors, nurses, and technicians that happen to hold various positions on the team at the time Mr. Tulkinghorn is treated. There is, however, a need to make much clearer what makes any particular collection of medical practitioners a team. One hears of a group "beginning to function as a team." Imagine one of the members exclaiming, "At last we're a team!" Usually in such a case the use of "team" is only intended as a way of saying that awkwardness and unnecessary repetition of tasks has been eliminated during procedures. A team might not function much like a team at all. Witness the New York Mets of the early 1960s.

What makes a medical emergency team a team in the relevant sense, it seems to me, will have to be organizational structure. A happenstance collection of the finest medical minds, the deftest medical hands, and the best medical technicians gathered in an operating room over a patient will not necessarily make a team, regardless of whether or not their actions save the patient's life. A less-talented collection, however, could satisfy the conditions for being a team. If a true team is created, although individual accomplishment and failure can and ought to be recognized, it should make sense to treat the team itself as a primary subject of accountability.

Sentence 2 certainly praises the emergency team for saving a life. It does not say that a particular doctor, nurse, technician, etc., is responsible for the praiseworthy outcome. We may imagine that each team member simply did his or her assigned tasks in a rather perfunctory, ordinary, though competent, way. Looked at individually, there is nothing particularly praiseworthy about anyone's actions. Had anyone done less, failed to perform to normal standard, of course, he might be held accountable if his actions caused the end result to be unhappy, if the patient were to die. But, in fact, even if one of the team members does not perform quite up to standard and matters proceed to a successful end, sentence 2 will be appropriate. There is an error factor in team play. Sometimes an error will have no effect on the outcome, and hence, it is either forgiven or made a personal matter among team members who might be concerned about its repetition on another occasion. Other times an error by a team member will decide the issue unfavorably. The team loses *and* the errant member will also be held accountable and possibly removed from the team. The loss, of course, is borne by the team. The team bears the responsibility for the success or failure of the enterprise. In other words, the accountability of the team with respect to the reason for its organization does not seem to be distributive among the members. But team members do not hang together so as to avoid hanging separately. They hang together and they may also hang separately for their failures as individuals to perform their team or role tasks. This account of teams then, appears to be very like that of conglomerates.

Sentence 2 should probably be read as nondistributive, as saying that the medical team is responsible for saving Mr. Tulkinghorn's life and that the team deserves full credit for doing so. It does not say that any particular member of the team deserves full credit. It does not even say that every member of the team deserves some credit. Team members, we may suppose, enjoy the glow of credit earned by the team, but the more sober among them will realize that they may only individually have done the minimum they were hired to do. They just did their job. In a baseball game, if the right fielder catches a routine fly ball to end the game, he would be thought more than a bit extravagant were he to claim the credit for the team's victory just because he did not drop the ball. Yet, of course, there is some sense to saying that he does share in the victory. It does, however, seem to me instructive that in sports histories team and individual records are never confused. (Witness the fact that both Ralph Kiner and Ernie Banks have been inducted into baseball's Hall of Fame for their individual accomplishments although both played on dreadful teams during their entire careers.) Much more, unfortunately, must be done on the analysis of teams, with respect to responsibility, than is presented here. Although it is clear that teams are not just aggregates, my intuitions caution against their treatment as full-fledged conglomerates. Nonetheless, the above account of sentence 2 seems to me correct on the assumption that the emergency team is a distinct, organized unit through time and not an ad hoc arrangement of practitioners. We may be able to assimilate medical teams, but not professional baseball teams, to the aggregate model on the grounds of the absence of conglomerate policy recognitors, the lack of a general policy of action that can be said to inform those decisions that are team decisions, that is instantiated in team actions, that licenses redescription of events as team actions rather than as the acts of aggregated human beings. That policy element is integral in a Corporate Internal Decision Structure. The question in the case of the team is whether a collective general intention to try to do whatever possible to successfully treat its patients constitutes a conglomerate basic policy. I am reluctant to say that it does, even though that leaves matters in a rather untidy state. It may be suggested that "team" is used metaphorically when it is used to refer to certain medical collectives. The metaphorical escape, however, is surely undermotivated here and has a suspiciously hollow right to it. In fact, I cannot see any strong reasons, laying aside neatness, in support of a claim that there is anything metaphorical about "emergency medical team" at all.

In summary, I think we may say that the analysis of types of collectivities has served us with a defensible, and I think correct, reading of sentences 1 and 3. Sentence 4 was not, from the point of view of the present concerns, problematic. Unfortunately, sentence 2 is not so clearly resolved by application of the theoretical apparatus.

In concluding this chapter I want to say something more about sentence 1. I want to say that it is true. The medical profession is responsible for the inequitable delivery of health care in the United States. That does not mean that the profession is solely responsible, but, as argued above, what it does mean is that the individual members of the profession bear the moral burden for the problem.

If one is concerned with the rectification of the inequity, then it is to the behavior of individual component members of that aggregate that one must direct attention. The medical profession is not a shield that hides individual medical practitioners from responsibility for the general state of health care. Quite the contrary. The use of the name of the aggregate in such a responsibility ascription puts each and every one of them on call.

CHAPTER TEN

What Is Hamlet to McDonnell–Douglas
or
McDonnell–Douglas to Hamlet:
DC–10

On March 3, 1974, on the outskirts of Paris, France, a Turkish
Airlines plane carrying 346 passengers and crew fell from the sky
killing all aboard. The plane was built by the McDonnell–Douglas
Corporation, with major design subcontracts to the Convair Division of General Dynamics. It was ship 29 of the DC–10 line. It
became clear shortly after the event that the crash was no mere
accident, not an act of God nor due to pilot or crew error. Ship 29
fell from the sky when its cargo-hold door blew open at approximately 10,000 feet, causing the floor of the passenger compartment to collapse, thereby breaking the electrical and hydraulic lines
that run under that floor. Without electrical or hydraulic power
the airplane is unflyable.

The Paris crash was not the first cargo-door failure on an in-
flight DC–10. Some two years earlier over Windsor, Ontario, an
almost duplicate accident occurred, but not all hydraulic lines were
severed. The pilot of that plane, owned by American Airlines, mi-
raculously managed to land the airplane in Detroit, without fatal-
ities. The history of DC–10 door failure and floor collapse, however, dates back to July 1970, when ship 1 of the line, while under
pressurization tests outside a hangar at the Douglas factory, blew
its cargo door, and the floor collapsed.

There can be little doubt that many engineers and managerial personnel at McDonnell–Douglas (and Convair) knew, well before the Paris crash, of the potential for a class IV hazard. (A class IV hazard is a hazard involving danger to life.) due to defective design of the DC–10 cargo-door latching system and the floor structure. Not unexpectedly, McDonnell–Douglas tried to blame Turkish Airlines and its ground personnel for the Paris disaster. When that did not stick, it then suggested that some relatively low-ranking members within its own corporate structure had been contributorily negligent in the manufacture of ship 29. There is, indeed, strong evidence that some employees of McDonnell–Douglas, through negligence, carelessness, or sloppiness, contributed to the design and manufacture of a defective airplane, but the authors of one of the books that provide the history of the corporate development of the DC–10 have also written:

> Some part of the blame [for the Paris disaster] must lie with the major subcontractor for the DC–10, the Convair division of General Dynamics. But the *central responsibility*, at least in terms of morality, must lie with McDonnell–Douglas and in particular with its Douglas division.[1]

Evidence supporting that claim will be our primary concern in this chapter, but the moral responsibility of some individuals within the broader context of corporate responsibility will also be examined. I am not here concerned with legal responsibility. The standard legal notions of strict liability, enterprise liability, and, the traditional ambit of corporate legal responsibility, vicarious liability, provide adequate legal basis for recovery for wrongful death. The usual interpretation of such notions, however, steadfastly sidesteps full-fledged corporate *moral* accountability and blameworthiness and hence does not locate a ground upon which a viable theory of corporate criminality and punishment may be built.

In order to examine some of the morally significant aspects of this case, it will be necessary to introduce what I take to be rather commonly held views about the accountability of moral persons. A first condition of accountability (or moral responsibility) is what Bradley called "selfsameness." Bradley wrote:

If when we say, 'I did it,' the I is not to be the one I, distinct from all other I's; or if the I now here is not the same I with the I whose act the deed was, then there can be no question whatever but that the ordinary notion of responsibility disappears.[2]

This condition is deeply grounded in our intuitions. It is, simply, the statement of the need for identity through time of moral subjects. If moral persons lack identity through time, in other words if there were *no* grounds for identifying one moral person now as the same person who existed at some previous time and did certain things, all sense of holding persons accountable for their deeds would be lost. The selfsameness condition, as we saw in chapter 2, can be met by corporations.

In Book III of the *Nicomachean Ethics*, Aristotle argues that only voluntary actions are properly praised or blamed. When behavior is involuntary, "we are pardoned and sometimes even pitied." For Aristotle, behavior under constraint or compulsion or because of ignorance is involuntary. Let us concentrate on ignorance. Aristotle distinguishes two primary senses of ignorance. The first is ignorance of moral principle, which he tells us is not pardonable. He writes, "Ignorance in moral choice does not make an act involuntary—it makes it wicked. Aristotle's second major sense of ignorance is "ignorance of the particulars which constitute the circumstances and the issues involved in the action."[3] Aristotle maintains that exculpability and pardon depend on what aspects of the circumstances are those of which the person is ignorant.

Consider Hamlet. Let us stipulate that he knows his moral principles, that he knows that intentionally killing an innocent human being is murder, is morally wrong. We also know that he is certainly ignorant of the fact that the person hiding behind the arras in Gertrude's room is the rather harmless Polonius and not the murderous King Claudius. In fact, when he stabs that person, he believes he is stabbing the King. In keeping with Aristotle's point, it is clear that a person may be ignorant of many of the true descriptions of his action that are different from the one under which he intended the action. An action may be intended under one description, but not intended under another. Hamlet intends to kill the person hiding behind the arras, and he intends to kill the King who he believes is hiding there, but he certainly does not intend to kill Polonius. Hamlet's ignorance of the identity of the person he intentionally stabs even may be offered in support of the claim that it is false that Hamlet *murdered* Polonius. (You can kill but you cannot unintentionally murder someone.) Of course, there is much more we should want to say about Hamlet's deed before we consider letting him off the moral hook. At the very least, however, it is clear that when accountability is at issue, it is crucial to know what a person intended as well as to know what actually happened. Insofar as ignorance limits what a person can actually intend, we see why true descriptions of a person's actions that are unknown or unforseeable by him are not properly praised or blamed. Suppose Hamlet had stabbed into the arras thinking he was killing a rat, and lo and behold, the King, who had been hiding there, is dispatched on his way off this mortal coil. Would Hamlet deserve praise for so efficiently avenging his father? Not very likely!

These considerations may be captured in what I have elsewhere called the strict or Primary Principle of Accountability (PPA): a person can only be held accountable for that person's intentional acts.[4]

PPA however, is counterintuitive. It does not even satisfy intuition in the Polonius stabbing case. A few minor modifications need to be made.

First, we do want to hold persons morally accountable, at least to some degree, for some of the unintended effects of their actions, those they should have or did know would occur. Suppose you know that you have inadequate skill for the performing of some task that when performed by the unskilled usually results in harm to someone else. The first time you perform the task, if you are unaware that harm will result and harm does result, we are likely to write off the harm as an accident or a misfortune and not hold you accountable. If you perform the task again, without sufficiently improving your skill, even if causing the harm is not your intention, you were willing to have the harm occur. In such cases you can be held morally accountable for the harm.

This explains why we are inclined to hold Hamlet morally accountable for Polonius' death. When he stabs through the arras with the intention of killing the person behind it (though he believes that it is the King), he is willing to kill Polonius if, as it happens, Polonius is the person in hiding. Polonius cries out from behind the arras, "Oh, I am slain!" The Queen asks Hamlet: "What hast thou done?" And Hamlet, somewhat befuddled responds: "Nay, I know not. Is it the King?" When he discovers it is Polonius, however, he says without apparent remorse: "Thou wretched, rash, intruding fool, farewell! I took thee for thy better." (His lack of regret at having killed Polonius is again manifested when he carts off the corpse.) It seems not unfair to describe Hamlet as having at least been willing to kill Polonius, though he certainly had no intention of doing so. Being willing to do something then does not entail intending to do it, but that means that moral accountability involves more than PPA allows. Not having intended the outcome, of course, might be treated as mitigatory in some cases. Holding Hamlet morally responsible for Polonius' death is not necessarily equivalent to accusing him of murder.

The second modification of PPA takes into account obliquely or collaterally intended second or nonoriginal effects that involve other persons. Suppose we have two persons: John and Mary. Suppose John does a, and Mary does b at some time later but in direct response to John's doing a, and suppose an outcome of Mary's doing b is harmful, and John was aware of that when he did a. Should John or Mary or both be held accountable for that harm? If Mary's doing b is a natural or (within some organizational structure) a required response to John's doing a, we usually hold only John primarily accountable for the harm (or John and the organization) by reason of what we may call oblique intention of a nonoriginal effect. (We assume that John knows that to get Mary to do b, he has to do a or that he can get Mary to do b if he does a.)

If Mary's doing b, although a response to John's doing a, is something she knows to be morally wrong and she can be truly described as willing for the harmful event to occur, even if not intending to cause harm, then Mary and not John may be held primarily accountable for the harm, ceteris paribus. But, if John's doing a is a clear temptation for Mary to do b, and if John should know or does know it is such a temptation and John does a (even if he does not intend that Mary do *b*) and harm occurs, then the moral responsibility for the harm would be distributed to both, though perhaps it would fall more heavily on John than Mary, ceteris paribus. Within certain organizational structures, however, Mary's doing *b* may be an established and automatic response to John's doing *a*, and that should be or is known by John. In such cases, when harm results, John is held more to account and Mary less so for the results of Mary's doing *b*. The historically more automatic Mary's response, the less she is held morally to account.

The principle of accountability that satisfies all of these considerations could be put in the following form: A person (presupposing Bradleyian selfsameness) may be held morally accountable for his intentional actions and for those actions that he was willing to perform under different descriptions of his intentional actions. Also he may be held accountable for those nonoriginal or second effects that involve the actions of other persons that he obliquely or collaterally intended or was willing to have occur as the result or under different descriptions of his actions. Let us call this the Extended Principle of Accountability (EPA). Armed with EPA, which may still need further modification but will suffice for present purposes, let us examine the ascription of moral responsibility to McDonnell–Douglas in the case of the Paris air crash.

What might justify such an ascription? There are at least three solid contenders: (1) McDonnell–Douglas would have to have decided to build ship 29 intending that its design be defective such as would predictably result in a crash that kills hundreds of people; or (2) McDonnell–Douglas, not intending ship 29 be defective or crash, would have to have taken such steps in the development, design, and construction process of the airplane that it knew or should have known to be inadequate with regard to safety and highly likely to result in an in-flight class IV hazard; or (3) it would have to have established policies and performed actions that it knew or should have known would prompt rather automatic responses by persons associated with the corporation that would increase the likelihood of the manufacture of a defective product, ship 29.

Clearly McDonnell–Douglas did not design, manufacture, and sell DC–10's with the intention that they crash. It surely did not build ship 29 and sell it to Turkish Airlines with the intention of killing 346 people. We will have to focus on the other two possibilities: one puts forth the claim that without intending to produce a defective airplane, McDonnell–Douglas was willing to do so, and the other claims that McDonnell–Douglas was willing to have a harmful outcome occur as the result of the predictable actions of other persons made in response to actions or policies of McDonnell–Douglas. In both claims appeal is made to EPA and not to the strict PPA. Surprisingly (and sadly) the facts support both claims.

Before we examine those facts, it will help if we are clear about a few rudiments of DC–10 design.[5] We need concern ourselves only with cargo doors and passenger floors. The cargo doors on a DC–10 are rather large and cannot utilize the same plug design that secures the passenger entry doors. Instead, a latching system needs to be installed. There are two alternate types of systems that might be used. One is electrical, the other hydraulic. An electric latch actuator system is lighter, has fewer parts, and is easier to maintain than an hydraulic system. An hydraulic system, however, continuously exerts pressure on the latching device, holding it in place. An electical system exerts pressure only when it is switched on. Electrically driven latches are prone to slip back if they are not made irreversible. When they achieve maximum force they must be fixed until the electric switch is again activated.

> An electric latch will behave very differently from an hydraulic one. An hydraulic latch, though positive, is *not* irreversible. If it fails to go over-center, it will in the nature of things "stall" at a point where the pressure inside the cylinder has reached equilibrium with the friction which is obstructing the travel of the latch.
>
> Thereafter, quite a small opposite pressure will move it in the reserve direction—and what this means in a pressure-hull door is that if the latches have not gone quite "over", they will slide open quite smoothly as soon as a little pressure develops inside the hull and starts pushing at the inside of the door. Thus, they will slide back and the door will open, well before the pressure inside the aircraft hull is high enough to cause a dangerous decompression. The door will undoubtedly be ripped from its hinges by

the force of the slip stream but, at low altitude, that poses no threat of structural damage to the plane and no danger to its passengers. The crew will immediately become aware of the problem because the aircraft cannot be pressurized and can simply return to the airport.

However, if an irreversible electric latch fails to go over-center, the result will usually be quite different. Once current is switched off, the attitude of the latch is fixed, and if it has gone quite a long way over the spool, there will be considerable frictional forces between the two metal surfaces, holding the latch in place. Pressure building up inside the door cannot *slide* the latches open. It can only force the fixed, part-closed latches off their spools. This, typically, will happen in a swift and violent movement, occurring only when pressure inside the airplane has built up to a level when sudden depressurization will be structurally dangerous.[6]

The underside of the passenger floor of a wide-bodied jet liner is laced with the electrical and hydraulic lines that are absolutely necessary for the airplane to fly. The stability of that floor is crucial. In the event of a sudden decompressurization of the cargo area, enormous unoffset pressures from the passenger compartment are exerted on the floor. Without sufficient support, it will buckle and break and in so doing sever the electrical and hydraulic lines. The DC–10 was designed both with an electric cargo-door latching system and with relatively few passenger floor supports, given the wide-bodied nature of the craft. Why? Certainly not because Mc-Donnell–Douglas intended to build a dangerous airplane.

McDonnell–Douglas seems to have believed that by using technology that had proven successful during its long tradition of building passenger aircraft, it was manufacturing a safe product. DC–10 engineers, under express management orders, utilized the existing Douglas technology gained on the DC–3, DC–8, and DC–9 as the basic design for the wide-bodied DC–10.[7] That technology, though not clearly inappropriate to the jumbo craft, in the case of crucial systems, had been superseded by engineering advancements pioneered by Boeing and Lockheed on the 747 and the Tristar. The "state of the art" had developed, before McDonnell–Douglas had committed itself to its DC–10 design, beyond the design constraints with which McDonnell–Douglas had saddled its engineers, and the relevant technology was not proprietary.[8]

McDonnell–Douglas has an oft-stated company policy of technological caution that, combined with its severe financial straits in the 1960s, was apparently interpreted by its engineers and manufacturing staff to dictate that corners be cut and existing Douglas technology be used[9] even if that meant that some systems that were rejected as inferior by its competitors would be designed into the DC–10. It is of note that another engineering result of policy and financial constraint is less redundancy of key systems in the DC–10 than on 747s and Tristars. Both its competitors have four hydraulic systems, each of which is capable of providing sufficient power for a landing. (Manual power is ineffective in moving control surfaces on a wide-bodied airplane.) The DC–10 was engineered with only three redundant hydraulic systems, all running in parallel under the cabin floor. Its competitors can weather the loss of one more system than the DC–10. There is, of course, a point somewhere along the line where redundancy, even in essential systems, is waste. It probably is not reached, however, at three of four systems.[10] The DC–10 simply did not achieve the minimum state of the relevant engineering art. In the case of some products, that might be only quaint, but not, we should all allow, when the transportation of millions of people is involved.

The evidence supports the claim that McDonnell–Douglas designed an airplane that they *should have known* did not meet the engineering standards of the industry with respect to certain crucial systems. Manufacturing that airplane is arguably redescribable as being willing to produce a class IV in-flight hazard, regardless of what McDonnell–Douglas might have intended. This sounds extremely harsh; unfortunately for McDonnell–Douglas matters are worse. Not only *should they have known* of the extreme hazard to life they were manufacturing, they *did* know. The evidence seems incontrovertible.[11] As it happens, in order to make the DC–10 case analogous to Hamlet's killing Polonius, we would have to imagine that Hamlet in fact knows that the chances are the person hiding behind the arras is not the King, yet he stabs away intending to kill the King, but willing to kill whoever is there, perhaps because he wants, at least, to terrify his mother.

In 1969 Convair was asked by McDonnell–Douglas to prepare a Failure Mode and Effects Analysis (FMEA) for the DC–10's cargo-door latching system. The FMEA is an assessment by the design engineers of the likelihood of failure of the system and its consequences for the airplane. FMEA's on the critical systems of a new airplane must be given to the Federal Aviation Administration by the manufacturer when the airplane is certified. Convair's FMEA for the cargo-door latching system shows that there were at least nine possible failure sequences that could result in life-endangering hazards. Four of those sequences would produce sudden depressurization in flight and the almost certain crash of the airplane. One of those sequences in the FMEA reads as follows:

> Door will close and latch, but will not safety lock. Indicator light will indicate normal position. Door will open in flight—resulting in sudden depressurization and possibly structural failure of floor; also damage to empennage by expelled cargo and/or detached door. Class IV hazard in flight.[12]

Approximately five years later that is exactly what happened over the outskirts of Paris. (It may also be of note that McDonnell–Douglas never submitted that Convair prepared FMEA to the FAA.[13] If the FMEA were not enough evidence for McDonnell–Douglas to be said to *know* of the defects of its DC–10 design, one year later, in 1970, the cargo door blew and the floor collapsed on ship 1, the prototype of the line, while it was undergoing standard pressurization tests.

If we apply EPA to the facts, it is clear that on the basis of this evidence alone McDonnell–Douglas can be held morally accountable for the Paris crash. Its knowledge of the defective class IV hazard design of the cargo-door latching system well before ship 29 was built for Turkish Airlines provides us with adequate grounds to support the claim that McDonnell–Douglas was willing to manufacture and market an airplane that had a higher probability than the Boeing 747 or the Lockheed L-1011 of creating a class IV hazard in flight. Again notice that I do not believe McDonnell–Douglas wanted or intended to manufacture a defective airplane. Its intentional actions regarding design decisions, however, clearly have a high probability, as shown in its own FMEAs, of certain consequences which, though unintended, ought, nonetheless, given the information available to McDonnell–Douglas to have been expected by the manufacturer. There is even evidence, in the form of company memos, that high-ranking engineering personnel expected class IV hazards to occur on in-flight DC–10s.[14] It is as if Hamlet did not expect it was the King in hiding, hoped it was, and stabbed anyway.

In this analysis I have not tried to locate within the McDonnell–Douglas corporate structure any individual human beings who were significant contributors to the series of corporate decisions that resulted in the design and manufacture of the DC–10. Finding the corporation morally accountable surely ought not to exculpate such persons. In cases such as this, however, it is difficult to identify the relevant corporate employees.[15] The effects of what have been called the "Law of Diminishing Control" and "Cognitive Dissonance," as well as unintentional blocking of information, etc., in such large decentralized firms as McDonnell–Douglas, belie any simple reductionism to the beliefs, reasons, and intentions of human beings associated in the corporation. Australian corporate legal theorist W. B. Fisse has (with a nod to my work) recently written:

> The conventional assumption has been that corporate crime reduces to the willed acts of individual actors. However, this assumption fails to account for corporate behavior which cannot be explained exclusively in individualistic terms . . . corporate policy is not merely the sum of individual intentions but a collective choice influenced and constrained by organizational factors, including bargaining and teamwork. Nor are corporate acts simply the aggregation of individual acts: organization is a *sine qua non*. Accordingly, there is no oddity about regarding a corporation as a criminally responsible actor (or a moral person) where the act alleged has a sufficient organizational nexus.[16]

There is, however, another aspect of the unhappy history of ship 29 in which both individual and corporate responsibility, in accord with EPA, may be assessed.

After McDonnell–Douglas admitted possible difficulties with locking the cargo doors following the Windsor incident, an agree-

ment with the FAA was reached that called for a modification of
the doors. In July 1972, ship 29 was in the "Rework for Delivery"
area of the Long Beach plant of McDonnell–Douglas. Included in
the work to be done on ship 29 were modifications to the cargo
door. The plant records for July 1972 indicate that three inspectors stamped the work records for ship 29 to indicate the modifications had been completed and that the plane was in compliance
with FAA guidelines. None of the work on the cargo doors had
actually been done. All three inspectors identified the stamps on
the work record as theirs, but none of the three remembered having worked on ship 29. There is no evidence that the stamps of all
three, however, were stolen or borrowed during July 1972. It is
company policy that: "You are responsible for any work that your
stamp appears on the record for accepting."[17] One inspector, Edward Evans, conjectured that his stamp appears on the records of
ship 29 either because "it was high summer,"[18] and he had become confused between airplanes because of the summer heat and
had stamped the wrong document, *or* that he had been interested
in some other aspect of the reworking and had not carefully in-
spected the cargo-door-latching system. The other inspectors could
not even offer conjectures as to how their stamps appeared on the
records of ship 29.

The president of the Douglas division of McDonnell–Douglas,
John Brizendine, who was responsible for "engineering, flight development, and production" of the DC–10, when questioned by
attorneys, claimed no personal knowledge of misuse of inspection
stamps. In fact, he insisted that he had nothing to do with insur-
ing that design reworking actually was done. After the Paris crash
he did reprimand the inspectors for misuse of stamps.

We could give two alternate accounts of what happened with regard to the inspections of ship 29. The first is that three inspectors, whether singly or in concert, lied or conspired to lie about
the inspections of ship 29. But for what reasons? The second is
that the McDonnell–Douglas system that is supposed to assure that
individual responsibility is exercised by personnel at various stages
of production to "insure quality in the tradition of the company"
is fundamentally weak and easily compromised by employees who

have fallen into a rather automatic pattern of behavior encouraged by that company policy and procedure. It is certainly impractical to insist that President Brizendine or any other high-ranking corporate officer make all of the necessary inspections, etc., himself. The assumption of an uncompromised verification of inspection procedure, however, was not responsible.

The evidence supports the view that over the years McDonnell–Douglas established an inspection procedure that invites or tempts inspectors to be lax and careless,[19] and some of those inspectors, either through inadvertance or because of conditioning to laxness, cursorily performed tasks that, given the basically poor design of the aircraft, called for the closest attention to detail to insure safety. McDonnell–Douglas policies and procedures constituted a temptation to carelessness, even though managerial superiors were unaware of such a temptation and that safety was at stake. Those corporate officers, we may say with some confidence, should have expected that their inspection procedures would be unintentionally compromised by inspectors.

The actions of the three inspectors are not excusable (if inadvertance is proved that may be exculpatory), but it would be a grand offense to our moral intuitions, in the absence of any evidence of intentional sabotage, etc., to hold those inspectors primarily responsible for the crash of ship 29. We are brought back to the principal actor in the design, manufacture, and sale of ship 29, McDonnell–Douglas Corporation.

When recently discussing this DC–10 case with certain economists and management professors, I was surprised to learn that they thought the whole matter should be resolved as a risk issue. On their account, McDonnell–Douglas, operating in the best of market traditions, simply had taken a not unreasonable, calculated risk in the manufacture of the DC–10. All machines are liable to failure or breakdown, and any manufacturer of a machine needs to take the probability of failure into account when marketing the product. For example, it buys product liability insurance. Also, any consumer of the machinery, I was told, can be presumed to know that machines are liable to breakdown. Turkish Airlines and

its passengers can be presumed to have had such general knowledge of machinery. What then is the problem? If all that is meant
by "taking a risk" in a business context is that the corporation,
fully cognizant of certain product deficiencies, produces and markets the product in the hope (probably supported by statistically
based predictions of failure) that sales will offset any actual liabilities due to inadequate design, then evidence that such calculated
risks were taken can only serve to strengthen the ascription of moral
responsibility to the corporation on the occasion of harm. "It was
a calculated risk" has no exculpatory or even mitigatory power. In
fact, in cases of this sort, if anything, it is inculpating. There is,
however, another side to the risk issue that is often confused with
the matter of whether the corporation took a reasonable or calculated risk when it decided to manufacture and market its product.
That is the matter of putting persons using the product at risk in
cases where ordinarily they would be presumed to have taken or
accepted the risk.

Clearly, risk, in this sense, is, in most cases, negotiable. A reasonable person will accept a certain amount of risk if the compensation is satisfactory. Everyone, we might say, has a risk budget.
But risk cannot be negotiated in a unilateral contract, nor can it
be said to have been negotiated in the absence of knowledge by
the parties of the relevant data. For risk to have been negotiated,
the facts relevant to the potential for the causing of harm must be
known by the parties, at least in general terms. Certainly every
passenger who enters a commercial airliner should realize that there
is a certain probability that the aircraft will develop a malfunction
that could result in his death. In the case of most American commercial airplanes that probability is remarkably low. The benefits
of fast travel far outweigh the risk in the minds of many travelers.
The passenger pays for his ticket and boards the airplane. In effect, there is a certain, generally understood, risk to life involved
in the use of a commercial airliner. Passengers can be presumed to
understand that the risk is about the same for any craft on which
they might fly.

None of this rather unexceptional business is, however, relevant
to the DC–10 case. The DC–10 design was such as to drive it out

of the risk probabilities of its sister craft. Risk budget calculations made in ignorance of the faulty design are not necessarily going to be the same as those that would have been made if the facts were known. The relevant design information was, of course, not widely known or easily accessible to consumers. In the case of ship 29, Turkish Airlines clearly should have known of the previous cargo-door latching failures, but it also had the assurances of Mc-Donnell–Douglas that FAA required modifications had been made.

Risk is simply not a unilateral matter. McDonnell–Douglas' decision to take a risk with the DC–10 supports the uncontested view that McDonnell–Douglas had no intention of building a defective airliner. The fact is McDonnell–Douglas was just wrong in its calculation of the risk it was taking with respect to product liability. It was creating a far greater risk for the passengers on its aircraft than they could have taken into account when deciding to fly the DC–10, and it should have known (indeed it did know) that it had miscalculated the risk. If the information about the defective design of the DC–10 had been public knowledge, it is unlikely McDonnell Douglas would have been able to sell the airplane. (After the Chicago crash of 1978, attributed to engine-mount failure, the entire DC–10 fleet was grounded for reworking and inspection. The resumption of DC–10 service, despite bargain rates and other allurements [compensations], was greeted with less than enthusiasm by the flying public. For years, many Americans evidenced a preference to book flights on planes other than DC–10s. That is, of course, a good example of risk bargaining at work in the marketplace. No such circumstances surround the Paris crash.)

In short, the introduction of the notion of risk in the DC–10 case is totally irrelevant to the concern of moral accountability. Even if all 346 people who boarded ship 29 in Paris on March 3, 1974, knew they were entering a machine and that every machine has a statistical probability of breakdown for any moment of its operation, they cannot reasonably be said to have struck a bargain to accept the realistic risk probabilities of the *crash of ship 29* for the compensation of the convenience of less in-travel time between Paris and London. McDonnell–Douglas' failure to engineer to the state of the art again enters the picture of our analysis because it accounts for the fact that the probabilities of harm generally understood to apply to American commercial aircraft were inapplicable to the calculation of the risk passengers were taking in the case of DC–10s. The facts are that McDonnell–Douglas knowingly exposed DC–10 passengers to a significantly higher probability of death than they would have been exposed to on other aircraft. The fact that McDonnell–Douglas performed acts that constituted creating such a risk and concealing pertinent evidence from the public and the regulatory agency only supports the moral indictment.

In the absence of admission of corporations like McDonnell–Douglas to citizenry in the moral world, the moral responsibility for the Paris air disaster cannot reasonably be finally assessed. The aggregate of justifiable individual responsibilities for the production of ship 29 simply does not add up to an individual's responsibility for its crash. Without a theory of the corporation as a moral person upon which to base the accountability ascriptions I have made in this analysis, the real villain of the piece will escape moral detection. A. A. Berle has written:

> The medieval feudal power system set the "lords spiritual" over and against the "lords temporal." These were the men of learning and of the church who, in theory, were able to say to the greatest power in the world: "You have committed a sin; therefore either you are excommunicated or you must mend your ways." The "lords temporal" could reply: "I can kill you." But the "lords spiritual" could retort: "Yes that you can, but you cannot change the philosophical fact." In a sense this is the great lacuna in the economic power system today.[20]

The theory of the corporation as a moral person is intended to supply the missing link that brings the corporate giants, today's "lords temporal," into the scope of morality.

CHAPTER ELEVEN
The Principle of Responsive Adjustment: The Crash on Mount Erebus

On the morning of November 28, 1979, flight TE-901, a DC-10 operated by Air New Zealand Limited, took off from Auckland, New Zealand, on a sightseeing passenger flight over a portion of Antarctica. The following are paragraphs from the official Report of the Royal Commission appointed by the Governor-General of New Zealand that inquired into the events surrounding that flight.

12. The personnel at McMurdo Station and Scott Base were expecting the arrival of an Air New Zealand DC-10 aircraft carrying sightseeing passengers. The flight plan radioed to McMurdo from Auckland had named the pilot in command as Captain Collins. . . . It was expected that the DC-10 would fly down McMurdo Sound. . . . The aircraft would come in from the north and in the vicinity of Ross Island would descend to a low level so as to afford the passengers . . . sightseeing. . . . The aircraft would probably fly down the Sound at an altitude of somewhere between 1500 feet and 3000 feet . . . a perfectly safe altitude at which to fly over flat ground in clear weather, and the cause of no concern to the United States Air Traffic Control.

13. . . . When the DC-10 was about 140 miles out from McMurdo, Mac Centre transmitted a weather forecast . . . to the effect that there was a low overcast over Ross Island and the McMurdo area. . . . Mac Centre suggested that once the aircraft was within 40 miles of McMurdo Station, the entrance of McMurdo Sound, it would be picked up by radar and its descent through cloud guided down to an altitude of 1500 feet. This suggestion was accepted by the air crew. At 1500 feet, under the cloud layer

in the McMurdo area, visibility would be unlimited in all directions. . . .

15. By 12:35 P.M. it was confirmed between Mac Centre and the DC–10 that the aircraft was now descending to 10,000 feet and was requesting a radar let-down through cloud. The request was accepted by Mac Centre. . . .

16. At 12:42 P.M. the aircraft informed Mac Centre that it was flying VMC (visual meteorological conditions) and that it would proceed visually to McMurdo. This message indicated to Mac Centre that the aircraft had found an area free of cloud through which it would descend before level-ling out at an altitude less than the cloud base. Thus the aircraft would be approaching under the cloud layer in clear air at an altitude of about 2000 feet. . . .

17. There followed further transmissions between the aircraft and Mac Centre and then at 12:45 P.M. the aircraft advised Mac Centre that it was now flying at 6000 feet in the course of descending to 2000 feet and that it was still flying VMC. . . . This was the last transmission from the DC–10. . . .

22. The United States Navy sent out aircraft on intensive searches and ultimately after several hours, the reason for the long radio silence from the aircraft was discovered. A United States Navy aircraft found the wreckage of the DC–10 on the northern slopes of Mount Erebus at a point about 1500 feet above sea level. The aircraft had been carrying 20 crew and 237 passengers. There were no survivors.[1]

Those familiar with the unhappy history of the DC–10 naturally would suspect that another engineering fault had been responsible for the disaster. The Mount Erebus crash, however, was not the result of any airplane engineering errors or faults. This DC–10 performed perfectly. The simple fact is that the plane was flown in broad daylight in clear air at approximately 2000 feet above sea level directly into the side of a 12,000 foot mountain. "Simple facts" in the case of airline disasters are, however, notoriously complex. Photographs taken by the ill-fated passengers indicate that just seconds before the crash the view from the plane was unob-structed for many miles. The report notes that:

28. It followed [from the photographic evidence] that as the aircraft had approached Mount Erebus it was flying in skies in which there was perfect visibility for at least 23 miles. It was also apparent that the aircraft had been flying well under the cloud base when it collided with the mountain.

Air New Zealand Limited released a statement proclaiming that the cause of the crash had been pilot error. The airline maintained that Captain Collins had become disoriented or confused or distracted and had flown TE-901 directly into the mountain. They added that he had no business flying that airplane at 2000 feet. The flight, they said, should have remained at no less than 14,000 feet, a claim that the Royal Commission Report disputes by pointing out that the very nature of the flight necessitated relatively low altitude. At 14,000 feet the passengers would have seen nothing but clouds. They would certainly not have witnessed the advertised splendor of Antarctica. And, it is important that clearance to fly at 1500 feet down McMurdo Sound was granted by the Mac Centre controller and was generally regarded as a safe altitude for such flights over the flat terrain of the Sound.

The bald fact is that Captain Collins had flown far off course, some 27 miles, and that he was flying into Lewis Bay not the McMurdo Sound. Lewis Bay is a much smaller body of water than the Sound and from its shore on Ross Island rises Mount Erebus. Captain Collins was no fledgling pilot. He had a long and distinguished flying career. The pilot error theory called for him to have made a monumental miscalculation as to his location and also to have failed somehow to see the impending doom of the slopes of Mount Erebus rising up directly in front of him.

The evidence collected by the Royal Commission established quite a different scenario than provided by the airline. In order to understand their version we need to take a brief digression to explain something about the navigational systems on the DC–10. DC–10s are navigated by a computer system known as the Inertial Navigation System (INS). DC–10s proceed to their destinations by a series of waypoints. The INS "31. . . . operates by typing into a computer system on the aircraft [the AINS] the latitude and longitude of each waypoint. . . . Once this series of coordinates has been fed into the aircraft's computer, the aircraft will then fly its own course from one waypoint to another." This flight path is known as the aircraft's "nav track."

TE-901 was, its recovered black box revealed, flown on its programmed nav track almost the entire distance of the flight. It is also important to note that INS systems are widely regarded in the industry to be highly accurate (¶ 33).

How then did TE-901 end up in wreckage on the slopes of Mount Erebus when it should have been cruising at 2000 or 1500 feet above McMurdo Sound, passenger cameras clicking wildly at the spectacular vistas of Antarctica?

The primary cause of the disaster, the Commission reported, was a direct result of the administrative and communication system of Air New Zealand Limited. In order to see how they reached this conclusion it is necessary to briefly canvass some of the facts uncovered by the Commission.

Captain Collins and his First Officer attended a briefing on Antarctic flights nineteen days before their TE-901 assignment. At that meeting they were provided with printouts of the flight plan used by a sightseeing flight that had just returned from Antarctica. The coordinates on that flight plan, they were informed, would be the standard ones for all of the airline's sightseeing flights. The Commission learned that Collins had written the coordinates in his notebook and that on the night before TE-901 was to depart, he had plotted the track of his forthcoming flight on his atlas and a map. That track showed that the plane would head directly down McMurdo Sound with Mount Erebus approximately 27 miles to the east.

The Report reads:

> 36. When the flight crew assembled on the morning of the flight and were handed the flight plan for 28 November 1979 extracted from the ground computer earlier in the morning and when the flight crew inserted into the computer on the aircraft the series of latitude and longitude coordinates on that flight plan they believed, in accordance with ordinary and standard practice, that they were inserting the long-standing coordinates.

The tragic fact was that they were doing nothing of the kind. A set of figures different than those provided at the briefing had been substituted and that change had the effect of moving the destination waypoint for McMurdo Sound 27 miles to the east, directly at Ross Island and collision with Mount Erebus (if the plane were flown at less than 12,450 feet). Collins, according to standard operating procedure, holding to his computerized nav track, had flown the plane directly into the mountain, in the mistaken belief the plane was heading down a wide and open expanse of water.

The computer coordinates were changed in the airline's Flight Operations Division. That division is comprised of four subunits: Navigation Section, Computer Section, Flight Dispatch Section, and the RCU Briefing System. The Navigation Section directed the Computer Section to reprogram the computer when it received a verbal direction to do so from Captain R. T. Johnson, operations manager for DC–10 aircraft at Air New Zealand. There is no record of any direction to the Flight Dispatch Section to inform Captain Collins of the change nor any to indicate that the change had actually been made. There are no records of any kind in Flight Operations Division. It is standard operating procedure in the airline that none of the decisions in the division are committed to writing.

As it happens, the alteration of the nav track was a very reasonable thing to do. Captain Simpson, who piloted the Antarctic flight prior to TE-901, had noticed that the programmed waypoint for McMurdo was approximately 27 miles to the west of the tactical air navigation system (TACAN) of McMurdo Station (¶ 242). (The TACAN allows a pilot to determine his distance from it and hence is a useful navigational aid.) Simpson informed Captain Johnson that crews of future flights should be aware of this discrepancy, but he now claims that he did not suggest that a change in the flight plan be made (¶ 243–45). Johnson, however, believed that Simpson had told him there was a serious error in the flight plan and that the relevant waypoint ought to coincide with the location of the TACAN. Johnson testified that he believed that when the coordinates were changed in the computer there would be no need to inform Captain Collins because the alteration amounted to only a 2.1 mile movement of the final waypoint. In this calculation he was woefully wrong.

The Commission explained the nav track change in a radically different way. Frankly, they did not accept Captain Johnson's claim that Simpson's information had been misinterpreted. Instead, they argue:

> 245. . . . Both Captain Johnson and the Navigation Section knew quite well that the McMurdo waypoint lay 27 miles to the west of the TACAN and that since his track had not officially been approved by the Civil Aviation Division, it should therefore be realigned with the TACAN and then someone forgot to ensure that Captain Collins was told of the change. Such an interpretation means that the evidence as to the alleged belief of a displacement of only 2.1 miles is untrue.

This nav track alteration and the pilot's reliance on the AINS combined with the expected practice of descending to a low altitude to allow better views, indeed any view at all, took TE-901 directly into Mount Erebus. The Commission held that it would not be just to hold Captain Johnson fully responsible for the disaster. Although Captain Johnson probably ordered the alterations in the computer to put the Antarctic flights on a course that provided the pilots with a better set of navigational checks than did the path down McMurdo Sound, it is clear that he had no knowledge of the other key factor that brought TE-901 to disaster.

Certainly an experienced pilot, even if he believes himself to be flying over a relatively wide body of water, would quickly correct his descent from 16,000 feet when he saw a 12,450-foot obstacle in his direct path. Nav track or no nav track, an experienced pilot can be expected to take manual control and ascend to a safe altitude, fly over Mount Erebus and circle east to the Sound. Why had Captain Collins not corrected his descent when the face of Mount Erebus loomed up before him?

Although the answer is quite straightforward, it took some detective work for the Commission to discover it. They learned that in clear air in Antarctica a pilot can experience a visual difficulty called a "whiteout." The whiteout is an atmospheric effect that produces a loss of depth perception, flattening out even mountainous terrain. "165. . . . Only two conditions are necessary to produce whiteout, a diffuse shadowless illumination and a monocoloured white surface. . . . The condition may occur in a crystal clear atmosphere or under a cloud ceiling with ample comfortable light." It is likely that TE-901's pilot and flight crew experienced a whiteout. The Commission itself experienced the phenomena while on an investigative trip to the crash site. The crew of TE-901 never saw Mount Erebus or rather they never recognized what they saw as a 12,450 foot mountain. Their belief that they were flying over the waters of McMurdo Sound was apparently confirmed for them by what they thought they saw out of their windows.

The commission listed ten factors or circumstances which they believed contributed to the crash. They are as follows:

1) 387. . . . Captain Collins had complete reliance upon the accuracy of the navigation system of his aircraft. . . .
2) There was not supplied to Captain Collins, either in the RCU briefing or on the morning of the flight, any topographical map upon which had been drawn the track along which the computer system would navigate the aircraft.
3) Captain Collins plotted the nav track himself on the night before the flight on a map and upon an atlas.
4) The direction of the last leg of the flight path to be programmed into the aircraft's computer was changed about six hours before the flight departed.
5) Neither Captain Collins nor any member of his crew was told of the alteration which had been made to the computer track.
6) Checks made in flight . . . demonstrated to the crew that the AINS was operating with its customary extreme accuracy. . . .
7) McMurdo Air Traffic Control believed that the destination waypoint of the aircraft was 27 miles west of McMurdo Station. . . .
8) Mac Centre invited the aircraft to descend to 1500 feet in McMurdo Sound for the reason that visibility at that altitude was 40 miles or more.
9) Captain Collins accepted this invitation and made the decision to descend to that altitude.
10) The nature of the cloud base in the area and the unrelieved whiteness of the snow-covered terrain beneath the overcast combined to produce the whiteout visual illusion.

The commission maintains that had any of these factors (or what Mackie would have called INUS conditions[2]) not been present, TE-901 would not have crashed into Mount Erebus.

Despite the fact that the ten factors in this case were all necessary, though individually insufficient, parts of the set that were sufficient though not necessary to result in the crash. The Commission felt it was able to identify two acts, (2) and (5), both omissions on the part of the airline, upon which to found or justify ascriptions of moral responsibility for the crash to the corporation. It was concluded that, "392. . . .The dominant cause of the disaster was the act of the airline in changing the computer track of the aircraft without telling the aircrew." From the point of view of the Commission (5) was the INUS condition with a difference.

This lengthy, though sketchy version of the details of this case is justified if we want to understand what the commission thinks their identification of the "dominant and effective cause" of the Mount Erebus crash entails. Why had they not simply laid the moral responsibility for the disaster at Captain Johnson's doorstep? He, as the Simpson testimony seems to reveal, ordered the change in the computer track and failed to insure that the information about the new track was communicated to the captain on board. The Commission, however, refused to lay responsibility squarely on Johnson's shoulders. It concluded its report by maintaining that the crucial mistakes regarding the reprogramming and the failure to inform are "393. . . . directly attributable, not so much to the persons who made (them), but to the incompetent administrative airline procedures which made the mistake(s) possible." In other words, the Commission concluded that the cause of the Mount Erebus disaster that founds an ascription of moral responsibility has an organizational nexus, and that it would be unjust to attribute the crucial failure to individuals within the company. In an important and irreducible way, they held that the standard operating procedures of Air New Zealand were causally responsible for the crash. Is this justifiable? And, more important, can it be translated to an ascription of moral responsibility to the corporation?

The Commission's investigation focused on the standard operating procedures of the Flight Operations Division of Air New Zealand. Four major defects in the administrative structure of the division were identified. The flaws described by the Commission were:

(1) Operational pilots held executive positions in the Flight Operations Division;

(2) None of those operational pilots had been given a training course in administrative management;

(3) There exists no written directives from Flight Division that spell out the duties and administrative responsibilities of the executive pilots;

(4) There exist no written directives in Flight Operations that specify the way various duties are to be performed, e.g., there exists no written directive that specifies the steps to be taken by the various subsections when adjustments are made to flight plans or changes are made in navigational procedures. (See ¶ 365)

The structure and practices of the Flight Operations Division depended upon a tradition of verbal communication. There is, in fact, a general policy in Air New Zealand against written memoranda. The chief executive officer (CEO) of the airline testified before the Commission that he had always "366. . . . controlled the airline on a verbal basis." Communications regarding inter or intradepartmental business were almost never written. The fatal alteration in the coordinates was, according to standard practice, verbally directed to the Navigational Section by Captain Johnson. If any confirmational or informational messages passed from one subsection of Flight Operations to another or to the flight crew, they would have been verbal.

It might be argued that the CEO or the board of directors should have expected their verbal communication policy to result in serious breakdowns. The fact that active pilots also wore administrative hats and hence, on many occasions, had split duties and subsequently split attentions, should have also alerted some concern. A pilot with a number of his own flight problems on his mind could easily forget, misunderstand, or confuse information passed to him verbally, especially when that information concerned flights other than those he regularly flew. The Commission, however, did not make such an argument.

The Commission holds the view that the board and the CEO could not be expected to investigate the daily administration of Flight Operations and that there was a long history of excellent, safe airline service at Air New Zealand to justify whatever smugness might have been manifested regarding the lack of written documentation of administrative communications. The CEO's verbal policy may have been intended to foster a family-like atmosphere in the company, or, conversely, one that functioned along military-like verbal command lines. Also, the policy may have been the result of more than a modicum of confidence in the personal care taken by each of the company's executives to accomplish the various tasks of his office. It is likely that a breakdown of the magnitude of the Mount Erebus crash could not have been foreseen by the board or the CEO. The CEO, in fact, believes that many other corporations operate with the kind of verbal communication practices he encouraged at Air New Zealand. Whether or not that is true, or is true for corporations of a similar size and engaged in similar activities, is a matter to be determined by further investigation.

It is important that the existence of a policy of verbal communication as adopted by Air New Zealand, in itself, hardly constitutes a willingness on the part of the board or the CEO to have such events as this crash occur. It would be grandly unjust to suggest that anyone calculated the trade-offs and opted for the possibility of a disaster such as the crash on Mount Erebus rather than a formalizing of the organizational communication system. The fact that the board and CEO adopted and encouraged the less formal communication system, though having certain of its own problems, is surely an inadequate basis upon which to find them morally responsible for the disaster on Mount Erebus even though causal responsibility focuses on the organizational breakdown.

Let us explore a different tact. Strict liability, in the criminal law, is usually applied on the basis of causal identification alone. (That in some jurisdictions it may be understood in terms of a limited range of conditions of defeasibility will not concern us here.) Strict liability, we should say, is both blind to the reasonableness of beliefs and morally uninterested. Strict liability can, of course, be used to direct us to the party or parties about which objective liability and moral responsibility questions might be raised, even though they may not be raised in the criminal context. For moral responsibility we need agency, intentionality. For objective liability we need a standard of reasonableness of beliefs. Air New Zealand's organizational and communication structure surely was causally responsible for the crash, as argued by the Royal Commission, and the corporation can be held strictly and possibly objectively liable under the law for damages. The matter of the corporation's moral responsibility, however, cannot be resolved by either causal identification alone or by causal responsibility and an appeal to the reasonableness criterion that is embedded in objective liability.

The examination of the corporate moral responsibility for the Mount Erebus disaster, however, ought not rest at this level. Commonly, when an untoward event occurs and when the facts will not support an ascription of moral responsibility to the causally responsible party because the event was not intended under the relevant descriptions, the subsequent behavior of the perpetrator is observed to determine whether measures are taken to insure nonrepetition of events of the same kind as the earlier untoward event. If appropriate behavioral changes are not made, a kind of moral reevaluation of the earlier event is made and the perpetrator is held morally responsible for the untoward event regardless of the fact that at the time of its occurrence the perpetrator did not have the morally relevant intention. (Certain excuses, primarily those that claim continuing incapacity or diminished responsibility defeat the moral reappraisal.)

Suppose, as in the landmark strict liability case of *Regina v. Prince*,[3] that a man, named Prince, contrary to law, took a girl under sixteen years of age away from her parents, and suppose at the time he believed that she was older than sixteen and she gave him every reason to believe so and any reasonable person would have guessed that she was over sixteen. We stipulate that it was no part of Prince's intentions to commit an act under the description for which the law rightly holds him strictly liable. On the basis of a straight rule of accountability, Prince ought not to be held morally responsible for his illegal assignation. An intuitively appealing, behaviorally oriented, principle of accountability will, however, under certain conditions, license a radical alteration of the finding that

Prince ought not to be held morally responsible. I shall call it the Principle of Responsive Adjustment (PRA).

PRA captures the notion that the causally responsible party for an untoward event should adopt specific courses of future action calculated to prevent repetitions. We have strong moral expectations, identified by Aristotle, regarding behavioral adjustments that correct character weaknesses, bad habits, and ways of acting that have previously produced untoward events. But PRA, as I construe it, is more than just an expression of such expectations. It allows that when the expected adjustments are not made, and in the absence of convincing evidence supporting an exculpating excuse for nonadjustment, the party in question can be held morally responsible *for the earlier* event. PRA does *not*, however, assume that a failure to mend one's ways after being confronted with a harmful outcome of one's actions is strong presumptive evidence that one had intended that earlier event. The question of the intentionality of the past behavior is settled: under the appropriate description it was not intentional and nothing subsequent to it can make it intentional at the time it happened. PRA incorporates quite another idea. It might be expressed by saying that a refusal to adjust one's harm-causing ways of behaving has a second-level effect of associating oneself, morally speaking, with the earlier untoward event. I take it that refusal in this context is an intentional act or acts and that refusal may take a myriad of forms from practiced indifference to blatant repetition. The intuition to which PRA must appeal is that a person's past actions (even if unintentional) can be and usually are taken into the scope of the intentions that motivate that person's present and future actions.

F. H. Bradley wrote, "In morality the past is real because it is present in the will."[4] I construe PRA as providing an expression of this elusive notion. The idea is that certain moral considerations, primarily those that stress the integrity of a lifetime, require adjustments in behavior to rectify flaws of character or habits that have actually caused past evils or, on the positive side, to routinize actions that have led to worthy results. Bradley's idea takes, however, a further reading that exposes the metaphysical foundation of PRA. PRA entails that the intention that motivates a lack of responsive corrective action (or the continuance of offending behavior) affirms, in the sense that it loops back to retrieve, the actions that caused the evil. By the same token, failure to routinize behavior that has been productive of good results divorces the previously unintentional action that had good consequences from one's moral life.

Let us try to grasp what this means. Surely, intentions reach forward (as J. L. Austin's miner's lamp),[5] but PRA allows that they also may have a retrograde or retrieval function such that they illuminate past behavior that was unintentional in the relevant moral way. But how can a present intention to do something, or to do it in a certain way, draw a previous action into its scope?

Consider Prince's illegal affair with the girl under sixteen. Suppose after serving his punishment, Prince intentionally, and quite deliberately, seeks out other young girls and makes no special attempt to discern their true ages. (Remember he has a penchant for young teenage girls, a penchant, but not an uncontrollable obsession.) In other words, imagine that Prince decides to take himself down to the local high school and pursue another teenage girl to whom he has taken a fancy. Prince's intention with regard to this continuation of his behavior with such girls is formed within a personal history that includes his conviction in *Regina v. Prince*. Prince is aware of his past, indeed, in a Lockean sense, his past behavior and its subsequent punishment is, we should expect, a part of his current consciousness. The memory of those events is co-conscious within his mental history and that mental history constitutes, in conjunction with his concerns for his well-being in the future or his life plan, his identity as a person, at least in a relevant moral and legal sense. If, subsequent to the commission of the crime, Prince had taken precautions to insure that he learn the ages of the girls he courts, we would allow his ignorance of the age of the girl in the legal case as an exculpating excuse for moral purposes (although he must bear the punishment for the strict liability offense). But in our extension of the story, Prince makes no responsive adjustments in his behavior that would have the effect of not putting him in the position of repeating the offense. In fact, he embarks upon a course that could very well lead to another violation of that same law, though whether or not it does is immaterial to PRA. By PRA, we are permitted to claim that Prince's subsequently manifested intention to continue his romantic pursuits of underage girls constitutes an affirmation of the strict liability violation behavior. In other words, by virtue of a retrieval function in the subsequent intention, Prince may be legitimately held morally responsible for the strict liability offense.

A second example may help to fortify the intuition. Suppose that Sebastian gets drunk and drives his car onto Quincy's property. Let us assume that Sebastian had no intention of damaging Quincy's property or of getting drunk. After regaining sobriety and learning of his misadventure, Sebastian, who is not yet an alcoholic, subsequently and quite deliberately returns to the local pub and proceeds to get himself roaring drunk. Again we should say that Sebastian's past is known to him, at least he is aware of the fact that he got drunk on a certain occasion and destroyed Quincy's property. Yet, he embarks upon a similar course again. Though we would have excused him from moral responsibility for the damage he did on the first spree had he subsequently modified his behavior, he did not do so, and by PRA, he is making the crucial past behavior not an out-of-character happenstance but very much in character and hence something for which, as Aristotle would say, he may be held morally accountable. Seen in this light, PRA captures (at least to some extent) the Aristotelian idea that we do not blame people for unintentionally "slightly deviating from the course of goodness,"[6] as long as they do not subsequently practice behavior that makes such deviations a matter of character.

PRA insists that moral persons learn from their mistakes. "It was inadvertent or a mistake" will exculpate only if corrective measures are taken to insure nonrepetition.

The most radical element of this analysis surely is that which provides for a retrieval of past unintentional behavior in a present intention to do something. Although this strikes me as quite consistent with common intuitions, a more technical account is surely wanted. That account, however, is easily at hand. Intention, as noted in earlier chapters, is an intensional causal notion. As such, it is referentially opaque so that the aspect of the event described makes all the difference. We intend under event or action descriptions, and we redescribe actions and events as licensed by certain rules. To say that someone intends to do something is to say that there is at least one proper description of some event under which that person acts. Act descriptions have a well-known feature that Joel Feinberg once called the "accordian effect." Like the musical instrument, the description of a simple event can be expanded in different directions to include causal and other related aspects that might themselves be treated as separate events for different purposes. For example, the act of pulling the trigger of a rifle might, through a series of redescriptions, be expanded to the description "the killing of the judge." Accordians, of course, can be drawn apart in both directions. The description of Sebastian's present act of getting drunk may be associated to this past action by the ordinary relations "like yesterday," "as before," or "again." It is the case that Sebastian, in our story, intends to get drunk *again*. The action intended under that description clearly retrieves the previous behavior, though it certainly does not make the previous behavior intentional at the time it occurred.

PRA, however, demands a bit more than this because Sebastian could offer the plea that he had not intended to get drunk under such an accordianed description at all. He only intended to get drunk simpliciter. We may, however, reject this plea on the grounds that unless he is of diminished mental capacity or suffering from amnesia, his grasp of what he is doing is made within a mental or personal history that is not present-specific. The descriptions of events under which he intends his actions are formed within that history. "I intended only to get drunk, not to get drunk again," is, in this context, unintelligible. There are limits on excludability by appeal to semantic opacity in intention. If Sebastian, quite intentionally makes his way to the pub in order to get roaring drunk, he intentionally goes to get drunk again, or like yesterday, etc., and his doing so affirms the previous episode insofar as it takes it into the description captured in the scope of the intention. That is what PRA requires.

The application of PRA to cases like our imagined extension of *Regina v. Prince* and drunken Sebastian can be generalized to the

position that although a person may not have access to the relevant
information at the time of an action that produces a bad or harmful outcome, that person may still be held morally responsible for
that outcome if he or she subsequently intentionally acts in ways
that can reasonably be said to be likely to cause repetitions of the
untoward outcome.

No strict set of temporal closures need be applied to PRA. There
is no statute of limitations. For example, many decades after an
event, moral enlightenment may demand reevaluation of an action
or an outcome that was not originally thought to be bad or harmful and PRA will require moral accountability of the perpetrator
if, after enlightenment, no behavioral adjustments are made. (This
was pointed out to me by Professor Lisa Newton.)

PRA has another important, intuitively appealing aspect. Suppose that we think of all of those acts for which a person can be
morally blamed or morally credited as exhausting that person's moral
life, the biography that can be morally judged or evaluated against
a standard of worth or virtue, as Aristotle would have it, "in a
complete life." PRA may incorporate originally nonintentional pieces
of behavior into a person's moral life because PRA does not let
persons desert their pasts. It forces persons to think of their moral
lives as both retrospective and contemporaneous, as cumulative.
Moral persons cannot completely escape responsibility for their accidents, inadvertent acts, unintended executive failures, failures to
fully appreciate situations, bad habits, etc., simply by proffering
standard excuses. PRA, in fact, defines the boundaries of acceptability of pleas of the form "it was unintentional." If I am right,
the ordinary notion of moral responsibility is far richer than usually described. It operates over more than isolated intentional acts
considered seriatim. The moral integrity of a person's life depends
upon a moral consistency that is nurtured by PRA.

Let us now return to the tragic crash of TE-901. The Royal
Commission reports, as already mentioned, that when Air New
Zealand became aware of the crash, it proclaimed the pilot error
theory. Its CEO also ordered that only one file be compiled, to be
kept in his possession, of all of the airline's pertinent information

regarding TE-901, and all other documents regarding the flight (duplicates, etc.) be shredded. (¶338 and 373). This may appear a suspicious move, but it is not indefensible, for the airline wished to avoid trial by the press that could affect future settlements with relatives of the victims. In fact, PRA does not direct immediate attention to those and other seemingly irregular activities of the airline management immediately after the crash. The Royal Commission, I think, is most unkind in its description of the post-accident behavior of the senior executives of Air New Zealand. It refers to the testimony of airline executives as "377. . . . an orchestrated litany of lies." (That finding has, however, been recently overturned by the New Zealand Court of Appeal.)

The crucial question is, "Did Air New Zealand, when fully apprised of the extremely strong case made in the Commission Report, move to make adjustments in its internal administrative systems?" Has Air New Zealand restructured its standard operating procedures, especially in the Flight Operations Division, to correct the deficiencies outlined in the Report? The answer is "No."

Rather than redesign its policies to incorporate a way to ensure that information within and among the sections of the Flight Operations Division is placed in the proper hands, Air New Zealand has continued in court, interviews, and company documents to defend its old procedures, structure, and verbal-communication policy. Rather than accept the findings of the Commission Report, Air New Zealand continues to insist that the primary cause of the disaster was pilot error.* They have, it should be noted, discontinued all flights to the Antarctic, but it is not solely to such nonregular flights that attention should be drawn. The Flight Operations Division still functions just as it did before November 28, 1979, for all scheduled flights.

PRA is brought into the analysis of the moral responsibility for the crash if we (1) substantially accept the findings of the Commission, and (2) confirm that Air New Zealand has taken no responsive adjustment measures to correct the organizational flaws

---

*This remains true at the time of this writing, as reported by Professors John Braithwaite and W. Brent Fisse who have recently interviewed Air New Zealand executives while researching a forthcoming book on the effects of publicity on corporate policy.

identified by the Report as "399. . . . the single effective cause of
the crash," regardless of whether they have had any more recent
serious crashes. On PRA and given a fair reading of the facts, it
seems clear that Air New Zealand should be held morally responsible for the Mount Erebus crash. Its post-crash and post-Report
behavior manifested the intention to continue its crucially prone-
to-defect structural and procedural policies, and that intention retrieves within its scope the corporate actions (or the actions of corporate personnel in its Flight Operations Division) that "494. . . .
programmed the aircraft to fly directly at Mount Erebus and omit-
ted to tell the aircrew." Again the Commission Report is quite ex-
plicit. "393. . . . That mistake is directly attributable, not so much
to the persons who made it, but to the incompetent administrative
airline procedures which made the mistake possible." Air New
Zealand's failure to adjust, on PRA, provides the basis for the jus-
tification of an ascription of moral responsibility for the tragic crash
to the airline.

The Mount Erebus case may be paradigmatic of a large class of
cases in which questions of corporate moral responsibility arise, not
because it is dramatic and involves great loss of life, but because
the focal event is not originally corporate intentional. Although I
think that PRA is a basic principle of morality and hence is applicable to all persons, it seems to be particularly appropriate in morally evaluating corporate actions. Corporations, through their standard operating procedures, may actually have a greater capacity for
reactive adaptation than do human beings. (But that is only a matter of degree and, I think, not a matter of any consequence.) Often
corporate personnel or subcorporate units at all levels of an organization, do things that result in untoward events and a higher
subcorporate unit, or the corporation itself, must decide on a responsive course of action. PRA allows the incorporation of the actions of personnel in the intentions of the corporate body and hence
a finding of corporate moral responsibility. But by the same token,
the appropriate corporate internal adjustment in response to the
revelation of the unintentional (at least at the level of corporate or
subcorporate unit) causing of an untoward event preserves corporate moral blamelessness in the event. PRA gives us an explication

of the corporate excuse that it was just a foul-up in the organization, or the selfish dealings of an individual, or a misdeed by someone, who, though he may have believed he was acting for the corporation, was actually pursuing his idiosyncratic conception of the corporate interests and corporate policies.

Organizational defects are one of the most common causes of corporation-caused untoward events, and they are also responsible for many criminal violations (particularly in the advertising area). A case in point is reported in Andrew Hopkins' study for the Australian Institute of Criminology on *The Impact of Prosecutions Under the Trade Practices Act* (April 1978). The Sharp Corporation of Australia falsely advertised that its microwave ovens were approved by the Standards Association of Australia (SAA). The ovens had been approved by the New South Wales Electricity Authority according to standards set for electrical equipment by the SAA. But no SAA standards existed at the time for microwave ovens. Sharp's sales manager, who authorized advertisements, claimed that although his technical staff would have been aware of the distinctions in the standards and authorities, that staff is not, in the standard corporate procedure, consulted on such advertising, and he was ignorant of the relevant distinctions. "Sharp's failure was a failure to involve the appropriate technically qualified people in checking the advertising copy before publication . . . the offense was not intentional" (p. 5–6).

In response to prosecution, Sharp changed its advertising procedures to insure that technical staff check copy before it is published to prevent any recurrence of the false advertising. Sharp's response is sufficient to rule out a finding of moral responsibility in the matter, whereas a failure to alter the corporate procedures, given PRA, would have provided a clear ground on which someone might claim, as one judge in the case did, that the advertisement was a "gross and wicked attempt to swindle the public," an intentional corporate action meriting moral reprobation and animadversion.

CHAPTER TWELVE

Intention and Corporate Accountability

The Principle of Responsive Adjustment (PRA), unearthed in the previous chapter, has an important upshot for the theory of the corporation as a moral person. A slight, but significant, modification of the crucial concept that underlies the theory originally developed in chapter 3 is needed to bring it in line with PRA. The required modification has also the happy consequence of providing a decisive response to a frequent criticism of the theory, while it more firmly cements the status of corporations in the moral world.

Our intuitions and prephilosophical reflective practices subscribe to PRA. That principle is not infrequently utilized when the character and worth of persons is assessed and evaluated. PRA, in fact, may be understood as functioning as one of our most common constraints on forgiveness.

PRA and EPA do, I think, constitute the superstructural principles of moral accountability. EPA captures Bradley's insistence that a deed cannot belong to someone unless it can be properly said to "issue" from his will and Aristotle's view that virtue and excellence depend upon the voluntary nature of actions.[1] PRA embodies Aristotle's conviction that persons are "themselves by their slack lives responsible for becoming men of that kind and men make themselves responsible for being unjust or self-indulgent . . . ; for it is activities exercised on particular objects that make the corresponding character" (p. 66).

If something is to be counted as a moral person, it must, minimally, have the properties or attributes that would justify its being treated as a proper subject of both EPA- and PRA-type judgments. Simply, to be a moral person is to be both an intentional actor and an entity with the capacity or ability to intentionally modify its behavioral patterns, habits, or modus operandi after it has learned that untoward or valued events (defined in legal, moral, or even prudential terms) were caused by its past unintentional behavior. Actually, a full-blooded conception of intentional action will involve or include the requisite responsive ability, as Aristotle's theory certainly does. Surely, for example, Aristotle would say the initiative necessary to respond to events we have unintentionally caused "lies in ourselves . . . in our power" (p. 66). And hence, because continuing "a given kind of activity produces a corresponding character" (p. 66) and we are (generally) responsible for our characters, we can be held morally accountable for our failures to alter, as long as it is naturally possible to do so, habits, etc., that have proven to cause untoward events. Of course, as Aristotle allows, once the "stone is thrown, . . . the die is cast" (p. 66), and one's character is so fixed that one no longer has the power to alter it, it is not causally possible for a person not to be what he has become.

There are some philosophers who would insist that there are degrees or levels of intentionality or that intentionality is a rather anemic notion that can be exhibited by lower animals. They argue that my theory of the corporation as a moral person, because it involves the position that anything that can behave intentionally is a moral person, entails that dogs, cats, etc., are also moral persons. Thomas Donaldson, for example, has recently written:

> Some entities appear to behave intentionally which do not qualify as moral agents. A cat may behave intentionally when it crouches for a mouse. We know that it intends to catch the mouse, but we do not credit it with moral agency . . . One seemingly needs more than the presence of intentions to deduce moral agency.[2]

With the dash of a philosophical swashbuckler, Donaldson cavalierly leaps from a somewhat noncommital "may behave" to a very staunch epistemological claim about the way cats think. It can only be wondered on what such confidence with regard to knowing a cat's intentions is grounded. Suppose the cat remains in its crouch while a parade of mice sashays by. Should we then say that it did not intend to catch a mouse (or one of *those* mice), or that it changed its mind, or, perchance, that it suffers from a severe case of weakness of will? Rather than wasting time poking fun at Donaldson's example, we are in a position to offer our modification of the account of moral personhood to satisfy the concern that seems to have motivated Donaldson's comments, while yet preserving the basic theory of the corporation as a moral person.

Donaldson's cats and other lower animals are to be excluded from the class of moral persons because, although they *may* behave intentionally in some rather restricted way that I should not like to try to specify, they can neither appreciate that an event for which their intentional or unintentional behavior has been causally responsible is untoward or worthy nor intentionally modify their ways of behaving to correct the offensive actions or to adopt the behavior that was productive of worthy results. In short, they are just not full-blooded intentional actors. Simply, they are not intentional actors.

In this regard our account is less Aristotelian than Bradleyian, for Aristotle thought that infants and animals, at least sometimes, act voluntarily and so are responsible.[3] A popular cornerstone of such a view, though it is not particularly of Aristotle's construction, is the position taken by some philosophers that because children and animals are punished when they behave badly, they must be regarded, at least by those inflicting the punishment, as responsible moral persons. No argument (if that is what this is) could be weaker. In the first place, punishment of anyone or anything does not presuppose that the thing punished is a responsible person. Donaldson would certainly agree with that position, for clearly business corporations are regularly punished by the courts with fines, etc., for their misdeeds. If the efficacy of punishment were the index of responsibility, we would only have to look to the legal case history to find that corporations, at least some of them are responsible actors, and all of them are responsible actors according to the *Model Penal Code*, which I will discuss in chapter 13.

Furthermore, as Bradley noted, those who claim that animals

and children are punished for their wicked deeds generally confuse punishment inflicted as a just desert with something altogether different: discipline. Bradley writes: "The former [punishment] is inflicted because of wrong-doing as a desert, the latter is applied as a means of improvement."[4] He adds that the application of discipline is purely a practical matter. It is the parent's or the trainer's role to decide on the efficacy, the type, and the amount of discomfort to be administered to the child or the animal. The goal is to affect an alteration of behavior: it is not retribution.

The PRA modification allows, in the absence of strong evidence regarding their responsive adjustment to moral evaluation, exclusion of lower animals from the class of moral persons. As noted in the previous chapter, PRA is, however, especially applicable to corporations. The managerial organizations of most business firms provide the kind of decision procedures necessary for making responsive adjustments that are less clearly available to individual human beings who are often emotionally bound to previous commitments and have deep psychological difficulties when confronted with the need to break habits or give up old ways.

PRA does, however, require a certain type of managerial organization. Although I think the theory of the corporation as a moral person is neutral as between an economic man and an administrative man theory of decision-making, for responsive adjustment of the relevant sort, business corporations cannot be locked into purely programmed decision structures. The standard distinction between programmed and nonprogrammed decisions is cut on the automatic nature of the solution to problems. Decisions in an organization are "programmed to the extent that they are repetitive and routine because of existing definite, systematic procedures."[5] If a corporation operated purely on a programmed decision-making basis, it would be managed in what is often called a classical mechanistic manner, but it will be capable of dealing only with stable, predictable conditions, and its managers must be assumed to be guided solely by rational economic principles of the classical sort operating under conditions of certainty with ordered preferences governed by the profit motive. As a matter of fact, most cor-

porate decisions are routine so that the appropriate decisions under various controlled or known conditions can be programmed into
the standard operating procedures (SOPs). By the same token,
however, if the SOPs and the corporate preferences of the programmed corporation are in place and if morally untoward, but
not economically alarming, outcomes occur, the mechanistic structure can only be expected to continue in its routine fashion to crank
out decisions relatively similar to those that were productive of the
offensive events. There is almost a perfect analog here to the habits of human beings. Habits cannot be broken habitually.

PRA, of course, requires that habits that produce morally disvalued events be broken and replaced by behavior (or procedures)
that do not have such effects. In this regard, if a corporation is to
satisfy the PRA-related conditions of moral personhood, it must
be capable of making what are generally known as nonprogrammed decisions. Perhaps the most evident nonprogrammed
decision-making that goes on in most manufacturing corporations
concerns new products. Although adherence to clearly established
procedural steps is generally required, decisions pro or con new
products are not programmable in the way that computation of
employee salaries in accordance with labor contracts and product-
mix decisions are. Operations research may prove an aid to nonprogrammed decision-making, but neither it nor linear program-
ming can substitute for creative problem-solving. PRA decisions
not only cannot be programmed, they are commonly program or
procedural-corrective decisions. A place in the CID Structure might
well be designated as the watchdog or responsive adjustment office, in the sense that the structure can prepare itself for the even-
tuality of required adjustment, but the decision-making that characterizes such a practice cannot be routinized in the way the practices
of those controlling product-mix (under usual market and supply
conditions) can be.

In sum, only those corporations that have CID Structures that
facilitate nonprogrammed decision-making can meet the conditions of moral personhood.

Most business firms, as it happens, have very active nonprogrammed elements in their CID Structure. If they did not, they

would be incapable of innovation, growth, and development with regard to their most vital economic interests. By the same token, most corporations do not have CID Structures that mirror the intellectual structure of classical rationality. Corporate decision structures that must work only under conditions of certainty are certain to become moribund, unproductive, and fiscally stagnant in a remarkably short time.

The theory of the corporation as a moral person requires that corporations have the structural capacity to innovate and that capacity is demonstrable if a corporation is at least able to do such things as develop new products, initiate mergers, relocate plants, select new board members, acquire properties and other corporations, etc. It is unimportant to the theory that corporate managers may be primarily motivated by objective profit-maximization rationality or by a "satisficing"[6] rationality that recommends choice of the first alternative that meets some subjective minimum standard of satisfaction as they function in a CID Structure that is about the business of resolving nonprogrammable issues. The theory is not concerned with why the corporation should be moral and hence with trying to locate economically rational reasons for making the morally recommended adjustments. The theory is concerned with the foundational matter of whether the corporation satisfies the conditions of moral personhood, not with what a corporation's most basic aims, goals, or motives might be nor with the concept of rationality under which it directs its operations. We ought not forget that, according to the classical theory, utility maximization is the prime motive of human behavior, and no one would argue, regardless of how difficult that makes acquiescing to the recommendations of morality, that classical economic man was not a citizen of the moral world.

Donaldson makes another attempt to formulate a reduction of the theory of the corporation as a moral person. It is an appeal to our intuitions about rights. He tells us "If, morally speaking, corporations are analogous to persons, then they should have the rights which ordinary persons have."[7] The idea is that we will be aghast at this notion and give up the theory as having an absurd corollary. But does it? What rights has Donaldson in mind? He admits that such legal rights as owning property, entering into agreements, and making profits are clearly shared by corporations and human beings. But then he claims that it would be implausible for corporations to have the right to vote and to draw Social Security benefits. Yes it would definitely be implausible, indeed it would be stupid.

But that proves absolutely nothing. Twelve-year-old human children do not have either the right to vote or the right to draw Social Security benefits. And why not? Because legislated rights are not always, in fact rarely are they, nonrestrictive. The fact that a perfectly competent sixteen-year-old woman does not have the right to vote says nothing at all about her moral status. I have argued elsewhere that rights are institution specific, that they are created within the operations of certain kinds of institutions in accord with the rules of those institutions.[8] All of the rights mentioned by Donaldson are of this sort. "X has the right to draw Social Security" does not entail "X is a moral person." Certain human beings who are utterly incapable of intentional action may nonetheless possess the right to Social Security benefits.

Donaldson might have argued that corporations cannot be said to have natural rights. That, of course, is unexceptionable. To have natural rights something must be natural. Corporations clearly are not, that was the point of many of the previous chapters, but especially chapter 6. I certainly would not want to attempt an argument in favor of natural rights, that is, an argument that conclusively shows that there are such things and what they are. I do not happen to think there are any such things, but if there are, then they attach to the natural kinds, and "person" and "moral person" are not natural-kind terms. Donaldson's argument from rights is utterly beside the point, misguided, and irrelevant. No one ought to worry about Exxon drawing Social Security or voting for President of the United States, or serving as Secretary of State. The lesson to be learned from Donaldson's argument is that philosophers ought to be rather more conservative with regard to what they claim is to be unpacked from moral personhood. To be a moral person is to be a proper subject of certain kinds of judgments, moral responsibility ascriptions, moral blaming, and praising statements.

In the previous chapter it was suggested that failure to routinize corporate unintentional behavior that was productive of good results defeats the assignment of moral credit to the corporation. Professor Lisa Newton has developed a case that nicely illustrates this point. I am grateful to her for drawing it to my attention and giving me permission to use it. Though I will not attempt to reproduce her case in full, the gist is:

> A new employee of a large electric alliances company is assigned the task of getting rid of half a ton of broken or unusable parts. His predecessor had left without providing instructions as to how such problems were to be handled. He asks a fellow employee for advice and is told that his predecessor always used a certain removal service. The employee then orders his secretary, who is also new on the job, to make the necessary arrangements. The name of the removal firm happens to be similar to that of a vocational high school. The secretary calls the school and says something on the order of, "Can you take away about a half a ton of discarded electrical parts? We need them removed tomorrow." The person from the high school, after moments of silence, responds with enthusiasm that the parts will be removed.

> The employee, after his secretary has hung up the phone, realizes he forgot to have her ask the cost, but a fellow employee tells him that the usual fee is $75. The employee writes out a $75 check, leaving blank the name of the firm (in case he has not gotten the proper name) and leaves the check for the yard supervisor to fill in and give to the people who come to remove the parts.

> The next morning two dozen teenagers in pick-up trucks and vans arrive and load the discarded parts and receive, if with some befuddlement, the $75 check.

> On the following day the local newspaper runs a banner story about how the electric plant had benefited the vocational school. Praise is heaped on the company from all quarters. The vice-president for policy management may well bask in the radiance of extended gratitude, but he is at a loss to explain how the company came to be such a donor. We may imagine that the new employee will be called to account for his actions.

The company, of course, consistent with long-standing moral principles, particularly those framed by Kant, ought not to be given moral credit for having benefited the school insofar as its doing so was but the result of a series of accidents, mistakes, and misunderstandings. No one can be moral by accident. The company, however, is confronted with a morally significant choice of action when it becomes cognizant of the facts. It can order its employee never to make such a mistake again, informing him that standard procedure is to have the discarded parts carted away by a commercial firm, one with whom it has a contract. Or, it can routinize the practice of donating its discarded parts and the usual removal costs to the vocational high school. If it chooses to do the former, it would offend our moral sensibilities if it were to receive moral credit for the earlier unintended beneficence. On the other hand, if it does the latter, we would be licensed by PRA to allow moral recovery of the earlier charitable action in its present intention to program the practice. Simply, to get moral credit for an unintended good deed, the company must adopt a standard policy of performing such deeds. In sum, PRA formulates a basic intuition about the moral need and value of consistency in the lived life. It is a principle of integrity, of probity, and hence, enforces the idea that there needs to be a certain unity to the life of a moral person.

CHAPTER THIRTEEN

Corporate Criminality and the Model Penal Code

Although it is not necessarily directly related to the theory of the corporation as a moral person, the ongoing debate in law over whether corporations should be held criminally liable is closely allied to the moral personhood issue. As shown in chapter 3, the fact that something is a legal person is no grounds for including it among the members of the moral community, and an argument that would defend the proposition that because something is a moral person it must be a legal one fails to grasp the institutionality of law. The rules that govern inclusion in the legal community are to be counted among the institution's constitutive rules, constituting in themselves a subset of the institutional grammatical rules. In short, moral personhood is a metaphysical matter: legal personhood is a matter of institutional rules and may be of a purely practical origin.

In the sphere of criminal law, historically there has been a very close association between the discussion of the conditions of moral personhood and those of criminal liability. Obviously, that is because criminal law is, by and large, concerned with the punishment of malefactors, and punishment is associated not only with causal responsibility but with intent and desert. Desert, of course, usually is taken to entail moral responsibility. Hence, Jones deserves to be punished for doing something only if Jones is morally responsible for doing it. Such a tight little formula, however, does not hold throughout the law. For example, it does not hold in strict-

liability cases. Nonetheless, it is a cornerstone of offenses that traditionally are thought to necessitate a mens rea. From the earliest
days that has been the major stumbling block for corporate criminality. Blackstone, speaking for a veritable army of legal theorists, wrote that a "corporation cannot commit treason, or felony,
or other crime, in its corporate capacity; though its members may
in their distinct individual capacities."[1]

Blackstone's lights, however, have not shown a straight and narrow path to the criminal legal theorists, jurists, or legislators in the
centuries that followed his pronouncement. In a relatively short time
the law has moved to the view that corporations can be found guilty
of most crimes, including those that require a mens rea. To be sure,
corporations cannot commit certain crimes by virtue of lacking the
relevant abilities to perform specific actions. Corporations cannot
be bigamists or rapists, but the fact that they do not have the capacities needed to commit those crimes has no general effect on
their status vis a vis the criminal law per se. Analogously, a man
who is severely disabled may not be able to commit rape, but he
may still be guilty of murder, theft, or manslaughter. The notion
of criminal liability has never been framed in such a way that those
who may be found guilty of some crimes may be found guilty for
all or any crimes in the corpus.

The criminal law, as it affects corporations, evolved from the
imposition of liability for nuisance and nonfeasance in seven-
teenth-century England to liability for felonies as serious as manslaughter and reckless homicide in this century. The nonfeasance
and nuisance cases of the seventeenth and eighteenth centuries were
brought against public corporations, counties, boroughs, and towns.
It was not until the nineteenth century that criminal responsibility
was imposed on private commercial corporations and those, probably not coincidently, were railroads.

In 1842 the English court found, in *Queen v. Birmingham and
Gloucester Railway Co.*, that corporations can be held criminally
responsible for their inactions. The railway was indicted for failure
to obey an order to remove a bridge over a public road after it had
been declared a nuisance. The court found that insofar as a statute

had created a legal duty on the corporation to perform certain acts, that the railroad could be punished for nonfeasance. The court maintained that a business firm's liability "was to be equated, so far as possible, with that of natural persons."[2]

A few years later, in *Queen v. Great North of England Railway*, a corporation was convicted, not of a failure to do something (non-feasance), but of doing something (misfeasance). The railway was indicted for obstructing the public highway. The nuisance in this case was created by railroad workers who, in their capacity as employees of the corporation, performed certain acts that had the effect of blocking the thoroughfare. *Great North of England Railway* is noteworthy on at least two counts. In the first place, the court adopted the concept of vicarious liability that became the ambit of corporate criminal liability in the eyes of federal courts in the United States. The court bound the corporation to the actions of its employees (as long as they had been performing in their corporate roles). In the second place, the court ruled against the railway's defense that although it could commit acts of nonfeasance (as in *Birmingham and Gloucester Railway Co.*), it could not perform affirmative acts for which it could be criminally liable. In the oft-quoted words of Lord Denman C.J., the court responded.

It is as easy to charge one person or a body corporate with erecting a bar across a public road as with the nonrepair of it; and they may as well be compelled to pay a fine for the act as for the omission.[3]

Early development of corporate criminal law in the United States also runs along the rails. In 1852, in one of the more famous cases, *State v. Morris & Essex Railroad Company*, a corporation was indicted for obstructing a highway and creating a public nuisance.[4] As in *Great North of England Railway*, the matter turned on whether a corporation could commit and be held responsible for an affirmative act of misfeasance and not merely a nonperformance or nonfeasance. The Morris & Essex Railroad was found guilty. The old chestnut corporate defense that it is incapable of affirmative acts was tested in *Commonwealth v. Proprietors of New Bedford Bridge* (1854) and again found wanting.[5] In this case the court wrote that the distinction between nonfeasance and misfeasance is artificial, and the doctrine that a corporation is indictable for the former but not the latter is absurd.

In both of those landmark cases, however, the court allowed that a corporation could not be "liable for any crime of which a corrupt intent or *malus animus* is an essential ingredient."[6]

In 1879 in the Supreme Court of Appeals of West Virginia the court was called upon to decide whether a corporation, the Baltimore and Ohio Railroad Company, could be indicted and convicted for Sabbath breaking, in violation of "the 16th and 17th Sections of Chapter 149 of the Code of West Virginia."[7] In its opinion, the court examined in detail the doctrines and precedent with regard to corporate criminal liability in both the United States and Great Britain. The court found that a corporation is "liable for torts, . . . willful acts of its agents though done within the proper range of employment, . . . a nuisance, . . . misfeasance . . . libel . . . malicious prosecution, . . . assaults and batteries committed by its agents in the performance of their duties (p. 373). From these latter liabilities the court deduced that it could not accede to the view that a corporation cannot be held liable for any offenses that derive their criminality from corrupt intent.

> The very basis of an action of libel, or for a malicious prosecution, is the evil intent, and malice of the party against whom such suit is brought; and I cannot now well see how it is possible to hold that a corporation may be sued for a libel, and punitive damages recovered and at the same time hold that such a corporation could not be indicted for such libel. The suits of libel and malicious prosecution are in their nature very like to criminal proceedings; and if they lie against a corporation, it would seem to follow, that there are cases for which indictments may lie against a corporation where the evil intention constitutes an element in the offense. (p. 380)

The court found that the statutory misdemeanor of Sabbath breaking fell well within the capabilities of a corporation. The court went on to discuss in some detail the Sabbath breaking laws and whether they applied to only those who can have religious duties to God, but although the full account is fascinating, it is rather outside of the current purview. (It may be worth noting that the court did not find that only those with a religious duty to God are liable to obey the statute.)

In 1909 the Court of Appeals of New York heard *People v. Rochester Railway and Light Co.*,[8] in which the corporation was alleged to have installed "certain apparatus in a residence in Rochester in such a grossly improper, unskillful, and negligent manner that gases escaped and caused the death of an inmate." The demurrer to the indictment raised the question of whether a corporation "is capable of committing in any form such a crime as that of manslaughter." To the corporation's surprise, the court found that "the proposition urged in behalf of the people that it may do so" (p. 22) is in no doubt. The court reasoned that corporations are generally liable in civil proceedings for all sorts of misconduct by agents and employees, and "it is but a step further in the same direction to hold that in many instances it may be charged criminally" (p. 23). Summing up the court's response to the demurrer's claim, the court wrote—quoting from the decision in *Telegram Newspaper Co. v. Commonwealth:*

> We think that a corporation may be liable criminally for certain offenses of which a specific intent may be a necessary element. There is no more difficulty in imputing to a corporation a specific intent in criminal proceedings than in civil. (p. 23)

The court, however, did not support a conviction of the corporation on the grounds that the section of the penal code that defines homicide is so written as to preclude all but natural human beings from committing the crime. The code read "the killing of one human being by the act, procurement or omission of another" (p. 24). The court maintained that the word "another" meant not a person, but a member of the natural kind named by "human being." The court, in fact, argued that had the law been rewritten to use the word "person" rather than "another," corporations would be included and could then be properly said to be capable of committing homicide in any of its varying degrees, including manslaughter. In short, the court's opinion may be read as containing the suggestion that the penal code be revised to define homicide as the killing of one human being by the act, procurement or omission of a person. That was the reading urged by the state, but the ambiguity of "another" was sufficient in this case to insure the affirmation of the judgment in favor of the Rochester Railway and Light Company. It is noteworthy that the court expressed the view that it did not shrink from the somewhat radical interpretation (at the time) that the corporation could commit homicide, if the law defining the crime had been written to make specific reference to persons.

The leading Supreme Court case of *New York Central & Hudson River Rail Road v. United States,* also in 1909,[9] upheld the constitutionality of the law that made corporations criminally liable for the acts of their agents, employees, managers, etc., as long as those acts were arguably within the general scope of corporate duties (The Elkins Act). The corporation's defense in this case involved the claim that to punish a corporation is to unjustly punish its innocent stockholders. The Court rejected that claim by noting that stockholders benefit from the illegal acts of the corporation's agents, employees, etc., and could therefore be penalized without damage to justice or fairness.

In more recent decisions the words "persons" and "whoever" in statutes consistent with Title I, Section 1 of the United States Code, are generally interpreted to include corporations, "unless the context indicates otherwise." (See, for example, *Western Laundry and Linen Rental Co. v. United States* 424 F.2d 441 [9th Cir.]) Although in *State v. Pacific Powder Co.* (226 Or. 502, 360 P.2d 530) in 1961 crimes of violence against persons were excluded from corporate criminal liability, that view has not been taken by the American Law Institute in the *Model Penal Code* and in the celebrated Ford Pinto murder case in Indiana, the corporation not only was indicted, it was tried. The acquittal of Ford turned on matters of evidence, fact, and interpretation unrelated to the old doctrine that a corporation cannot commit a crime of personal violence like murder.

The Model Penal Code

Section 2.07 of the American Law Institute's *Model Penal Code* reads as follows:

> Liability of Corporations, Unincorporated Associations and Persons Acting, or Under a Duty to Act, in Their Behalf
> (1) A corporation may be convicted of the commission of an offense if:
>> (a) the offense is a violation or is defined by a statute other than the Code in which a legislative purpose to impose liability on corporations plainly appears and the conduct is performed by an agent of the corporation acting in behalf of the corporation within the scope of his office or employment, except that if the law defining the offense designates the agents for whose conduct the corporation is accountable or the circumstances under which it is accountable, such provisions shall apply; or
>> (b) the offense consists of an omission to discharge a specific duty of affirmative performance imposed on corporations by law; or
>> (c) the commission of the offense was authorized, requested, commanded, performed or recklessly tolerated by the board of directors or by a high managerial agent acting in behalf of the corporation within the scope of his office or employment . . .
> (4) (c) "high managerial agent" means an officer of a corporation having duties of such responsibility that his conduct may fairly be assumed to represent the policy of the corporation.
> (5) In any prosecution of a corporation . . . for the commission of an offense included within the terms of Subsection (1) (a) . . . other than an offense for which absolute liability has been imposed, it shall be a defense if the defendant proves by a preponderance of evidence that the high managerial agent having supervisory responsibility over the subject matter of the offense employed due diligence to prevent the commission. This paragraph shall not apply if it is plainly inconsistent with the legislative purpose in defining the particular offense.[10]

Subsection 6 clarifies a point I have emphasized throughout this book: corporate responsibility is not substitutionary, except where the law allows only the corporation to be found guilty of the crime (and where human beings who are employed by the corporation are only liable according to complicity or accessory doctrines). The *Code* is quite clear that agents, employees, etc., are legally individually accountable "to the same extent as if it were performed in his own name or behalf."[11] In other words, corporate criminal liability, like corporate moral responsibility, is not a shield for individuals. In the words of L. H. Leigh, "corporate criminal liability is cumulative."[12] A cadre of cases can be cited to show that at common law a natural person whose actions are the basis for a finding of corporate liability is not excused from responsibility by the conviction of the employing corporation. Of particular note is *Rex v. Hendrie*, 11 O.L.R. 202, 10 C.C.C. 298 (C.A. 1905), *United States v. Wise*, 370 U.S. 405, 82 Sup. Ct. 1354 (1962), and the Canadian case of *Regina v. Continental Cablevision Inc.*, 18 C.P.R. (2d) 209 (Ont. Prov. Ct. 1974).

As Leigh points out, two rather different lines of authority have emerged with regard to corporate criminal liability (p. 266). The *Model Penal Code* formulates what might be called the principle of "corporate personal liability" and disassociates that principle from the more traditional assimilation of corporate liability to vicarious liability. The vicarious liability approach, as earlier mentioned, has been frequently taken by the federal courts and may be attributed to the court's realistic need to secure compliance with regulations.

> They have not assumed that crimes have necessarily originated in the boardroom, and have imposed liability in respect of the middle range of corporate officials . . . regardless of whether the offense reflected the policy of the corporation as seen by the highest levels of management. (p. 267)

Seldom has any attempt to prove complicity of the highest ranking officers been required. The landmark case in this regard is *Egan v. United States* (137 F.2d 369 [8th Cir. 1943]).

The operative rules governing corporate vicarious liability are to be found in *Standard Oil Co. v. United States* (307 F.2d 120 [5th Cir. 1962]). Those rules concern benefit and intent. "The court held that in relation to crimes of intent, a corporation cannot be charged with guilty knowledge acquired by employees outside the scope of their employment" (p. 268). Also, an employee is not to be understood as acting within the scope of his employment unless his actions are primarily intended to benefit the corporation or further its business interests. Of course, no benefit may accrue to the corporation though the employee's intention was to further the corporation's interests; so, Leigh tells us, the "purpose to benefit the corporation is decisive in equating the agent's action with that of the corporation" (p. 268).

The corporation can, however, be held liable even if its employee did not act with the purpose of benefiting the corporation, and did not in fact benefit the corporation, if their superiors were aware of their actions and did not take either corrective measures or report violations to the proper authorities. It is also noteworthy that the due diligence defense that is a cornerstone of the *Model Penal Code* has not been recognized by the federal courts when mens rea offenses are concerned. Leigh cites *United States v. Harry L. Young & Sons* (464 F.2d 1295 [10th Cir. 1972]) as a case in point where the fact that the employee disobeyed corporate instructions did not affect the imputation of his intent to the corporation (pp. 268–69).

It should be stressed that these federal court rules emerged, by and large, in the adjudication of cases where the main interest lay in attaining compliance with regulation. The attempt to determine actual corporate policy, interests, decision-procedure outcomes, etc., was evidently regarded as too cumbersome to be allowed to affect the resolution of such cases. Rather than offering a strong philosophical argument of a methodological individualist nature, the courts tended to deal at the level of practicality. If any philosophical argument underlies the rules used in these courts, it is probably one that focuses primarily on the efficacy of punishment with particular regard to deterrence. It may be assumed that if corporations are to be held criminally liable, in the broad sense defined by adoption of the rules, for the acts of their employees, that corporations will exercise especial care, beyond what might be generally regarded as due diligence, to supervise employee activity.

The *Model Penal Code*'s approach to corporate criminal liability is founded on principles that are consistent with the theory of the corporation as a moral person as I have developed it. The cornerstone of the *Model Penal Code*'s position is laid on the imposition of corporate personal liability, distinct from vicarious liability, and is based on the identification of the decision-making powers of certain offices within the corporate internal decision structure (its CID Structure). This doctrine of identification has roots in English law where it is frequently used to ground attributions of a mens rea to a corporation.

The standard case for the statement of the doctrine is *Lennard's Carrying Co. v. Asiatic Petroleum* ([1915] A.C. 7051 [1914–15] All E.R. Rep. 280 H.L.) In that case the corporation argued that only its board of directors could be identified with the mind of the company. The employee at fault was a managing director and the board of directors was not cognizant of the conditions that constituted the negligence in question. The House of Lords, however, rejected the company's defense. Viscount Haldane maintained that "a corporation('s) . . . active and directing will must be sought in the person of somebody who . . . is really the directing mind and will of the corporation."[13] Haldane went on to argue that actual corporate operations might not support the identification of the mind of the corporation with its board of directors. The board may or may not be the controlling mind with regard to certain corporate enterprises, tasks, etc., where individuals holding lower-managerial offices have better information and more direct executive power than board members.

Leigh notes that in *Rex v. Fane Robinson Ltd.* ([1941] 2 W.W.R. 235, 76 C.C.C. 1961, [1941] 3 D.L.R. 409 [Alta. C.A.]) the Canadian court applied the principle articulated in *Lennard's Carrying Co. v. Asiatic Petroleum* "to establish that corporate liability was truly personal liability and that a corporation could personally entertain the mens rea necessary for liability for criminal conspiracy."[14]

There need to be limitations on the application of the identification doctrine to bring it more in line with common sense and usual practice. Surely, there must be a level of corporate decision-making beneath which identification with the corporate mind and will is not only gratuitous but wrongheaded. On the other hand, identification cannot always be restricted to high officials and sometimes should not be interpreted to exclude non-officeholders.

may be concisely put: if a corporate mens rea cannot be proved with regard to the relevant action, then the corporation cannot be convicted of the crime.

Without reiterating the specific details, recall the 1980 Ford Motor Company reckless homicide case. Insofar as the crime requires a mens rea, it was incumbent on the prosecution to show that Ford harbored the motives and intentions that in common law would generally be regarded as sufficient to prove a mens rea in like cases when the defendant was a natural person. Ford certainly had no intention to kill the young women who were incinerated in the crash, but Ford might have been shown to be willing (by application of EPA) to have people die in such crashes rather than expend the capital necessary to modify a vehicle it knew was not safe. If such a willingness could be demonstrated, would that be sufficient to prove a corporate mens rea with regard to the specific case? That, of course, is a matter for the courts, though it should be useful to construct analogies to cases concerning individual human beings who demonstrate a willingness to jeopardize the lives of others by their actions, and someone put at risk dies.

Negligent omissions and commissions that do not require a mens rea will probably still constitute the bulk of corporate criminal liability cases. Such cases by their very nature are also, by and large, going to be more socially important than mens rea cases. We ought not to forget that isolated corporate homicides and corporate thefts are not as destructive to the fabric of social order as the pollution of the air, land, and water, and in such cases, in fact, justice is generally not served by the prosecution of some natural person who happens to work for the corporation. The corporate body itself needs to be brought before the bar. As Leigh puts it, "fairness and social justice: it is important that the public realize that powerful entities are not above the law." [17]

The Canadian case of *Regina v. St. Lawrence Corp.* ([1969] 2 O.R. 305, 5 D.L.R. [3d] 263 [C.A.]) is often cited as providing a clear formulation of the principle.

> If the agent falls within a category which entitles the court to hold that he is a vital organ of the body corporate and virtually its directing mind and will in the sphere of duty and responsibility assigned to him so that his action and intent are the very action and intent of the company itself, then his conduct is sufficient to render the company indictable by reason thereof. It should be added that both on principle and authority this proposition is subject to the proviso that in performing the acts in question the agent was acting within the scope of his authority either express or implied.

This doctrine has many practical as well as theoretical virtues. Most evidently, it does not provide the corporation with the automatic defense that the board of directors was ignorant of the offending actions. Furthermore, it reflects the general practice in large decentralized corporations in which various office managements exercise nearly autonomous control over specific aspects of the corporate enterprise. The corporate mind may reside in various offices in various locations throughout the corporate empire. The test should be that the manager or employee has a significant degree of autonomy with regard to making corporate decisions and instigating corporate actions. "The question is not whether the relevant human actor occupies a particular place within the corporation, but whether, whatever his title, he exercises substantially autonomous powers in respect of a significant aspect of the corporation's activities." [15] The procedural aspects of a CID Structure will, obviously, provide the first level of data in the determination of identification, but, as maintained in chapter 4, nonformalized decision structures do typically occur and may give rise to roles that are filled by employees whose actions should be identified with those of the corporation.

The policy recognitor tests stressed in chapters 3 and 4 remain crucial and are affirmed both in the identification doctrine and in the *Model Penal Code*. The code is less inclusive than the English-Canadian doctrine of identification in that it specifies "high managerial agent," and it does so because it is generally believed that the conduct of such an individual, acting within the scope of employment on behalf of the corporation will usually represent corporate policy.

The *Model Penal Code* and the identification doctrine advance the notion of corporate criminal liability well beyond the limits of vicarious liability and strict liability. This line of authority in law develops the basis for attributions of mens rea offenses to corporations. There are, however, certain difficulties with the *Model Penal Code* approach that should be examined.

It is one thing to identify the managerial level that is likely to harbor the mind and will of the corporation, but it is quite another to identify the actions and intentions of the persons in such offices as corporate even if they are performed to benefit the corporation or as a matter of fact benefit it. The *Model Penal Code* is far too dependent on the procedural and station aspects of a CID Structure. What is wanted is a statement that allows the corporation, on the basis of established internal policy, to rebut the attribution of corporate responsibility of any act of its high managerial staff members working within their defined corporate powers. In short, what is needed is a clear recognition that an act is corporate not only because of its form, but because of the policy it instantiates, displays, or manifests. The corporation should be able to use not only a due diligence defense, but also a nonreflection of corporate policy defense. This latter defense, however, will not be easy to support because the corporation will have to demonstrate the existence of either actual official policy statements and guidelines or internal precedents that are understood within the organization's management to be overriding with regard to the matters in question. A failure to have a policy—or the fact that in previous similar cases no corporate action was taken or conduct very like that in question was condoned at the relevant managerial levels—should constitute, at least, corporate complicity, and if the policy decision in question is made by a suitably high managerial officer, then that action will be properly attributable to the corporation, consistent with section 2.07. Evidentiary rules will be crucial to the establishment of such a defense. The matter is a practical one, but one that

must be carefully considered if the *Code* is to be a clear, rational, and fair legal interpretation of the doctrine of corporate agency.

A second objection has been formulated by Gerhard O. W. Mueller. Though Mueller, in general, finds section 2.07 to be "a rational interpretation . . . for the application of a rational theory of corporate criminal liability on the basis of the guilt-deterrence orientation of the common law of crimes,"[16] he insists, and with good reason, that the *Code* goes too far. Section 2.07 (4) concludes with the sentence, "This paragraph shall not apply if it is inconsistent with the legislative purpose in defining the particular offense."

The idea expressed seems to be that the legislature in its wisdom may identify certain actions or outcomes as corporate crimes even though the tests of attribution to the corporate mind and will are failed. It is of note, however, that subsection 4 expressly excludes what are called "absolute liability offenses." Those offenses, of course, do not require identification of a corporate mens rea. Social welfare and antipollution legislation are often written in such a way. Having already excluded strict or absolute liability offenses, what could then be included by the last sentence of the subsection? Either a criminal offense is one that requires a mens rea, or it does not. If it does not, it is a strict liability matter that is excluded from the subsection. If the offense is a common-law liability, then it requires a mens rea. A legislature cannot, for example, define murder in a way that allows no exculpation, for that would convert the crime from a common-law liability into an absolute liability and thereby offend against the grand tradition that underlies the very concept of murder: the tradition in which it is acknowledged that murders cannot be unintentionally, accidentally, committed.

If the legislature cannot play fast and loose with such common-law criminal liabilities as murder, what can it do? Mueller's answer is, as it should be, that the clause in subsection 4 is utterly unnecessary. "It is a poor legal system indeed which is unable to differentiate between the law breaker and the innocent victim of circumstances so that it must punish both alike" (p. 45). The rule that ought to govern mens rea offenses with regard to corporations

CHAPTER FOURTEEN
Punishing the Criminal Corporation

It would surely be regarded as remiss of me were I not to mention perhaps that most quoted line regarding corporation criminal liability in all the annals of discussion on the matter. That line is attributed to Edward, First Baron Thurlow, Lord Chancellor of England. The line, of course, is, "Did you ever expect a corporation to have a conscience, when it has no soul to be damned, and no body to be kicked?"

Baron Thurlow's interests lay in the efficacy of punishing criminal corporations for corporate actions that violated statute or common law and his concern is a pressing one to this day. No doubt we would not find so prosaic a way to frame the issue; nonetheless, we should be concerned with the value of or the rationale behind corporate criminal liability if the law (or the state) has no effective means to punish the corporation once it is properly found guilty of the commission of the crime. Baron Thurlow's dictum is firmly cemented into a foundation of retributivism that, by and large, has sustained our penal system. Although there are strong competitor theories of punishment, the utilitarian and the rehabilitativist for examples, the firm hand of retribution, with its biblical authority, still commands the high ground of our thinking about the punishment of criminals. If a corporation has no body to kick (leaving to God the business of souls and eternal damnation), how can it repay in kind for its felonious behavior? It has no eye to be exchanged for an eye that was blinded by unsafe working conditions. Or so the story is meant to go.

Retributivism does not, as most theorists will tell us, have to be

understood in such biblical blood-lust terms. To retribute is to repay, but payment need not always be made in kind. Capital punishment in the case of natural person murderers has in many jurisdictions been replaced with life sentences that have possible parole
stipulations. The old Anglo-Saxon notion of wergild is commonly
utilized in settling wrongful-death suits. The price of a human life
may not be cheap, but it is being set by the courts and paid by
corporations or their insurance carriers.

The idea that a corporation can pay a fine or a set sum to the
survivors of its victim in a homicide case and thereby expiate its
guilt is regarded as an affront to justice and fairness by many people. It may appear that the price of retribution is but another cost
of business and that cost may, in the normal course of things, be
passed on to the consumers of the corporation's products or services.

There is, of course, a way that capital punishment can be exacted on a corporation: revocation of charter, and there is also a
corporate version of removal from the community of the members
of society: revocation of license to do business in the state or city.
Charter revocation only will be viable in the state of charter, but
licenses and other business rights can be revoked in any place where
they are required. This sort of punishment generally arouses two
objections. The first is that innocent people tend to be the most
seriously harmed by revocations. Stockholders and innocent employees suffer financially. The second is that punished corporations can, with relative ease, reconstitute themselves, get new
charters, and get back to business as usual.

The trickle-down effect of corporate punishment, it seems to me,
is not to be given much attention. Stockholders, those who are
usually the primary concern of proponents of this argument, are
well-protected by SEC regulations, and if they suffer, that is a risk
they undertook when entering the market. In many cases, especially bribery cases, the stockholder stands to benefit from the un-
detected crime and may do so for a period of time. I see no reason
why the same stockholder ought not to bear some of the burden
of punishment. The stockholder, after all, is free to trade his holdings in the market and was never assured of a clear profit. Also,

the stockholder might consider pressing a civil suit against the corporation that cost him a significant value in stock due to its criminal behavior. A class-action suit by stockholders who claim damage under such conditions could have a second-level retributive result. If the corporation were forced to pay stockholders for losses due to corporate crime, its penalty might be significantly increased.

Such penalties are likely to be passed on to the consumer of the corporation's products or services in the form of higher prices. There is, however, a limit to that kind of recovery practice, and it is set by the marketplace. The only exceptions would be in public utilities or in other monopoly or semimonopolistic enterprises where consumers must deal with the criminal corporation or forego the service. Such public service corporations are generally directly regulated by government agencies, and pricing increases to offset penalties could be prevented if those agencies act in the best interests of the community at large.

The matter of reconstitution is hardly a stumbling block. If charter states are prepared to fully research charter applications and refuse reconstitutions that are no more than evasions of penalties, then only genuine reconstitutions will be chartered. This seems to be another red herring thrown in the pond of corporate criminal liability by those who either are convinced that state agencies are incapable, incompetent, or otherwise unable to do their jobs in an appropriate fashion or are philosophically committed to a view that excludes corporations from the criminal law, committed to some version of the old maxim *societas delinquere non potest*

A final point on the matter of harming innocent employees and others associated with the criminal corporation may be worth mention. When a natural person commits a felony and is convicted and punished, his or her associates, often family members and dependents, are frequently cast into dire financial straits. The harm done to them, though they may be totally innocent of any complicity in the crime, may, in fact, far outweigh that done to the incarcerated felon. After all, the convicted felon receives three meals a day and lodging. His or her family may be reduced to penury and may find that meals are only a sometime thing and then hardly nutritious. In many jurisdictions, little or no official interest is paid to these innocent sufferers. Certainly the law may entertain mercy pleas and pleas for reductions in sentences due to hardship, but if the crime is of a significant magnitude such pleas will generally be ignored. By analogy, the corporation that is punished may succeed in gaining a reduction in penalty if it can prove that a significant number of its innocent associates are directly harmed by the penalty, but for the most serious offenses, particularly those involving loss of or threats to life, indirect harm to corporate associates should not defeat penalty.

A number of legal theorists have put forth important accounts of corporate punishment consistent with the principles of the *Model Penal Code* or the doctrine of identification.[1] Many of their arguments are more than worthy of serious consideration. I am not, however, proposing to examine them. Instead, I want to offer what I regard to be one version, among a number of possibilities, of corporate retributive punishment that I believe has the generally desired *in terrorem* effects while being particularly suited to dealing with the corporate criminal. I must stress that in isolation from the other forms the punishment I have in mind will not likely have the significant reformative or deterrent effects a concerned citizenry would desire. Hence, I do not intend that my account be understood as offering a clear alternative to more traditional forms of retribution when corporations are criminally liable. Instead it should function as an augmentative device in sentencing and may be sufficient in a number of cases. I discuss it because it has not been considered as often or as seriously as is warranted,[2] and because it may open discussion of an important moral outlook or frame of reference.

The moral psychology of our criminal–legal system, as is frequently noted, is based on guilt. Herbert Morris provides useful studies of what he calls the "conceptual schemes" or "structures and features of a world" that is developed or created around the concept of guilt.[3] To be guilty is to have done something "in the wrong way" or wrongly. Wrongdoing, essential to the notion of guilt, Morris argues, depends on the concept of being harmed. Harm

can be caused in many ways and to many objects, animate and inanimate, but it is the personal injury of another that is keyed to
guilt. Someone may, of course, feel guilty for having harmed himself. (Some persons who smoke cigarettes report feeling guilty when
they do so because they recognize they may well be injuring their
health.) At any rate, when harm is related to guilt via the notion
of wrongdoing, it is usually not self-inflicted injury that is involved.

The wrongdoing that gives rise to guilt is conceptually related
to the idea of a union or community among persons. To have
wronged is to have behaved in a way that jeopardizes that unity.
"Wrongdoing . . . arises in a world in which apologies, forgiveness, and punishment exist and where they, as well as other forms
of conduct, have the significance of a rite of passage back to union
and restoration of the whole."[4]

Guilt is to be viewed as a form of separation and as debt either
to the specific victim harmed by one's wrongdoing or to the society as a whole. To expiate guilt the guilty party must pay (or rather
repay). Punishment is an institutional vehicle of repayment and
restoration. The idea of guilt traces to the notion of debt. The Latin
debitum in the Lord's Prayer and in Matthew 18:27 is translated in
Old English as *gylt*. In fact, the substantive sense of *gylt* as debt
has often been treated as the primary sense of the term. Hence,
the popular expressions are "the guilty must pay" and "paying one's
debt to society." Guilt is, however, more than simply debt, for there
are a number of things one can do with debts that one cannot do
with guilt. Most obviously, debts can be transferred: guilt cannot.
The family of the deceased may be bound to pay his outstanding
debts, but they cannot assume his guilt for the legal violations he
committed. That is not to say that they may not have a vicarious
liability for his actions if, under certain circumstances, he acted as
their agent.

Our notion of guilt, because it so directly associates with rule or
law violation, is what Morris calls a threshold notion. Guilt is not
amenable to scaling. The crime may have different degrees, such
as homicide, but the criminal is not partially guilty or 75 percent
guilty, etc. Either the defendant in a criminal case is guilty as

charged or not guilty. More important, the legal association of guilt renders it as primarily a minimum maintenance notion. Guilt avoidance involves meeting very basic standards of behavior as set by uniformly applicable rules or laws. As should be expected, guilt-based moralities are statute or rule dominated and stress the establishment of constraints of a nonharming variety over requirements that could call for heroic or out-of-the-ordinary efforts to aid others. The spotlight is on the boundaries of acceptable behavior, on the minimal level, not on maximal efforts to serve the welfare of others. "The law is concerned primarily with maintaining a certain balanced distribution of freedom and does this by ordering relationships among individuals through rules that set up a system of reciprocal rights and duties."[5]

In contrast to a guilt-based morality, certain societies, and in part our own, have emphasized the worth of the person to himself and in comparison to ideal models. In such systems of morality, the governing notion is shame. The poet W. H. Auden wrote:

> The first significant difference between the conception of man held by a shame-culture and that of a guilt-culture is that a guilt-culture distinguishes between what a man is to other men, the self he manifests in his body, his actions, his words, and what he is to himself, a unique ego which is unchanged by anything he does or suffers. In a shame-culture, there is no real difference between statements in the third person and statements in the first; in a guilt-culture, they are totally distinct.[6]

A key to understanding a shame conception of morality is that evaluation of behavior is done, not against rules or laws that set minimal constraints, but against role or type models. To feel shame or to be shameful a person must come to regard his or her behavior as having fallen below, or short of what is expected of or associated with the role, station, or type in which he or she belongs. As Morris points out, with this view of moral evaluation it is possible to talk in terms of degrees of perfection and success in realizing the ideal.[7] Focus, in fact, may fall on maximal efforts, on the accomplishment of the extraordinary, so that someone may be ashamed of not doing what no law would ever have required.

The crucial element in the shame-based culture is that of *model identity*. Shame then, does not relate so much to community as it relates to the individual's self-conception. To be sure, the model and that self-conception may be nurtured by the culture, as Auden claims was the case in ancient Greece.[8] The relevant model may be one in which a certain skill or style of interpersonal management is strongly emphasized. Under such models a person should feel shame when his or her actions damage the relationships that partially constitute the model. It is important that the failure that triggers the shame is defined in terms of personal estimation and not in terms of not meeting obligations to other persons or to the society.

Shame is a visual concept. The way one is seen, the way one's actions look to oneself and others, is most important. Even if one has broken no laws, violated no rules, one may believe that one is viewed as unworthy or that one should be so viewed because of a failure to do more than what is legally required. Although the law certainly does not hold the parents of a would-be presidential assassin responsible for his deed (and indeed he may be innocent of the crime by virtue of insanity), the parents may feel that they failed to perform as parents should in raising their son, and they may feel shame and seek to hide from community view.

A community may enforce certain laws that to some degree form the basis of various conceptions of model identities, but, by and large, those models are either personal constructs or the product of extralegal communal expectations and practices. A particularly adept penal system, however, would be one that could both induce shame when there has been a failure to achieve, in some significant degree, identification with a widely held model and utilize the visual and media capabilities of the society to heighten the sense of shame in the case of offenders. Felt shame is not purged by mere repayment. Shame is not a debt, it calls for positive creative responses to restore the personal sense of worth that has been damaged.

Moral and legal responsibility can be defined solely in terms of institutional and interpersonal obligations, but it can also be conceived, at least partially, in terms of character and worth. Responsive adjustment to failures might then be understood as creative

acts of worthy character building and not as or only as acts of restitution or atonement. A significant form of punishment in such a
system is what John Coffee has called the Hester Prynne Sanction.[9]

> The penalty thereof is death. But in their great mercy and tenderness of
> heart, they have doomed Mistress Prynne to stand only a space of three
> hours on the platform of the pillary, and then and thereafter, for the re
> mainder of her natural life, to wear a mark of shame upon her bosom. "A
> wise sentence!" remarked the stranger gravely bowing his head. "Thus she
> will be a living sermon against sin."[10]

As is evident in Hawthorne's prose, the Hester Prynne Sanction
is, at heart, a shame-based device. When effectively used, it will
not be so much a monetary penalty as one that threatens the corporate prestige, its image, especially as it or its high-level management perceives itself to be viewed by its many publics. This sanction will be fully effective only if the criminal (or the convicted
corporation) regards social stigmatization as a matter of grave concern, as a mark of internal failure that can be removed only by
creative actions to rewin communal favor and moral worth. To be
sure, adverse publicity can contribute to the achievement of monetary retributive effects by costing the corporation business when
customers refuse to purchase products or services. That cost, of
course, may be negligible and so not constitute a real retribution
of the crime. For adverse publicity to really work as a penal sanction the criminal must regard himself as shameful, his status in the
community significantly reduced. The criminal must think of himself as unworthy of community respect, as outlaw. He must come
to view the sanction as a damaging blot on his reputation, as a mark
of moral failure, as an indication of a justified negative finding with
respect to communal, social, and personal value, or as the grounds
for the disgust of others and of his own feeling of shame.

The Hester Prynne Sanction should be particularly suited to offenders of a corporate nature because the image of the corporation, corporate communal prestige, is at the very heart of the business of business. Reputation may not be everything, but little success
has ever been gained by a corporation with a bad reputation. Of-

ficial censure is not an inconsequential matter where corporate achievement depends on social acceptance. In fact, the Hester Prynne Sanction potentially could be far more effective in dealing with corporate offenders than with natural persons. For the corporation to survive it must garner and nurture a good image among the members of its society, the constituents of the marketplace. Furthermore, punishment by adverse publicity orders is more likely to minimize the kinds of unwanted externalities that plague other kinds of sanctions used by the courts against criminal corporations. Coffee has written:

> Little doubt exists that corporations dislike adverse publicity and that unfavorable publicity emanating from an administrative or judicial source has considerable credibility.[11]

This almost universal corporate aversion to a tarnished image is, however, insufficient to ground the Hester Prynne Sanction as a penal device. Bad press may be repugnant, but it is not penal and can be countered by corporate media campaigns intended "to put a different face on the issues." Quite simply, if this sanction is to be retributively penal the convicted corporation must regard the adverse publicity to be not only noxious, but a justified communal revelation of the corporation's failure to measure up.

But, it should be asked, measure up to what? Against what standard, what model identity, is a corporation to judge itself and be judged by the institutions of social order and justice? *The Scarlet Letter* provides only the structural or formal aspects of the matter. Hester is judged unworthy against a model of fidelity and womanly behavior that was characteristic of the puritanical society of early Boston. The articulated model was understood and internalized throughout her community. Its laws, to some extent, codified the key elements and provided for the inculcation of the model in the daily lives of the community members. Hester's punishment is understood as an external mark of her shame that is defined against the model identity that does not countenance adultery. It is not simply that Hester had violated a law and so must pay for her crime: it is not simply that she is guilty. It is that she should be ashamed.

Law itself does not generate shame. We expect the murderer not only to feel guilty, but to be ashamed of what he has done, whereas we would be thought rather eccentric if we expected the person caught driving an automobile at 60 miles per hour in a 55 miles per hour zone, under ordinary conditions, to feel ashamed of what he has done. The sanction is only effective against corporations in a manner that transcends something equivalent to the assessment of a fine, if there exists a shared conception of corporate excellence of character, a corporate model identity, against which the offender's behavior can be graded. The construction of that model is, of course, a dynamic enterprise and it has extensive corporately personal aspects. Each corporation, just as each human being, formulates its own conception of worthiness, builds its own model. All of the models do, however, share certain elements, take cognizance of certain societal facts and moral notions.

It is certainly no recent discovery of moral psychology that every person is disposed to be the kind of person that person values and that the model valued generally is consistent with the basic moral concepts held by the wider social unit. Such a basic disposition underlies the efficacy of the Hester Prynne Sanction. The court has the authority and the social credibility to force persons to confront their failures to realize that which they would acknowledge to be appropriate to them either as individuals or as members of a certain class or type. Adverse publicity orders provides an institutionalized revelatory apparatus, the modern substitute for the pillory, where the convicted is not simply to stand abandoned, contemptible before the community, but where the convicted is forced to confront the fact of his or her or its own shamefulness.

The suffering of adverse publicity is not a punishment that restores the object to communal grace. Hester is to wear the A not only as a "living sermon against sin," but to the grave and her headstone is to be engraved with it. This sort of punishment is not suffered to regain social status. Punishment alone does not relieve shame. Only positive corrective acts can do that. In short the imposition of the Hester Prynne Sanction on a corporation can institutionalize and broadcast the corporation's shamefulness, can insure social contempt for its contemptible behavior, but it can only be the spark to ignite the kind of responsive adjustment to its operating procedures and policies that is required for it to regain moral worth.

Although Coffee acknowledges that the Hester Prynne Sanction could have significant deterrent effects on corporations, he argues that as a primary penal device the adverse publicity strategy is prone to fail for a number of reasons.[12] Coffee's reasons are not philosophic. They focus on practical problems with the sanction that might be expected to arise if it were in wide use in contemporary American jurisdictions. A philosopher or theorist could easily enough beg off consideration of Coffee's concerns, but I think they are worthy of, at least, passing note because they reflect a number of currently expressed reservations about the whole enterprise of penal sanctions against corporations and because they can be remedied by certain kinds of administrative or juridical rulings or orders that clearly fall within the purview of the courts.

Coffee tells us that "government is a relatively poor propagandist. It has trouble being persuasive, rarely is it pithy" (p. 425). The idea is that governmental attempts to broadcast adverse publicity will not have the bite or the catchy sloganeering quality of the advertising agency prose the corporation uses to continue to sell its products. For adverse publicity order to have the desired *in terrorem* effects, that is for it to have a genuine impact on corporate prestige (and, it is hoped, sales), the court will have to employ writers and publicists equal to the task and not the run-of-the-mill bureaucratic scribblers who crank out the government's soporific prose. Coffee suggests that the price of the court's matching Madison Avenue in the attempt to persuade the people of the contemptible nature of a corporation's actions is "indecent" (p. 426). By that he seems to mean that the court is likely to soil its own image by descending to the advertising agency level in order to produce an effective penal sanction. (Little is ever said about the court's lowering itself to the level of the prison warden when it utilizes the incarceration sanction in criminal cases.)

There is, however, little reason for such concern. The court surely has the power to write its order in such a way that the cost of the adverse publicity is paid by the criminal corporation from its own advertising budget and to a competitive agency (other than ones that carry its accounts), and the adverse-publicity campaign is to be approved by an officer of the court (perhaps a college professor trained in advertising and marketing). The corporation might have to submit its previous year's advertising budget to be used as a starting line, a percentage of the advertising budget will be set aside for the adverse publicity campaign, and that percentage will be carried through all annual budgets until the expiration of the order. In this way, even if the corporation increases its advertising budget to attempt to entice sales, it will have to pay a higher adverse publicity cost. The court appointed overseer will be instructed to expend all funds in the adverse publicity budget annually and to do so in outlets roughly equivalent to those used by the usual corporate advertising agencies, e.g., that officer will not be allowed to place adverse publicity in obscure small-town newspapers if the corporation does not generally advertise in such ways.

Coffee's second concern is that the level of anticorporate noise in our society is so great as to devalue the effect of specific adverse-publicity orders. "Weak criticism tends to rob accurate censure of its expressive force" (p. 426). In this I think he is right. The newspaper editorialists, the campaigning politicians, the special interest groups, the conservationists, the Naderites, and the assorted movie and TV actors and actresses with one or another cause all contribute to a confusing cacophony of charges that are usually indirect, unsubstantiated, and certainly not properly adjudicated. Can this noise be controlled? Probably not, and it is probably not a good idea to pursue such a line. The offended corporate body always has the option of legal action to counter unfair criticism. Against this noise, however, a well-developed adverse publicity campaign against a particular corporate offender identified clearly as court ordered is still likely to draw special attention. The public may never be very discriminating, but generally the fact that the court has ordered a certain publicity campaign as punishment for a particular criminal offense should pierce the shield of apathy behind which the public hides from the onslaught of corporate criticism.

Coffee's third concern is that "corporations can dilute this sanction through counter-publicity" (p. 426). There is no denying the power of Madison Avenue advertising agencies to create clever and effective image building even in the face of severe public or government criticism. The Hester Prynne Sanction can be ordered in such a way as I have suggested to offset any corporate counterattack. Furthermore, the court has the power to order the corporation not to engage in any advertising directed specifically towards rebutting or diluting the sentence. If the corporation were to promote its own case after having lost in court and received an adverse publicity sentence, it would be in contempt of the court and sterner measures would be justified. Coffee reminds us that oil companies like Mobil mounted effective replies to the charges leveled against them during the energy crisis. Also corporations after *Central Hudson Gas & Electric Corp. v. Public Service Commission* (100 S. CT 2343 [1980]) clearly have First Amendment rights to express opinions on matters of public concern. Corporate rebuttals to adverse publicity orders, however, are not necessarily protected by *Central Hudson,* and the Mobil commercials were certainly not attempts to minimize the effectiveness of any adverse publicity orders. The oil companies were only charged in the court of public opinion, and their response was totally appropriate in that court.

Coffee continues by noting that the Hester Prynne Sanction may prove efficacious in fraud, public safety, and felony cases, but that it is not likely to be equally effective with regard to criminal offenses against governmental regulations. Gulf Oil, it will be remembered, was convicted of illegal campaign payments in connection with the Watergate scandals. The publicity was profuse, but there is little evidence that it hurt Gulf Oil sales. There are two things that seem appropriate in response. The first is to point out that in the regulatory cases adverse publicity occurred in the ordinary media coverage of the events. It was not court ordered in lieu of or in addition to some other penal sanction, e.g., a stiff fine. In effect, it was incidental, and as the story faded from the front page or the first fifteen minutes of the telecast, its intensity diminished. More important, Coffee may well be right that the Hester Prynne Sanction does not produce significant desired effects in the case of certain crimes. I have made no claim that adverse publicity orders will always suffice to achieve the retributive ends of the courts. A mix of sanctions will undoubtedly be required, if deterrence and retribution are to be accomplished. I would argue that adverse publicity orders are more likely than most other sanctions to produce what might be called rehabilitative outcomes, reformed corporations. Fines are too easily assimilated to business costs and revocations of licenses and charters are usually too severe to suit the crime.

Coffee further argues that despite the appearance that the sanction will not produce the same externalities as fines, if the sanction is really effective, it will lead to decreased sales and the corporation's employees at the lowest levels will be made to suffer layoffs, etc. (pp. 427–28). Undoubtedly this will occur, but it should not overly concern us. As previously argued, such externalities plague penal sanctions of all kinds. More to the point, however, the true question raised by this argument is whether the Hester Prynne Sanction is justifiable over the simple assessment of a fine when both produce basically equivalent externalities. I trust that the arguments of the preceding section provide firm reasons for the court to prefer, at least with regard to a number of crimes, the Hester Prynne Sanction rather than or in addition to a fine. The payment of the fine and the suffering imposed by the adverse publicity sanction are simply not equivalent punishments.

(It is worth briefly noting that in a recent study of seventeen major corporations that have suffered adverse publicity over an offense or serious incident [though such publicity was not court ordered], executives at the middle and higher levels of management reported that loss of corporate prestige was regarded as a very major corporate concern.[13] Indeed, the loss of prestige was regarded as far more serious than the payment of a stiff fine.)

The celebrated case of *United States v. Allied Chemical Company* ([1976] 7 Env. Rep. [BNA] 29; File CR-76-0129-R [U.S. Dist. Ct., Eastern Div. of Va., Richmond Div. 1976]), in which Allied Chemical was fined $13.24 million after a no-contest plea to 940 counts of pollution of the James River and other Virginia waterways, is often cited as an example of creative sentencing leading to the development of an alternative to the traditional sanctions. The Allied Chemical fine was reduced to $5 million when the company agreed to give $8,356,202 to the Virginia Environmental Endowment. Strictly speaking, the court did not order community service, but did accept the company's establishment of the endowment as mitigatory. In another case, *United States v. Olin Mathieson* (File N-78-30 [U.S. Dist. Ct., Dist of Conn. 1978]), the company pleaded no contest to the charge of conspiracy involving the shipment of rifles to South Africa. The judge imposed a $45,000 fine after Olin Mathieson agreed to set up a $500,000 New Haven Community Betterment Fund. (The maximum penalty could have been $510,000.)

Although neither of these famous cases really involves the imposition of a community-service sanction, some legal theorists have recently argued that the lessons learned in them indicate the desirability of providing the court with such a sentencing option.[14] There are certain practical problems with this approach that warrant only brief mention. Perhaps the most serious is that the corporation's costs in buying or performing community service are tax deductible charity contributions and standard court-imposed fines are, of course, nondeductible. Legislation could correct this deficiency. Also, the performance of community service is a positive, image-enriching action that generally will have the effect of elevating the public opinion of the corporation rather than punishing it. The results of corporate community service are more likely to make a favorable impression on the members of society while the reason why the corporation embarked on an altruistic venture is likely to be forgotten.

Although community service, particularly in a case like Allied Chemical, can have very direct or obvious retributive features, moral fairness speaks against making that sanction available to the sentencing courts. The retributive goals of punishment are adequately served in corporate cases by the traditional sanctions augmented by adverse publicity orders. Those types of sentences satisfy the generally accepted goals of retribution, particularly what Fisse has called the vindication of resentment and deliverance from guilt.[15]

The Hester Prynne Sanction, as we have seen, can satisfy the felt need to vindicate public and private resentment against the criminal corporation by a public display, and because its focus is to shame the corporation, it should be a wellspring of the very kinds of creative public projects that a community-service order would require. For such projects to have a true moral value with regard to the rebuilding of corporate worth, however, they must originate in the corporate decision process itself and not be an imposed penalty. Community service may well be one of the most productive and creative ways in which a shamed corporation can restore its prestige in the moral community, but to have such an effect, the projects undertaken should be voluntary. If the courts make a practice of requiring community service, they will be blocking an important route to restoration of moral worth by the voluntary creative actions of the corporation.

Notes

PREFACE

1. Rudyard Kipling, "Tomlinson," in *Barrack-Room Ballads* (New York: Grosset, 1933), pp. 28–30.

2. Kenneth Goodpaster, "Review of *Ethical Theory and Business*," *Ethics* (April 1981), 91(3):525.

3. Alfred F. Conrad, "Business Corporations in American Society," in Donald E. Schwartz, ed., *Commentaries on Corporate Structure and Governance*, (Philadelphia: ALI-ABA, 1979), p. 41.

1. TYPES OF COLLECTIVITIES: A PRELIMINARY SORTING

1. See Emile Durkheim, *The Rules of Sociological Method* (New York: Free Press, 1938), p. 1–13.

2. Karl R. Popper, *The Open Society and Its Enemies* (Princeton: Princeton University Press, 1962); F. A. Hayek, *The Counter-Revolution of Science* (New York: Free Press, 1955).

3. J. W. N. Watkins, "Ideal Types and Historical Explanation," in H. Feigl and M. Broadbeck, eds. *Readings in the Philosophy of Science* (New York: Appleton-Century-Crofts, 1953), p. 729.

4. Immanuel Kant, *Foundations of the Metaphysics of Morals*, L. W. Beck, tr. (Indianapolis: Bobbs-Merrill, 1969), p. 47.

5. Watkins, "Ideal Types and Historical Explanation," p. 729.

6. Hilary Putnam, *Meaning and the Moral Sciences* (London: Routledge and Kegan Paul, 1978), Lecture V, p. 63.

7. Watkins, "Ideal Types and Historical Explanation," p. 730.

8. See Peter A. French, *The Scope of Morality* (Minneapolis: University of Minnesota Press, 1979), appendix.

9. J. L. Austin, "A Plea for Excuses," *Philosophical Papers*, J. O. Urmson and G. J. Warnock, eds. (Oxford: Oxford University Press, 1970).

10. J. L. Austin, "Three Ways of Spilling Ink," *Philosophical Papers*, J. O. Urmson and G. J. Warnock, eds. (Oxford: Oxford University Press, 1970), p. 275.

11. Haskell Fain, "Some Moral Infirmities of Justice," in P. A. French, ed., *Individual and Collective Responsibility* (Cambridge, Mass.: Schenkman, 1973), p. 32; Kurt Baier, "Guilt and Responsibility," in P. A. French, ed., *Individual and Collective Responsibility* (Cambridge, Mass.: Schenkman, 1973), p. 61.

12. Virginia Held, "Can A Random Collection of Individuals be Morally Responsible?" *Journal of Philosophy* (July 1970), vol. 23, and "Moral Responsibility and Collective Action," in P. A. French, ed., *Individual and Collective Responsibility* (Cambridge, Mass.: Schenkman, 1973); David Cooper, "Responsibility and the 'System' " in P. A. French, ed., *Individual and Collective Responsibility* " (Cambridge, Mass.: Schenkman, 1973).

13. Karl Marx, *Capital* (London: Everyman, 1974), p. 864.

2. CROWDS AND CORPORATIONS

1. Walter Van Tilburg Clark, *The Ox Bow Incident* (New York: Random House, 1940).

2. Gerald Massey, "Tom, Dick, and Harry and All the King's Men," *American Philosophical Quarterly* (April 1976), 13(2):89–108.

3. Tyler Burge, "A Theory of Aggregates," *Nous* (1977), 11:97–117.

4. Letter from Arnauld, *The Leibniz-Arnauld Correspondence*, H. T. Mason, ed. and tr. (New York: Barnes and Noble, 1967), p. 108. I owe this reference to Jonathan Bennett.

5. Letter from Leibniz, *Ibid.*, pp. 121–22.

6. Alvin Plantinga, *The Nature of Necessity* (Oxford: Oxford University Press, 1974), p. 71.

7. See Peter A. French, *The Scope of Morality* (Minneapolis: University of Minnesota Press, 1979), ch. 1.

8. Saul Kripke, "Naming and Necessity," in D. Davidson and G. Harman, eds., *Semantics of Natural Language* (Dordrecht: Reidel, 1972), pp. 253–355.

3. THE CORPORATION AS A MORAL PERSON

1. Bruce Berner, "Letter to William Maakestad," published in "The Ford Pinto Case and Beyond." A paper presented by F. Cullen, W. Maakestad, and G. Cavender at the 1983 Meeting of the Academy of Criminal Justice Sciences, 1983.

2. John Locke, *An Essay Concerning Human Understanding*, P. H. Nidditch, ed. (Oxford: Oxford University Press, 1975) Book II, ch. 27, p. 346.

3. For a particularly flagrant example see Michael Jensen and William Meckling, "Theory of the Firm: Managerial Behavior, Agency Costs and Ownership

Structure," *Journal of Financial Economics* (1976), 3:305–60. On page 311 they write, "The private corporation or firm is simply one form of legal fiction which serves as a nexus for contracting relationships."

4. Daniel Dennett, "Conditions of Personhood," in A. O. Rorty, ed., *The Identities of Persons* (Berkeley: University of California Press, 1976), pp. 175–96.

5. John Rawls, "Justice as Reciprocity," in Samuel Gorovitz, ed., *John Stuart Mill, Utilitarianism* (Indianapolis: Bobbs-Merrill, 1971), pp. 244–45.

6. John Rawls, *A Theory of Justice* (Cambridge: Harvard University Press, 1970), p. 146.

7. Frederick Hallis, *Corporate Personality* (Oxford: Oxford University Press, 1930), p. xlii.

8. *Coke's Reports* 253, see Hallis, *Corporate Personality*, p. xlii.

9. Continental Tyre and Rubber Co., Ltd. v. Daimler Co., Ltd. (1915), K. B., p. 893.

10. Hallis, *Corporate Personality*, p. xlix.

11. *Continental Tyre and Rubber Co., Ltd. v. Daimler Co., Ltd.* (1915), K. B., p. 918.

12. *Continental Tyre and Rubber Co., Ltd. v. Daimler Co., Ltd.* (1916), 2 A.C., p. 340.

13. See in particular Otto von Gierke, *Die Genossenschoftstheorie* (Berlin, 1887).

14. See Gerald Massey, "Tom, Dick, and Harry and All the King's Men," *American Philosophical Quarterly* (April 1976), 13(2):89–108.

15. I am especially indebted to Donald Davidson, "Agency," in Robert Binkley, Richard Bronaugh, and Ausonio Marras, eds., *Agent, Action, and Reason* (Toronto: University of Toronto Press, 1971).

16. J. L. Austin, "Three Ways of Spilling Ink," *Philosophical Papers*, James Urmson and C. J. Warnock, eds. (Oxford: Oxford University Press, 1970), p. 275: See Joel Feinberg, *Doing and Deserving: Essays in the Theory of Responsibility* (Princeton: Princeton University Press, 1970), p. 134–39.

17. John Kenneth Galbraith, *The Age of Uncertainty* (Boston: Houghton Mifflin, 1977), p. 261.

18. H. L. A. Hart, *The Concept of Law* (Oxford: Oxford University Press, 1961), ch. 6.

19. G. C. Buzby, "Policies—A Guide to What A Company Stands For," *Management Record* (March 1962), 24.5–12.

20. Peter Drucker, *The Concept of Corporation* (New York: Crowell, 1972), pp. 36–37.

4. CORPORATE INTERNAL DECISION STRUCTURES

1. For a fuller account see Peter A. French, "Wittgenstein's Limits of the World," *Midwest Studies in Philosophy* (1976), 1:114–25.

2. Ludwig Wittgenstein, *Philosophical Remarks* (Oxford: Blackwell, 1975), #39.

3. H. L. A. Hart, *The Concept of Law* (Oxford: Oxford University Press, 1961).

4. Ronald Dworkin, *Taking Rights Seriously* (Cambridge: Harvard University Press, 1977), p. 21.

5. See for example, John Danley, "Corporate Moral Agency: The Case for Anthropological Bigotry," Bowling Green State University Conference in Applied Philosophy, 1980.

6. *(Second) Restatement of Agency* (1958), Section 34, Comment g.

7. *Marsili v. Pacific Gas & Electric Co.*, 51 Cal., App. 3d, 313, 124, Cal. Rptr. 313 (1975).

8. G. C. Buzby, "Policies—A Guide to What a Company Stands For," *Management Record* (March 1962), 24:5.

9. GAF Corporation, "Corporate Morality: Whose Responsibility?" corporate pamphlet, New York, N.Y., 1975.

10. Proctor and Gamble Corporation, "Your Personal Responsibility," corporate pamphlet, Cincinnati, Ohio, undated.

11. W. L. Gore, "The Lattice Organization—A Philosophy of Enterprise," publication of W. L. Gore & Associates, Inc., 1980, pp. 1–5.

5. THE POWER OF THE PEOPLE IN GROUPS AND CORPORATIONS

1. Alvin Goldman, "Toward a Theory of Social Power," *Philosophical Studies* (1972), 23:221–68.

2. There is a large and growing literature of legal theory on this matter. See for example: W. B. Fisse, "Responsibility, Prevention, and Corporate Crime," *New Zealand Universities Law Review*, 1973; pp. 250–79; W. B. Fisse, "The Social Policy of Corporate Criminal Responsibility," *Adelaide Law Review* (1978), 6:361–412; L. H. Leigh, "The Criminal Liability of Corporations and Other Groups," *Ottawa Law Review* (1977), 9:247–302; Brosnahan, Miller, and Foy, "Corporate Criminal Liability," *The Practical Lawyer* (September 1980) 26(6):23–29.

3. As, for example, in: *State v. Morris & Essex R.R.*, 23 N.J.L. 360 (1852); *New York Central & Hudson River R.R. v. United States*, 2.2 U.S. 481 (1909); *United States v. George F. Fish, Inc.*, F. 2d 798 (2d Cir.) 328 U.S. 869 (1946); *Western Laundry and Linen Rental Co. v. United States*, 424 2d 441 (9th Cir.) 400 U.S. 849 (1970).

6. KINDS AND PERSONS

1. Hilary Putnam, "Meaning and Reference," in Stephen P. Schwartz, ed., *Naming, Necessity, and Natural Kinds* (Ithaca: Cornell University Press, 1977), pp. 119–32.

2. Hilary Putnam, "Is Semantics Possible?" in Stephen P. Schwartz, ed.,

Naming, Necessity, and Natural Kinds (Ithaca: Cornell University Press, 1977), p. 104.

3. See Hilary Putnam, "Meaning and Reference."

4. John Locke, *An Essay Concerning Human Understanding*, Book III, ch. 6.

5. Julius Moravcsik, "How Do Words Get Their Meaning?" *The Journal of Philosophy*, (January 1981), 78:5–24; John Dupre, "Natural Kinds and Biological Taxa" *Philosophical Review*, January 1981, pp. 66–90.

6. David Wiggins, "Locke, Butler, and the Stream of Consciousness: And Men as a Natural Kind" in A. O. Rorty, ed., *The Identities of Persons* (Berkeley: University of California Press, 1976), pp. 139–73.

7. Putnam, "Meaning and Reference."

8. Wiggins, "Locke, Butler and the Stream of Consciousness," p. 160.

9. Hilary Putnam, *Meaning and the Moral Sciences* (London: Routledge and Kegan Paul, 1978), p. 62.

10. See Putnam, "Meaning and Reference," for a full account of this example.

11. Wiggins, "Locke, Butler, and the Stream of Consciousness," p. 161.

12. This approach is suggested and defended by Patricia Kitcher, "Natural Kinds and Unnatural Persons," *Philosophy* (October 1979), 54(210):541–47.

13. Hotchkiss v. The National City Bank, 200 F. 287 at 293 (S.D.N.Y. 1911).

14. See Moravcsik, "How Do Words Get Their Meaning."

15. See Peter A. French, *The Scope of Morality* (Minneapolis: University of Minnesota Press, 1979), ch. 1. Also Donald Davidson, "Agency" in Robert Binkley, Richard Bronaugh, and Ausonio Marros, eds., *Agent, Action, and Reason* (Toronto: Toronto University Press, 1971), pp. 26–37.

16. As an example see John Danley, "Corporate Moral Agency: The Case for Anthropological Bigotry," Bowling Green State University Conference in Applied Philosophy, 1980.

7. PLATO, BRADLEY, ROUSSEAU, AND THE CORPORATE PERSONALITY

1. 1. D. Weldon, *States and Morals* (New York: McGraw-Hill, 1947), pp. 34–45.

2. Plato, *The Republic*, Francis MacDonald Cornford, tr. (Oxford: Oxford University Press, 1941), pp. 55, 56.

3. Weldon, *States and Morals*.

4. Plato, *Republic*, p. 55.

5. *Ibid.*, p. 110.

6. Weldon, *States and Morals*, p. 37.

7. *Ibid.*, p. 39.

8. F. H. Bradley, *Ethical Studies* (Oxford: Oxford University Press, 1876, 1962), p. 164.

9. Weldon, *States and Morals*, p. 45.

10. Bradley, *Ethical Studies*, pp. 163, 169.

11. Proctor and Gamble, *Code of Conduct for Employees*, company pamphlet, 1975.

12. Wally Olins, *The Corporate Personality* (New York: Mayflower Books, 1978), p. 82.

13. Jean-Jacques Rousseau, *The Social Contract*, Maurice Cranston, tr., (Baltimore: Penquin Books, 1968), p. 58.

14. *Ibid.*, p. 74. (See also, Book II, ch. 4, ch. 9 and ch. 10 and Book III, ch. 11.)

15. *Ibid.*, pp. 72–73.

8. TRIBES

1. H. D. Lewis, "The Non-Moral Notion of Collective Responsibility" in Peter A. French, ed., *Individual and Collective Responsibility* (Cambridge, Mass.: Schenkman, 1972), p. 131.

2. Fred Miller and John Ahrens, "A Critique of Corporate Responsibility," American Philosophical Association, Eastern Division Meeting, Boston, 1980. Abstract in *The Journal of Philosophy* (October 1980), 77(10):657.

3. John Rawls, "Justice as Reciprocity" in Samuel Gorovitz, ed., *John Stuart Mill, Utilitarianism* (Indianapolis: Bobbs-Merrill, 1971), pp. 244–45.

4. Joel Feinberg, "Crime, Clutchability, and Individuated Treatment" in *Doing and Deserving: Essays in the Theory of Responsibility* (Princeton: Princeton University Press, 1970), ch. 10.

5. John Rawls, *A Theory of Justice* (Cambridge, Mass.: Harvard University Press, 1970), p. 146.

6. Sally F. Moore, "Legal Liability and Evolutionary Interpretation: Some Aspects of Strict Liability, Self-Help, and Collective Responsibility" in Max Gluckman, ed., *The Allocation of Responsibility* (Manchester: Manchester University Press, 1973), pp. 51–107.

9. THE MEDICAL PROFESSION

1. Kenneth Kipnis, "Professional Responsibility and the Responsibility of Professions," Paper, University of Hawaii, 1978.

2. J. L. Austin, "A Plea for Excuses," *Philosophical Papers*, J. O. Urmson and G. J. Warnock, eds. (Oxford: Oxford University Press, 1970), pp. 176–77.

10. WHAT IS HAMLET TO MCDONNELL-DOUGLAS OR MCDONNELL-DOUGLAS TO HAMLET: DC-10

1. Paul Eddy, Elaine Potter, and Bruce Page, *Destination Disaster* (New York: New York Times Books, 1976), p. 167.

2. F. H. Bradley, *Ethical Studies* (Oxford: Oxford University Press, 1876, 1962), p. 5.

3. Aristotle, *Nicomachean Ethics*, M. Ostwald tr. (Indianapolis: Bobbs-Merrill, 1962), pp. 52, 55–56.

4. Peter A. French, *The Scope of Morality* (Minneapolis: University of Minnesota Press, 1979), ch. 1.

5. For a complete account see Eddy, Potter, and Page, *Destination Disaster*.

6. *Ibid.*, pp. 176–77.

7. *Ibid.*, ch. 6, especially pp. 96–99.

8. *Ibid.*, pp. 85–99 provide a clear and adequate account of the "state of the art" at the time of the development of the DC-10.

9. *Ibid.*, p. 97. The authors of *Destination Disaster* quote from McDonnell-Douglas company literature references to Pope's "Be not the first by whom the new are tried/Nor yet the last to lay the old aside," and Carnegie's "Pioneering don't pay." Further accounts of corporate policy are cited in chapter 6.

10. *Ibid.*, p. 99.

11. *Ibid.*, especially ch. 10.

12. *Ibid.*, p. 178.

13. *Ibid.*, pp. 176–77.

14. *Ibid.*, ch. 10.

15. See Christopher Stone, *Where the Law Ends* (New York: Harper and Row, 1975).

16. W. Brent Fisse, "The Retributive Punishment of Corporations," *Michigan Law Review*, 1982.

17. Eddy, Potter, and Page, *Destination Disaster;* p. 223.

18. *Ibid.*, p. 224.

19. *Ibid.*, pp. 223-35.

20. A. A. Berle, "Economic Power and the Free Society," in A. Hacker, ed., *The Corporate Take-Over* (Garden City: Doubleday, 1964), p. 99.

11. THE PRINCIPLE OF RESPONSIVE ADJUSTMENT: THE CRASH ON MOUNT EREBUS

1. Report of the Royal Commission to Inquire into the Crash on Mount Erebus, Antarctica of a DC-10 Aircraft Operated by Air New Zealand Limited, 1981. Presented to the House of Representatives by Command of His Excellency the Governor-General of New Zealand, 1981. Hereafter references to this report will be made in the text by citing the paragraph numbers of the Report.

2. J. L. Mackie, "Causes and Conditions," *American Philosophical Quarterly* (October 1965), 2(4):245–64.

3. *Regina v. Prince*, 13 Cox Criminal Case 138 (1875).

4. F. H. Bradley, *Ethical Studies* (Oxford: Oxford University Press, 1962), p. 46.

5. J. L. Austin, *Philosophical Papers* (Oxford: Oxford University Press, 1961), p. 284.

6. Aristotle, *Nicomachean Ethics*, M. Ostwald, tr. (Indianapolis: Bobbs-Merrill, 1962), p. 51.

12. INTENTION AND CORPORATE ACCOUNTABILITY

1. F. H. Bradley, *Ethical Studies* (Oxford: Oxford University Press, 1962), ch. 1; Aristotle, *Nichomachean Ethics*, M. Ostwald, tr. (Indianapolis: Bobbs-Merrill, 1962), Book III.

2. Thomas Donaldson, *Corporations and Morality* (Englewood Cliffs, N.J.: Prentice-Hall, 1982), p. 22.

3. Aristotle, *Nichomachean Ethics*, p. 57.

4. Bradley, *Ethical Studies*, p. 31.

5. Gary Dessler, *Organization and Management* (Englewood Cliffs, N.J.: Prentice-Hall, 1976), p. 317.

6. The term is Herbert Simon's. See his *Administrative Behavior* (New York: Free Press, 1957).

7. Donaldson, *Corporations and Morality*, pp. 22–23.

8. Peter A. French, *The Scope of Morality* (Minneapolis: University of Minnesota Press, 1979), ch. 6.

13. CORPORATE CRIMINALITY AND THE MODEL PENAL CODE

1. W. Blackstone, *Commentaries* (1765), p. 476.

2. 114 Eng. Rep. 492 (3 Q.B., p. 223, 1842).

3. 115 Eng. Rep. 1294 (9 Q.B., p. 315, 1846), p. 326.

4. 23 N.J.L., p. 360 (1852).

5. 68 Mass. (2 Gray), p. 339 (1854).

6. *State v. Morris & Essex Railroad Company*, p. 370.

7. *State v. The Baltimore and Ohio Railroad Company* (June Term), pp. 362–93 (1879).

8. 195 N.Y. 102, 88 N.E., p. 22, 16 Ann. Cas. 837 (1909).

9. 212 U.S., p. 481 (1909).

10. The American Law Institute, *Model Penal Code* (Philadelphia: The American Law Institute, 1962), pp. 35–37.

11. *Ibid.*, p. 37.

12. L. H. Leigh, "The Criminal Liability of Corporations and Other Groups," *Ottawa Law Review* (1977), 9:275.

13. *Lennard's Carrying Co. v. Asiatic Petroleum*, p. 283.

14. Leigh, "Criminal Liability of Corporations," p. 253.

15. *Ibid.*, p. 255.

16. Gerhard O. W. Mueller, *"Mens Rea* and the Corporation," *University of Pittsburgh Law Review* (1957), 19:21–50, 41.

17. Leigh, "Criminal Liberty of Corporations," p. 287.

14. PUNISHING THE CRIMINAL CORPORATION

1. See for example Christopher Stone's *Where the Law Ends: The Social Control of Corporate Behavior* (New York: Peter Smith, 1975) and "The Place of Enterprise Liability in the Control of Corporate Conduct," *Yale Law Review* (1980); and "Large Organizations and the Law at the Pass: Toward a General Theory of Compliance Strategy," *Wisconsin Law Review* (1981); W. Brent Fisse's, "The Social Policy of Corporate Criminal Responsibility," *Adelaide Law Review* (1978); "Responsibility, Prevention, and Corporate Crime," *New Zealand University Law Review* (1973); "The Retributive Punishment of Corporations," *Michigan Law Review* (1982); "Community Service as a Sanction Against Corporations," *Wisconsin Law Review* (1982); John Collins Coffee's "Beyond the Shut-Eyed Sentry," *Virginia Law Review* (1977); "No Soul to Damn: No Body to Kick," *Michigan Law Review* (1981). See also Leigh, "Criminal Liability of Corporations."

2. But see W. Brent Fisse, "The Use of Publicity as a Criminal Sanction Against Business Corporations," *Melbourne University Law Review*, 1971, vol. 107.

3. Herbert Morris, *On Guilt and Innocence* (Berkeley: University of California Press, 1976) pp. 59–64 and "Guilt and Punishment," *The Personalist* (Spring 1971), 52(2):305–21.

4. Morris, "Guilt and Punishment," p. 310.

5. *Ibid.*, pp. 319, 320.

6. W. H. Auden, "Dingley Dell & The Fleet," in *The Dyer's Hand and Other Essays* (New York: Random House, 1968), p. 413.

7. Morris, "Guilt and Punishment," pp. 319–20.

8. Auden, *Dyer's Hand.*

9. Coffee, "No Soul to Damn, No Body to Kick," p. 424.

10. Nathaniel Hawthorne, *The Scarlet Letter* (1850), p. 63.

11. Coffee, "No Soul to Damn, No Body to Kick," p. 425.

12. *Ibid.*, pp. 425–28.

13. W. B. Fisse and John Braithwaite (Albany: State University of New York Press, 1983).

14. See W. Brent Fisse, "Community Service as a Sanction Against Corporations," *Wisconsin Law Review*, 1982.

15. W. B. Fisse, "The Retributive Punishment of Corporations," Manuscript; see also Sir Peter Strawson, *Freedom and Resentment and Other Essays* (London: Methuen, 1976).

INDEX

Aggregate collectives, 5, 7-13, 17-18, 20-26, 67-75, 123; identity of, 5, 20-23, 24-26; medical profession as, 123-24; and moral responsibility, 7-10; power of the people in, 67-75; selection-exclusion principles of, 24-26; types of, 11-12
American people, 10, 11, 12, 17, 18
Aristotle, 40, 131, 156, 158, 160, 165, 166
Arnauld, 23
Arusha Masai tribe's collective responsibility system, 117-18
Auden, W. H., 192, 193
Austin, J. L., 6, 39, 124, 157

Baier, Kurt, xiv, 8
Berle, A. A., 144
Blame, 5-11; as fixing causes, 6-7; as holding responsible, 7-11; senses of, 6
Bradley, F. H., 94, 99-101, 105, 107, 108, 156, 164, 166 67
Braithwaite, John, 161n
Burge, Tyler, 23
Business ethics, xii
Buzby, G. C., 43, 58, 59, 60

Clark, Walter Van Tilberg, 19
Coffee, John, 194, 195, 197, 198, 199, 200; objections to the Hester Prynne Sanction, 197-200
Coke, Sir Edward, 35
Conglomerate collectivities, 13-17, 27-30; characteristics of, 13-14; identity of, 13, 27-30; responsibility of, 13-16
Conrad, Alfred F., ix, x
Cooper, David, 12

Coordination problem and collective power, 69-70
Corporate criminal liability: and federal court rules, 180-81; history of, 174-78
Corporate Internal Decision Structure (CID Structure), 39, 41-47, 48-66, 77, 109-11, 124, 127, 168-69, 182, 183, 184
Corporations: CEO's power in, 75-77; criminal liability of, 174-78; as fictions, viii, 35-37; identity of, 27-30; image and personality of, 101-5; intentionality in, 39, 41-47, 164-71; juristic treatment of, 35-37; as persons, 39-47, 91, 168-69; policies of, 41, 45-46, 48-62; power of the persons in, 75-77; procedures in, 41, 44, 48-62, 168; punishment of, 187-202

Danley, John, x, xiv
Davidson, Donald, xiii
DC-10: crash near Paris, 1974, 129 44; crash on Mt. Erebus, 145-63
Dennett, Daniel, 33
Doctrine of identification, 182-84, 190
Donaldson, Thomas, xiv, 165, 166, 169, 170
Drucker, Peter, 43
Dupre, John, 80
Durkheim, Emile, 1
Dworkin, Ronald, 52

Edward, First Baron Thurlow, 187
Event redescription, 39-41, 44-47
Extended Principle of Accountability (EPA), xii, 134, 138-39, 164

Fain, Haskell, 8
Feinberg, Joel, 114, 159
Fiction Theory, 35-36, 37
Fisse, W. Brent, xiv, 139, 161*n*
Ford Pinto case, 31, 57-58, 78-79, 186;
  dismissal motions, 78-79

Galbraith, J. K., 42
Goldman, Alvin, 68, 71; and the analysis
  of individual and collective power, 68-71
Goodman, Nelson, 22*n*
Goodpaster, Kenneth, ix
Gore, William, 62-66
Gore Associates, 62-64
Groups, 67-75
Guilt, 190-92

Hallis, Frederick, 35
Hand, Learned, 88
Hart, H. L. A., 43, 52, 53
Hayek, F. A., 2
Hegel, W. G. F., 94
Held, Virginia, 12
Hester Prynne Sanction, 194-200, 202
Hobbes, Thomas, 101
Hopkins, Andrew, 163
Hume, David, x

Individualism: Methodological (MI), 2, 3,
  5, 7, 8, 11, 13, 15, 16, 19, 55, 108; tradition, viii, 2
Intentionality, 38-40, 155-60; corporate,
  39, 41-47; an intensional notion, 39; and
  moral personhood, 38-39

Jie and Turkana tribe's collective responsibility system, 116

Kant, Immanuel, vii, 1, 2, 100, 171
Kipling, Rudyard, viii
Kipnis, Kenneth, 122
Kipsigis tribe's collective responsibility
  system, 116-17
Kitty Genovese case, 7-8, 9, 10, 12
Kripke, Saul, 29

Lango tribe's collective responsibility system, 116-17

Lattice model, 63, 64, 65, 66
Legal Aggregate Theory, 35, 36
Leibniz, 23, 24, 26, 30
Leigh, L. H., 180, 181, 182, 186
Lewis, H. D., xi, xiii, 112-15, 118-19
Locke, John, x, 32, 80, 83, 84, 101

Mackie, J. L., xiii, xiv, 151
Massey, Gerald, 21
Medical profession, 120-28; as an aggre-
  gate, 122; as a collectivity, 121-24
Miller and Ahrens, 112-13
Model Penal Code, 166, 179-86, 190
Moore, Sally F., 115-19
Moral community, vii
Moravcsik, Julius, 80, 88
Morris, Herbert, 190, 191, 192
Mueller, Gerhard O. W., 185

Natural kinds, 79-81, 88; defined, 79-80;
  terms as rigid designators, 80
Newton, Lisa, 163, 171
Nixon, Richard, 59

Olins, Wally, 103-5
Ox Bow Incident, The, 19

Penal sanctions, 187-202; adverse publicity, 194-200; community service, 200-2;
  fines, 187-90
Person, 32-47, 78-93, 164-70; corporation
  as, 39-47, 91, 168-69; as an empirical
  generalization's governed kind, 88-90;
  legal, 32-38; metaphysical, 32-34, 40,
  79; moral, 32-34, 38, 39, 79, 91-93, 164-
  67, 170; as a natural kind term, 79-87,
  170; senses, 32
Plantingan Principle, 24, 25, 30
Plato, 94-99, 100, 105
Popper, Sir Karl, 2
Predicates: collective, 21; multigrade, 21
Primary Principle of Accountability (PPA),
  132-34
Principle of Responsive Adjustment
  (PRA), xii, 155-57, 158-60, 161, 162,
  163, 164, 167, 168, 172
Putnam, Hilary, 3, 81, 82, 83, 89, 90

Random collectives, 12
Rawls, John, 33, 34, 35, 114
Reality Theory, 36-37
Recognition rules, 41-47, 52-56
Risk, 141-44
Rousseau, J. J., 105-8, 110-11

Scarlet Letter, The, 194, 195, 196
Shame, 192-93
Standard Operating Procedures (SOPs), 168
Stone, Christopher, xiv
Strict liability, 154, 155-56

Suku tribe's collective responsibility system, 117

Ultra vires, 46, 56-57; and the business judgment rule, 57-58

Von Gierke, Otto, 36, 37

Watkins, J. W. N., 2
Weldon, T. D., 95, 96, 101
Wicker, Tom, 31, 43
Wiggins, David, 81, 82, 84, 85, 86, 87
Wittgenstein, Ludwig, 48